LAST BASTION

By the same author

BERMUDA—THE STORY OF A NAVAL BASE
MALTESE MEMORIES

Valletta: Late Eighteenth Century

LAST BASTION
Sketches of the Maltese Islands

ERIC BROCKMAN, C.B.E.
Captain, R.N. and Knight of Malta

DARTON, LONGMAN & TODD LTD.
LONDON

DARTON, LONGMAN & TODD LTD.
29a Gloucester Road
London, SW7

Printed in Great Britain by
Jarrold & Sons Ltd, Norwich

FOR CALYPSO

CONTENTS

CONTENTS

LIST OF ILLUSTRATIONS

LIST OF ILLUSTRATIONS

INTRODUCTION

My first impressions of the Maltese Islands are now almost forty years old. During that time those islands have sustained the most concentrated and the most savage attack in all the long tale of their embattled resistance. They have also suffered, like the rest of us, a revolution as complete as any in history.

That social upheaval, like the original of which it is, as yet, an incomplete copy, has been very English in character. It has so far been bloodless, if we discount a few broken heads and a dent or two in a policeman's helmet. It has retained the semblance of constitutional genesis and democratic execution. But, in England, the social mechanism has ground out its answers slowly, by compromise and by precedent, and on the whole fairly noiselessly and with a minimum of blood-letting over a period of a thousand years. When we export that cold, Nordic brand of democracy, we are often surprised to discover that it advances by sudden, painful jerks and sometimes refuses in an alien air to work at all; at others it actually goes into reverse. The same is true of our English social conventions, our customs, and our patterns of thought.

Malta, like many another land to which we have, by accident or design, exported our way of life is not automatically rendered happier because of it. It is true that, in Malta, there is less squalor, less poverty than forty years ago. But these things are relative. There is also less contentment, less gaiety.

The writings which I have here put together are a poor patchwork without conscious design; but in so far as they may help towards a clearer understanding of the Maltese scene, they have an aim. Consequently, I have tried to arrange the patchwork so that something like a composite picture of the islands and the people I love might emerge.

I have been less than kind to the Garrison and some of its shibboleths. No impression of Malta could be complete without some reference to this phenomenon of the English overseas, and to have glossed over my irritation with some aspects of it would have been disingenuous. Nevertheless, I am not unaware of the other side of this picture. Where one race is inevitably dominated by and dependent upon another whose culture and traditions are different yet, as in Malta, not sufficiently different to make mutual segregation seem reasonable, the dominant caste is invariably wrong, whatever it does. Let zealous individuals interest themselves in welfare and social services and there will be voices enough to accuse them of impertinent interference. Let them be content with their cricket, their polo, and their coffee-parties and seek, like so many travellers, only 'the satisfaction of pointing out the deficiencies of foreign countries as compared with one's own[1] and they are insular and arrogant.

The familiar cries of 'Independence! Malta for the Maltese!' have been heard, and for those of us who love Malta and all her people the future remains anxious and doubting.

Nevertheless, Malta is not naturally a land of humourless rioters and bleak revolutionaries. The Maltese can laugh at himself —and at us—and he will not be miserable or resentful for long. I certainly do not despair, although I must deplore the errors of some of my compatriots. In these essays I have tried to avoid taking sides; though where my sympathies lie will be sufficiently obvious.

There are lasting things in Malta which will outlive Integration, Dominion Status, Royal State, Crown Colony, Independence, or whatever other political solution may be found for the well-being of her people. Not the least lasting are the essential kindliness and human-heartedness of that ancient, little people in the sun. I have never found them difficult to live with and do not expect them to become monsters overnight.

The short pieces called 'Festa' and 'Songs' first appeared in a collection called *Maltese Memories* (Allen and Unwin) in 1938, and the note on the 'Sovereign Order as a Naval Power' is an expanded version of 'The Navy of the Order of St. John' which appeared in *The Mariner's Mirror* in 1930, together with a similar article in the *Rivista del Sovrano Militare Ordine di Malta*, of 1958.

It remains for me to record my gratitude, first to Sir Hannibal Scicluna, Knight Grand Cross of Malta, my father-in-law, whose

---

[1] Jasper More, *The Land of Italy*.

illimitable library and whose electronic memory have always been at my disposal; then to Chevalier Joseph Galea, K.M., F.S.A. (Scot.) of the Royal Malta Library, who has never failed to produce chapter and verse on any matter touching the Maltese Archives; to my kinsman Guido Lanfranco, F.R.E.S., F.Z.S., F.B.S.E., whose delightful writings and drawings on Maltese Natural History have kept my amateur's imagination within bounds; to Mr. Charles Zammit, F.S.A., Director of Museums and Mr. J. C. Pollacco, Director of the Malta Tourist Board, both of whom took immense pains to produce many of the photographs with which this little book is embellished.

ERIC BROCKMAN

Kensington,
1961

I

FIRST IMPRESSIONS

FIRST IMPRESSIONS

> 'Our need is not to restore a vanished or to revive a
> vanishing culture under modern conditions, but to grow a
> contemporary culture from old roots.'
>
> (T. S. Eliot)

I FIRST saw Malta through the eyes of a midshipman of the
nineteen-twenties. A not very travelled midshipman whose
passing glimpses of countries other than his own had been
limited to a few ports in Norway—splendid, snow-capped
mountains mirrored in glass-quiet fjords, blonds in red, peaked,
and tasselled caps; Spain—sultry, malodorous but exciting;
Gibraltar—a citadel peopled by soldiers, a few natives and, in
those days, a lot of sinister-looking Moors.

Though the phrase had not, I think, been coined, we had all
learned that Niggers began at Calais. Norwegians, big, blond
Lutheran and Viking, were approved, but Spaniards were full of
darkness and the Inquisition. Gibraltarians were Rock Scorpions
and the rest of the Southern world might be inhabited by Wogs,
Wops, Malts, and the like.

I do not know whether the process of falling in love at first sight
can as rightly be applied to a place as to a person. Something of the
sort—indeed of both sorts—certainly happened to me in Malta.
We secured in the Grand Harbour of Valletta during Carnival—
the five days of merrymaking and uninhibited skylarking which
used to precede the austerities of Lent. Of recent years, a self-
consciously secular government has tended to celebrate Carnival
after Easter—a proceeding which has shocked the traditionalists;
but in those days I do not think that even Lent itself meant much
to me, nurtured as I had been in a sort of liberal agnosticism.
Some of my messmates, more loyal to the strictly Protestant,
Nelson tradition, affected to be shocked by the whole proceeding
and glibly retailed the fables that the 'Maltese ring their Church
bells incessantly to keep the Devils away and have false clocks on

3

their Church towers to deceive Satan.' I do not remember whether I ever believed these tales; but I certainly quoted Byron's 'Yells, Bells, and Smells' as glibly as any. Nevertheless, I remember noting an unexpected proportion of big, almost blond Maltese with Teutonic eyes and naïvely recording it to their credit.

Since the ship in which I was then serving (H.M.S. *Ramillies*) did not belong to the Mediterranean Fleet, we were not 'in Mediterranean Fleet Routine', and, quite improperly as it later transpired, the Gunroom officers were granted late leave during Carnival, a privilege denied the 'young gentlemen' of the Mediterranean Fleet because of the danger of 'incidents' with the local populace. We escaped incidents—of an unpleasant nature, anyway—but certainly enjoyed a unique introduction to the Maltese scene.

The streets of Valletta, narrow, stepped, medieval, and exciting, were crammed with dancing, singing people of all shapes, sizes and ages. Groups in fancy dress of countless variety and vast ingenuity were dancing the *parata*—supposed to represent the repulse of the Turks; but suspiciously like a Morris Dance or something even older. Young women, with masked, laughing eyes beneath the black hood of a *faldetta* and a tantalizing froth of white lace above silk-clad ankles, bombarded their cavaliers with handfuls of coloured rice and fled, laughing, into the jostling throng. The great moment of the procession arrived. I saw it from a seat on a lamp-post which a charming young Maltese had invited me to share with him. There were the usual float-loads of pretty girls, the giant figures of fabulous and less fabulous beasts and birds, and a company of stilt-men who marched and danced with great virtuosity, while they exchanged greetings with the spectators in the upper-storey windows. Everything was immensely gay and immensely good-humoured and everyone seemed to know everyone else. One float remains firmly in my memory. It was peopled by gigantic and very lifelike papiermâché figures of Malta's leading politicians—Sir Gerald (as he then was) Strickland, 'Gustu' Bartolo, 'Nerik' Mizzi. The figures talked, nodded, and gesticulated in an unmistakably political manner and were greeted with suitable noises by the crowd. I think the new breed of politician takes himself rather too seriously to permit such lampooning; or perhaps some of the good humour has gone out of the crowd.

Sunlight on golden stone, a childlike gaiety, courtesy, the

smell of roasting coffee and black cheroots: all and much else has remained with me as a lover's earliest memories of the beloved.

I was to return to Malta many times. In peace and in war, in happiness and in mourning and, in the end, to come to know that little rock as my second home; but it was some years before I quite ceased to think of the Island as just another British fortress with a dockyard, inhabited by natives who were exclusively engaged in ministering to the needs of the Fleet when they were not priests, monks, or nuns. If I thought much about them as a people, I put them into the popular category of a mixed race of Italian-Arabic stock, suffering from all the defects inherent in the misfortune of not being English.

Neither I nor my contemporaries were much to be blamed. The better sort of Maltese, the nobility and the professional classes of those days, had little time for the usual run of British officers. Their homes and their clubs were the inviolate strongholds of an exclusive Latin and Catholic culture. In particular, they were anxious to protect their daughters from what they regarded as dangerous contacts with a foreign and amoral way of life. Thoroughly authenticated English Catholics of good family were excepted from the general suspicion; but these were, naturally, in a minority in the Garrison and Fleet population. A not inconsiderable number of human disasters has attended the breaking down of these barriers, and it may be that the older generation of Maltese parents were right.

For similar reasons our sailors and soldiers knew little of the homes of the people and, forty years later, their impressions of the Maltese are largely gleaned from bars and the haunts of the least reputable.

It was, curiously enough, through the medium of a kind of bar that I began to learn something of the real Malta which lay behind the latticed, Spanish balconies of *Città-Vecchia* and the great, leather *portières* of the church doors. But this was a special sort of Bar. Proclaiming itself a 'Smoking Divan' it retained the atmosphere of the Victorian retreats to which gentlemen who were addicted to nicotine habitually resorted. Here the good Brothers Marich dispensed cigars and their own exclusive blends of tobacco and cigarettes which their father and their grandfather had supplied to King Edward VII, to the German Emperor, and the

Houses of Savoy and Battenberg. Every customer who essayed these princely portals was most carefully, albeit politely, examined, and should he fail to measure up to the standards set by three generations of service to the 'gentry', steps were taken, in the subtlest possible manner, to indicate that he was, perhaps, in the wrong shop. Coffee and a very special orange cocktail were dispensed on the clear understanding that they were simply concomitant to tobacco. There were other liquors, it is true, including absinthe which was kept for one customer.

I have never quite understood how I came to be admitted to the confidence—and friendship—of the Brothers Marich. It was during my second commission in Malta when, together with three other impecunious and not notably well-conducted young officers of the Commander-in-Chief's staff, I shared a bachelor flat in the Strada Forni, and we grew into the habit of calling in on our way back from the Auberge de Castille (where the Commander-in-Chief had his offices when we were disembarked from the flagship) or on a free Sunday forenoon for one or two of those deliciously cool, gaily coloured orange concoctions.

Those were fine and spacious days for a young Gunroom officer. We worked fairly hard, played a great deal, and were seated in that happy mean where membership of the rather pompous Union Club was barred to us, and 'poodle-faking' with the wives of our seniors and their train of predatory young women of the 'Fishing Fleet' could easily be evaded.

We were accepted—at first, I think, as an interesting new animal—by the Brothers and by the little nucleus of their steady customers who used the Divan as a club. There was a distinguished Canon of the Church, remarkable for his beautifully polished shoes, his silver buckles, and his very beautiful hands. He used to sip lemon-squash and smoke interminable Egyptian cigarettes, while he dilated, with what seemed to me an unclerical breadth, upon any topic which offered itself. An aristocrat and a priest by family tradition rather than from vocation he had, nevertheless, served in the Indian Missions where much of his private fortune had been invested in the souls of Tamils. He sat always in a corner out of sight of the door, so that he might not give cause for scandal for the more conservative of the Faithful who held that it was not seemly for a priest to smoke in public.

There was an artist, of French sympathies and education, whose views on life anticipated Sartre and the Existentialists. A kindly, good fellow who was, we learned, not *persona grata* in the best Maltese houses because he was known to employ nude models—from the only source available to him, the ranks of the foreign demi-mondaines who made a brief stop in Malta on that sad route towards Tangier, Port Said, or Buenos Aires. He made a great deal of his quite undeserved reputation and had built himself up into a sort of local Faust. It was he who drank the absinthe and engaged in endless and complex arguments with the Canon.

There were two Maltese Barons. One who was quite penniless and had an authentic pedigree descending from the Byzantine Paleologi. The other cultivated roses and always wore a fresh and a different bloom in his coat.

There were younger men, too. Maltese officers of the Royal Malta Artillery, products of English public schools and Sandhurst, who used unaccented English as fluently as Italian and Maltese.

It was in the Divan that I first heard of the Casino Maltese: in those days surely one of the most exclusive clubs in the world and not, as Englishmen still sometimes suppose, a gambling haunt. Not all the habitués of the Divan were members. The Brothers themselves, unquestionably gentlemen, kept a shop and were ineligible. The Byzantine Baron had been asked to resign by a long-suffering committee, tired of waiting for the settlement of his bills which in turn awaited the demise of a Venetian aunt. The artist's anti-clerical opinions and supposedly profligate way of life were unacceptable. So, here, on a sort of neutral territory, the friends could meet and talk. Talk incessantly, smoke and drink a little, arrive at no conclusions, and watch the Maltese world pass to and fro, across the Palace Square which was in those days the centre of Maltese life.

One other figure completed the little circle—surely a typical cross-section of Malta—to which we, two or three young Englishmen, were eventually admitted. He was the boot-black and odd-job man, clothed in a sailor's flannel and a pair of 'hospital-blue' trousers, with three medals of the First World War pinned to his flannel. He spoke no English, and had an impediment which made even his Maltese fairly incomprehensible. He was known as 'Booble-eyes', because his sole reply, if addressed in English, was to pat his bemedalled chest and announce 'Me Booble-eyes!'

—which we learned to understand as a proclamation of the fact that he had been mobilized!

Booble-eyes was a great purveyor of rumours, and I distinctly remember his forecasting the movements of the Mediterranean Fleet—it was one of those perennial crises in the Middle East— some weeks before they were known to the Commander-in-Chief. Whether he merely collected intelligent guesses or had some dark and secret source, I never knew.

The habitués talked usually in Maltese—a Maltese interlaced with phrases and sentences in Italian, French, or English. In our presence, they used English, unless the discussion grew heated, when they would lapse into Maltese, apologizing and translating for us as soon as the climate had cooled sufficiently. Sometimes, the translation itself provided fuel for a new argument. Was the sense exact? Perhaps there was no English word for it? The Canon might offer Latin as a go-between and then they were off again, he and the artist—the secret languages of the priestly hierarchy— mysteries veiled from the people—Babel and the need for an international tongue.

We listened and learned a great deal.

We found most common ground, of course, with the young gunners, who could be as English as we when occasion demanded. Yet they made no fetish of their Englishry, no exaggerated parade of it, as some of their sons now tend to do.

Then, as now, most of the better sort of Maltese affected to despise politics; but there was then a Second Chamber, the Senate, and in it and on the Governor's Council, the Nobility, the Church, and the men of culture were represented. And in that phase of a bewildering number of variations on the theme of self-determination which Malta has suffered, the interest of all classes was strong, though not at all amenable to clear-cut social definition. Paternalism is in the blood and your cook or your gardener voted like you and carried your arguments into his own class. Today, issues are clear cut between class and class. Men of the kind who used to gather in the Divan might think professional politics beneath their dignity, and I do not exonerate them from a charge of sloth; but they held sincere convictions and were not to be bribed or bullied in other directions. The generation which has followed them seems to me to have surrendered to expediency and to have few convictions of any kind.

In those days, the language question loomed largest, effectively obscuring the deeper social and economic issues of which it was but a symptom.

The protagonists of Italian as the official language enjoyed the support of a large part of the literate electorate: the Clergy, with the professional classes and the Italianate landowning families. Almost all of them had been educated by Italian-speaking priests, and the Church herself, not unnaturally, lent her weight to the side which seemed most likely to perpetuate 'Latinity' and the Catholic, European roots of Maltese culture. Only the Archbishop himself, a saintly Benedictine from Fort Augustus who missed his golf, Dom Maurus Caruana, seemed to favour the English school and spoke his Latin with a Scots accent, though he was of undiluted and distinguished Maltese stock.

The champions of English as the 'first language' were led by that very great Anglo-Maltese patriot, Gerald Strickland, Count della Catena, later Lord Strickland of Sizergh. His followers were drawn from the not negligible ranks of families with English or Irish affinities, education, and commercial interests. They saw danger, too, in identification with a politically unstable and over-populated Italy.

Between these irreconcilable extremes, a third element battled for the survival and revival of the native tongue which had, during centuries of Romance influence, degenerated almost to the level of a kitchen argot, without literature and with a decaying syntax. The loyalties of this little group of idealists swung between the two major parties, depending at any moment upon which of them seemed most likely finally to relegate Maltese to the kitchen. Since their impetus was primarily emotional and sentimental, purely sociological or economic factors tended to pass over their heads; but their influence was to reach far beyond their original aims and their crusade was to be joined by the most unlikely allies, with results which must have astonished most of them.

I was to learn a great deal more about the Maltese language and, in the end, to read it and speak it, after a fashion (it is excruciatingly difficult to the English ear and tongue). It is probably the oldest language still spoken, in the world; but in those days I dismissed it as a hybrid patois of Italian and Arabic with an admixture of Teutonic words and constructions. I had never seen it written, and I easily fell into the trap of assuming that Italian was more widely spoken and read than was the fact. The street-names were Italian, as were public notices and traffic signs. Italian newspapers were more common than English ones, and you would often overhear groups of young students loudly massacring the *lingua di Dante*.

Nostalgically, I prefer Strada Reale—Strada Mezzodi—Molino a Vento—Strada Forni—to Kingsway—South Street—Wind-mill Street—Old Bakery Street, and the committee which Englished the street names can scarcely be forgiven for such monstrosities as 'Curate Don Bosco Street', 'Saint Lucy Street', and 'Alley No. 1'.

In those days of Strada Reale, an urban Maltese of any social pretension invariably wore a dark suit, a stiff collar, cravat, tie-pin, and black Trilby. On occasions of ceremony, be it winter or high, sizzling summer, he wore morning-coat and top-hat. At the Palace, Court dress—knee-breeches, silk stockings, and dress sword—was still worn and anyone, even an English Serviceman, wearing shorts in the street, would have been arrested as a dangerous lunatic.

Like all townsmen, the urban Maltese led a life of fixed routines, varied but slightly by the seasons. He was an early riser and went to Mass daily, never later than seven o'clock. Thence to his barber —he never shaved himself—and to his favourite café or the Club, for coffee. He would be in his office by eight o'clock and never ate breakfast. In the hotter months, work ended at two o'clock. Lunch was a heavy meal by Mediterranean standards, often of five or six courses, for the Maltese table is cosmopolitan. An Italian basic cuisine has had grafted upon it specimens of French, Spanish, English, German, Greek, Turkish, and Arabic dishes. The housewife vied with her friends in producing something strange and wonderful: a wave of refugees from Smyrna would produce a fashion for Greek sauces and Turkish sweetmeats. The Russian Revolution had popularized Georgian and Tartar dishes. That excellent generation of cooks who patiently mastered each fashionable recipe has, alas, departed. Roast beef and the tin-opener, deep freeze and patent breakfast foods have invaded those ancient kitchens.

After lunch, the siesta was the rule, in summer, and shops and offices were closed until the cool of the late afternoon. English five o'clock tea was a recent innovation and a good hostess invari-

ably offered coffee as an alternative. The menfolk rarely frequented
the tea- or coffee-parties which followed each other in a regular
rota of 'at home' days, when the important matters of clothes,
babies, and the sins of the male were thrashed out. Cocktail-
parties had not then become the universal menace which they
now are; but the ladies would sip sweet, sticky liqueurs and the
men, when they came to collect their womenfolk, would—alone
at that time amongst Mediterranean men, I think—drink a glass of
whisky.

Ladies did not smoke. The men smoked cigars or cheroots and
Turkish or Egyptian cigarettes. They shook hands whenever they
met, had they parted but an hour earlier. There was a whole
protocol about the manner of kissing a lady's hand: unmarried
woman, wife, widow, spinster of uncertain years, all qualified for
slight variations of the salute.

Men raised their hats and women bowed on passing an open
church door. Manners and mannerisms were universally Latin.
As in Rome, there were

> gestures reserved for emotional occasions . . . crouching, placing the
> fingers bent against the forehead and suddenly extending them, hitting the
> breast and flinging the arms wide, turning swiftly away as if parting for
> ever, but whipping round suddenly with a pointing finger, bunching the
> fingers in front of the mouth: and that very insulting one, I imagine, of
> shrinking the neck into the shoulders and shrugging with extended arms,
> slowly and despairingly, as if one were addressing a hopeless and incom-
> prehensible moron.[1]

A moustache was still the symbol of adult status and Maltese
Naval ratings were permitted, by special dispensation of the King's
Regulations, to wear moustaches. Only priests were clean-shaven.
A few monks wore beards.

Incomes and wages were appallingly low by English standards.
A permanent Civil Servant, the Head of a Government Department, received a salary little higher than that of an English
sergeant and the average pay-packet of the wage-earners did not
exceed thirty shillings per week. There were beggars in most
streets; but the universal habit of charity ensured, as the Chinese
put it, that 'no man's rice bowl was broken'.

The incidence of disease was high and mortality from quite
mild complaints was widespread. Families, in all classes, were
large and the infant mortality rate one of the highest in the

[1] H. V. Morton, *A Traveller in Rome.*

Empire. Hospitals, orphanages, homes for the aged and disabled, were maintained by the Church, as were all the social services which we have now come to regard as a State liability.

Englishmen were apt to point critically at the numbers of priests, monks, and nuns to be seen in the streets. Few of them understood that these people were the doctors, lawyers, nurses, welfare workers, teachers, and civil servants and the like, who operated a Welfare State based upon voluntary offerings and dedicated service. If all the operators of the National Health and Education Services and the multiplicity of State-aided organizations given over to 'welfare' in England, were to wear a recognizable uniform, we should get a rude shock. But the notion of the Welfare State was unknown to us, then, and we used to play a game called 'Priests'. Four of you sat in a *karozzin*, two on each side, and scored points for the numbers of priests and nuns you could identify on each side of the road. We were ignorant of such Popish distinctions as Secular, Regular, Dominican, Franciscan, Augustinian, or Lay Brother and we scored one for a Black Priest, two for a Brown Monk, three for a White Monk, and so on. The side which sighted its own ship's parson lost the game.

The score sometimes ran into treble figures, and I hope we may be forgiven for thinking Malta 'priest-ridden'.

And it seems to me that the Maltese were happier, then. The literate classes led a life bounded and circumscribed by convention and tradition; but there was dignity and grace, kindliness and a sense of responsibility towards the less fortunate. The poorer folk, too, had their traditions, their fair share of leisure, and their sense of solidarity and mutual loyalty with those whom they served.

Poverty, it is true, was the general lot; but if there were few vast fortunes there were few who were destitute. The strong sense of family and of filial duty extended beyond the limits of close relationship—an old servant, a nurse, even a familiar tradesman, would be provided for if he or she fell upon evil days—and in the poorer classes, the very size of the family and its widening ramifications acted as a kind of insurance. If only one son emigrated and made good, all were automatically the sharers of his good fortune.

Disease, death, misfortune were the will of God. There was no blaming others, no envy of the more fortunate or the more able and small wish to make comparisons with the English, whose way of life was not greatly admired or much approved.

What it is now fashionable to call the Privileged Classes lived in and about Valletta. Only the old Aragonese, Spanish, and Norman nobility still clung to their ancient fastness in the old capital of Città Vecchia (now known as 'Mdina—its older, vernacular name) where they maintained a fair semblance of the feudal state of their ancestors.

Those great, old, knightly houses of Valletta were not very comfortable. The rooms were vast and all communicated with each other. Cold in winter—few had fireplaces—and stifling in the summer, the hanging arras, the leather curtains, and the charcoal braziers for winter, the fan-bearing pages, the Sicilian ice for summer, which had made them tolerable for their seventeenth-century builders had long gone out of fashion. Yet they retained much of the structure and pattern of the *auberges* of the Knights of Malta. Their great studded doors, shutting out the busy squalor of the narrow streets, opened upon a patio in which a fountain played and the shadows of tall palms fretted the mosaic pavement. As if to emphasize the Saracenic image which the Knights seem so often and so perversely to have conjured up, there would be Negro pages, in painted plaster, to greet you as you entered. At this level were the servants' quarters, the kitchen, laundry, bake-house, storerooms, and wine-cellar.

The house ascended, then, to three or more floors, all built around the central court, with wide doorways and verandas facing inwards to the shade. Each floor was allocated to a generation. The youngest, to be seen rarely and then not heard, were relegated to some remote eyrie near the roof where they kept pets, or made pets of the domestic fowls and beasts destined for the table, who lived on the vast, flat roof.

The whole family gathered at lunch and, sometimes, at dinner. Otherwise they went their separate ways and the children spent much of their earlier years in the company of nurses and servants. Mamma was much too busy managing her barrack of a household and Pappa was a remote demigod whose presence too often betokened doom or crisis. It was a self-sufficient *ménage* and moments of crisis united the tribe solidly behind the injured or troubled member—be he or she no more important a unit than the youngest scullion. Generations of servants grew up in the same family, sharing its joys and its sorrows and being, in the end, pensioned off to die in comfort. They were housed and clothed and sometimes educated by the family. Their dowries were found when they married, sons were set up in business or helped to emigrate. It was a primitive, patriarchal set-up, yet more warm and human than anything which has replaced it.

In the summer, the great houses of Valletta were evacuated for a villa in the countryside, where it was cooler and the children could run wild for a little. Like the English, Edwardian trek to the sea, this annual migration was a great event. Since cars were rare (and the roads were, in any case, unsuitable for them) the whole household migrated in *karozzini* complete with such impedimenta as Mamma dictated.

These country villas were often true villas, in the Italian style, a family property surrounded by fields and vineyards with two or three farmhouses attached to them. Others were literally castles, bare and crumbling, but splendid places for a summer holiday. Yet others were mere converted watch-towers or abandoned farmhouses. No matter how primitive the country retreat, it was not socially possible for the *Senjuri* to remain in the 'town house' during summer, and the extent of northward migration was some measure of worldly success. England was the Ultima Thule of summer travel; but only the anglicized, and they were few, made a habit of it.

Indirectly, I suppose, this feudal, patriarchal economy of the established families was as dependent upon the Fleet, the Garrison, and British commerce as the livelihood of the Dockyard workpeople, and as precarious; but you could easily have mistaken it for a balanced, self-supporting economy as remote from the British connexion as that of any Greek island or Sicilian seaport. Rents were as low as wages. Taxation was negligible (except in certain notable directions such as Succession Duty, aimed at preventing the accumulation of too much by too few). Paradoxically, the cost of a high standard of living was low; but standards were very different from the English measure: life was simpler, more static, tastes in leisure preferred excellence in a few things to mediocrity in many.

A Maltese lady of the days of Strada Reale led a full life; but her interests were essentially domestic and feminine. She concentrated on being a woman and was largely protected against the pains and discomforts of trying to be an individual in a man's world. While she took quite seriously St. Paul's injunction to be

1. Grand Harbour: outer anchorage, 1937

2. Carnival

3. Stilt Man and Giants

4. St. John's Conventual Church and co-Cathedral, Valletta

5. Poultry Seller: nineteenth century

6. War Damage: the Opera House

7. Reconstruction: St. John's Square

'subject to her husband', she gained rather than lost in stature thereby and most Maltese families were, in practice, matriarchies.

Educated in an Italian or, sometimes, an English convent, she was chaperoned on all public occasions. She 'came out', in white gown and long white gloves, at a suitable Winter Ball at the Governor's Palace, usually when she was eighteen. She went to Rome and had an audience of the Holy Father, visited the Seven Churches, and joined the pilgrims at the *Scala Santa*. In the Maltese 'Season' she appeared with her parents at the opera. A glamorous occasion when Pappa wore tails and decorations and the boxes and the foyer were filled with the glittering regimentals and the gilded Naval uniforms of the Services. Those were expansive times. The Opera House (a victim of the blitz and not yet replaced) itself was not, admittedly, La Scala; but it attracted some of the best companies in Europe and a presentation of 'Aïda' to an audience splendid in blue and gold and red, beribboned and bejewelled like Habsburg courtiers, was an unforgettable experience.

Our young lady would leave her box, with Mamma or a married sister, at the intervals and make a dignified, shy tour of the foyer; tacit signal of her marriageable status and any male acquaintance amongst the bravely caparisoned young Englishmen would do well to approach with caution. More than one admirer would already have approached Pappa and attentions paid to her without that formal approach were little short of insulting.

Early marriage was the rule, usually within the family's own circle, to a young man whom she had known from childhood or, perhaps, a kinsman who had been her playmate. There were few difficult adjustments to be made, little change in the tempo of life, except the sudden freedom of a married woman, which must have contrasted sharply with the almost cloistered existence of the maid. These marriages were successful. Perhaps too placid, unexciting, sustained by mutual respect, duty, and affection rather than upon the stormier ocean of a great love; but they had ample compensations—a competence, a stable background, and a good home, children in plenty and few of the economic penalties nowadays imposed upon child-bearing.

She could bear her children in her own home, assured of every attention, and of the affection of a husband to whom no child was ever unwanted, knowing, too, that her children could grow up in an environment of loyalty and affection. Only a great love—or a foolish infatuation—would gladly cast all this away for the changes and chances of a foreign marriage to a Serviceman. Hence, as well as from parental prejudice, the comparative rarity of such marriages. Nevertheless, there were 'mixed' marriages. The Maltese nobility, in particular, seem to have been prone to dilute their Norman blood. There was considerable intermarriage, at all levels, with Italians, and something like eighty per cent of Maltese family-names are Italian, though this is no proof of Italian blood, since it was as fashionable, before the Second World War, to italianize a name as it has since become to anglicize it. Italian names themselves are misleading. The famous artists' models of the Piazza di Spagna in Rome came from the village of Saracinesco and had names like Almansorre—originally, *Al-Mansour*. Similarly the Maltese (and Sicilian) 'Scicluna' may have been *Sheikh-al-Ghaijun* and 'Salamone', *Suleiman*. Of recent years this latter would more likely become 'Sullivan'.

But marriage with an Italian, or, indeed, any other Latin, contained none of the seeds of misery which lay beneath the romantic façade of an alliance with an English Serviceman. It was well enough against the background of the shining brass and enamel of battleships, brave in the sunlight upon the deep blue waters of the Grand Harbour, of the glittering parade of nights at the opera and a girlish vision of a distant England full of fairy-tale castles and forests and green fields and fox-hunting; but the drab reality had to be faced and conquered.

Uprooted from her environment of routine and convention, amongst a warm-hearted and demonstrative people, the Maltese girl might find herself in furnished rooms in the drizzle of an English port, amongst a people reserved and suspicious of her foreign ways. Or in a country village, miles from a Catholic Church, stared at for her 'smart' clothes and vainly seeking a kindred soul. The novelty of green fields and the blackbird's song would soon wear thin. Only the mud and the seemingly incessant rain and the curious, hostile faces of the English, ostentatiously minding their own business, remained. Small wonder that so many of these marriages ended in disaster. If the English partner were Protestant, the disaster need not be final for him; but for his Catholic wife it was irreparable.

It was in these nineteen-twenties that the tide of Maltese

'Latinity' began to turn. Mussolini and the language question served to hasten a process which had been quietly at work from the beginning of the British occupation, and one of the by-products of the process was a notable increase in the number of Anglo-Maltese marriages. A generation which spoke Italian and thought as European continentals, had children who spoke English and thought as Anglo-Saxons.

It ceased to be fashionable to insist on chaperones. Some bold young women even appeared in Church in coloured head-scarves and short-sleeved frocks. Ladies of fashion gave up the *faldetta* and wore hats. Young men paid court to their *namrati* without parental blessing and girls in their teens began to demand latch-keys. Cheap Virginian cigarettes replaced cheroots. The game of *morra*—the Roman *micare digitalis* of which the English 'match game' is a version—ceased to be the universal pastime for an idle moment. The younger generation did not shake hands so frequently, and males no longer raised their hats as they passed church doors. The English virus which seemed, for more than a century, to have made little headway suddenly began to spread. Reaction against Fascist Italy was the chief cause. As long as the English affection for nineteenth-century Italy—Rome—Florence—Naples—cradle of European culture—home of artists, musicians, Garibaldi, and happy peasants strumming guitars, survived, there was no call for the Maltese to question his Latin affinities.[1]

But Fascist propaganda was loud and fierce. Some Maltese fell for it; but the majority opted for England and the protagonists of Italian culture found themselves—unjustly it seems to me—tarred with the brush of treason.

The young men of the privileged classes were educated, for the most part, by local Jesuits, Augustinians, or Dominicans. There

[1] 'Italianity' was more than a passing phase or the fad of an eccentric minority, and there had been an 'Italian Question' for many years.

From the eighteen-twenties onwards the *Carbonari* and the Grand Orient Freemasons, with whom Garibaldi's movement was so unhappily associated, began to export political *emigrés*, many of whom fled to the shelter of British Malta, counting on English sympathy for any enemy of the Scarlet Woman.

Governor More O'Ferral was, however, a Catholic and little disposed to underwrite a colony of anti-Catholic and anti-Monarchist revolutionaries. He was unpopular with the Home Government as well as with some of his local Council of Government when he insisted on repatriating the *Carbonari*.

Garibaldi himself visited Malta and addressed a crowd from the balcony of a house in Strada Santa Lucia. He was howled down; but succeeded in recruiting a handful of 'Freedom Fighters'. Amongst them was a kinsman of my wife, one Colonel Giuseppe Camenzuli who fought with Garibaldi to the end and enjoys a hero's tomb in Messina.

was then no local English public school like St. Edward's (founded by Lady Strickland) and the already anglicized families sent their sons to English Catholic public schools—Stonyhurst, Beaumont, Downside, Ampleforth, Douai, and Fort Augustus. Some went on to the Royal University of Malta—founded in 1769 by the Grand Master Pinto—and some to the older English universities. They enjoyed, of course, far more freedom than their sisters, and were a good deal more mature for their years than their English contemporaries.

As a university student, the boy sowed his wild oats as circumspectly as possible, for he lived in a close-knit community where news travelled fast. Escape from the Island and from the critical eyes and ears of Mammas—to Rome, Sicily, Tunis, or further afield—was his ambition.

Opportunity was limited for a young man of education. If he did not emigrate he had a choice of the family business—the Royal Malta Artillery—the Church—Law—Medicine—the Civil Service, and little else; and for a hundred candidates there would be one vacancy. Though he might wish to emigrate, the strong tie of the family held him. An eldest son, inevitably, felt a duty to step into his father's shoes as protector and manager of the family affairs.

While the Malta University had a standard and a reputation second to none in the humanities, any sort of scientific or engineering training was in those days almost impossible to come by. Even now, a Maltese boy who wishes to qualify as an accountant must travel to England for each of the several examinations which are necessary to reach a recognized status. And in the twenties, a science or an engineering degree was suspect. The one was vaguely pagan and the other not quite gentlemanly. One advantage, however, was enjoyed by any Maltese who emigrated. They are all natural linguists and, although the illiterate massacre every language including their own, a boy of education would have fluent Italian, French, English, and make shift in several Arabic dialects.

There was, of course, a tragic waste of potential. It was too easy for a boy with Beaumont, an honours degree, and a Blue behind him (my penniless Baron friend had been one of these) to sink back into the rut of sunshine and security, of family duty, the Casino, boyhood friends, and complacent tradespeople. Thinking himself above politics or commerce, he might soon deteriorate into a gigolo or a high-grade beachcomber.

Yet many of these boys succeeded in casting off the shackles of environment and achieved honour and success in straight competition with men of many nations. A Maltese officer was amongst the last men off the beach at Dunkirk[1] and another died in the advance into Belgium.[2] Yet another commanded all the Native troops in Malaya. A Maltese was head of the Medical Services of the United Nations and another of its Legal Branch. Two permanent Secretaries in the Italian Civil Service are of Maltese birth. A standard authority on Maritime International Law is a Maltese lawyer. Artists, sculptors, musicians, and film stars may be added to the tale of local boys who have made good. In religion, not unnaturally a favourite national *métier*, the tale of distinguished bishops, abbots, and *monsignori* is long, as is the list of internationally famous historians and archaeologists.[3]

It is more surprising that Malta—with a quarter of a million souls of whom sixty per cent were quite illiterate—should have produced so notable a crop of successful men when one reflects that patronage was long the accepted door to any career.

The tradition that all advancement stemmed from the Grand Master via some influential Bailiff Grand Cross, the Grand Prior, or some feudal overlord, had survived—I daresay, been gladly inherited—well into the British era. Access to the Governor and his immediate entourage and thence, down the scale, to any officer or petty official with influence to wield had long been accepted as the normal method of achieving a desired post,

[1] Captain Arrigo of the Durham Light Infantry.

[2] Major Denaro of the Leicestershire Regiment. These officers were cousins and came of a group of families with a noteworthy military tradition, many of whose members were decorated for gallantry in one or both of Britain's two world wars.

[3] The fulsome praise lavished upon the people of Malta for their heroism during the Siege of the Second World War has had unhappy consequences. Within a year of the award of the George Cross to the people, a whispering campaign was current, suggesting that the people hadn't really been heroic at all and disgruntled and disappointed Maltese were murmuring that 'you couldn't eat the George Cross'. English Press propaganda served, too, to divert attention from the war effort of the Maltese elsewhere: from the hundreds of Maltese Merchant Seamen whose names embellish the Merchant Navy memorial on Tower Hill and in all the seaports of Great Britain: from the Maltese Naval ratings who perished in the 'little ships' off Crete: from the Maltese officers who rallied the forces of the Italian Partisans and the Maltese priests (who must remain nameless) who worked in the anti-Fascist, Italian Resistance. A Maltese lady, too, the wife of a Vichy Frenchman, was a key figure in the North African Resistance. She was Madame de Caumont (*née* Zammit-Cutajar) and the French gave her the Cross of the Legion of Honour. The British gave her an M.B.E.

appointment, scholarship, or preferment. The Maltese attachment
to patronage should not shock us, for we have not eradicated it
completely from our own system where the 'Old Boy Frequency'
is still powerful.

The lives of the poorer sort of Maltese fitted into the same,
general, conventional pattern as that of the literate classes. They
were bound by the same strong sense of family. The mother was
almost always the matriarch, father the remote figurehead. They
had, in a sense, more freedom because their lives were not so
strictly bound by social taboos. For this reason they reacted more
rapidly to foreign influences 'and since the labouring and artisan
classes were brought into closer contact with those influences
they were ready prey to every new idea. Their living conditions
were bad, though considerably better than those of the comparable Italian, and few of them could read or write (the public
letter-writer was still a familiar figure in the nineteen-thirties).
Opportunities for technical training existed only in the Royal
Dockyard and were strictly limited. The majority, when it came
to emigration, had to be classified as unskilled.

As everywhere, the best stock were the peasant farmers and it is
they who have tended to emigrate most.

The townsman who spoke some English had probably travelled
abroad and had had some contact with foreigners, was less anxious
to leave his beloved Island than the peasant who might never have
travelled beyond the next village. And it was not always poverty ·
which drove the peasant overseas, for he often had more real
wealth than his landlord. I suppose that the unskilled townsman,
when he did emigrate, more often found life harder and the
scramble more competitive and returned, disappointed, to advise
his friends and relatives to stay where they were. The peasant
went to the sugar plantations of Queensland, the coffee lands of
Brazil, or the wheat lands of Canada and applied his tough, patient
temperament to amassing a fair capital with which he bought land
and prospered. He would return to the village of his birth, dis-
pensing largesse and tales of the new lands where every man was
his own landlord, and take a wife back with him. In due course,
their relatives followed.

From the Australian and Canadian point of view they were not
ideal settlers. They did not assimilate and they remitted money
out of the country by one means or another.

There was, in 1945, a village not ten miles from the centre of Sydney which might have been picked up bodily from some remote corner of the Maltese Islands and planted in New South Wales. The sight of a barefooted Maltese peasant woman, wearing an *ghonella* gave me a pleasant start; but I was aware that she was not the Australian's notion of the best sort of potential 'Digger'.

The whole life of the Maltese centred and to a somewhat less extent still centres, on the Church.

Crops were planted, rents were paid, it would rain, be overcast, blow, people were born, married, died not by dates and months but on the Feast of St. Martin, at Santa Maria, Santa Barbara, St. John's Eve, Pentecost, The Ascension. The whole cycle of living followed the Church's calendar as it did in the England before Elizabeth which has left us such vestiges as Lady Day, St. Swithin, and Michaelmas.

Public holidays were still Holy Days—the nine Holy Days upon which Catholics are under spiritual obligation to hear Mass as well as on the Sabbath. Towns and villages enjoying the patronage of a major Saint or dedicated to a major Feast of the Church were less fortunate in this respect than those under the tutelage of a less famous personality, for, by tradition, everyone earned the holiday of his local village as well as the main national feasts.

As well as the prescribed religious exercises, the *Festas* were enlivened by fireworks, processions, football matches and peculiar toys and sweetmeats. The manufacture of fireworks was a considerable cottage industry, and many country houses possessed stout stone structures in their grounds where the local expert vied with his neighbours in producing the most eccentric, colourful and—sad to relate—loudest, pyrotechnics. Fatal casualties were common (and are not unknown today). A blackened ruin and some shreds of cloth was often pointed out as the memorial to Grandfather—a noted firework manufacturer!

The Church and its fasts and festivals, its careful fabric of duties and pleasures filled the place of book-learning, cinemas, television, the theatre—and the people were content that it should be so.

Superficially, Malta in the twenties presented a picture of a feudal, Latin upper class, entrenched within a medieval, theocratic society, maintaining a gracious and cultured way of life at the expense of an under-privileged, illiterate, and superstitious lower class, living on the fringe of absolute poverty.

In so far as this was a true picture, the British accepted and acquiesced in it, content only to interfere if the security of the fortress seemed threatened. Once or twice, clumsy and ill-judged attempts were made to subvert the Maltese from their Catholic loyalty; but at no time had the English repeated the French error of violent and official anti-clericalism—a fortunate error, as it transpired, for the English. If they interfered at all in local matters outside the immediate needs of the Imperial interest, the British invariably did so on the side of the established order. Under a Crown Colony system they could do little else without risking accusations that they were handling a civilized, European community as if they were backward savages.

But the picture of a feudal society—an anachronism and a fossil —which had survived because it had escaped Reformation, Counter-Reformation, and Industrial Revolution was incomplete. Far from being a people held in subjection by an oligarchy in the pay of foreign overlords, the Maltese of all classes had a long tradition of united revolt against any attack, or imagined attack, upon their ancient rights and privileges.

Their bishops and priests had led them repeatedly in peaceful protests and more than once in armed insurrection: and not only when the Church herself seemed threatened. Democracy, freedom, equality of opportunity, were not new thoughts to the Maltese, to be imported with the British Parliamentary system.

They had elected their leaders under the Carthaginians and the Romans. They had rebelled against an Arab tyrant and expelled him. They had unseated Grand Masters and starved a French garrison into submission.

The feudal structure of Maltese society was a deliberate choice, evolved through centuries of domination by alien Powers. The close-knit structure of Church, Barons, people, had been found the most effective defence against alien exploitation and the most effective method of ensuring that the voice of a numerically insignificant people could be heard in the councils of the nations.

Malta's geographical location and the configuration of her coastline, furnishing excellent anchorages at the centre of the civilized world and astride the main trade routes was bound to lend her an importance quite disproportionate to her area or her meagre resources; but it had always been the clannish, close-knit sense of community which ensured that the people enjoyed their fair share of the 'rent' which great Powers were willing to pay for exploiting the Islands' geography.

If a venal Carthaginian government imposed a crippling tax on sail-cloth, the Maltese called in the Romans. If a corrupt Roman Governor squeezed the people too far, they appealed to Caesar, and an advocate of the calibre of Cicero could be found to plead the Maltese case. They called in the Normans to expel an oppressive Arab Caid, and the French to destroy the aristocratic Republic of the Sovereign Order. Disappointed by the failure of French promises, the *Giurati*—direct descendants of the Elected Council which had called in the Romans—were able to persuade a reluctant England to accept Malta as a fief of the British Crown.

I do not know the genesis of the curious constitution which created a dyarchy—two governments within an island of one hundred square miles in area—but the idea was in essence little more than a recognition of the immemorial structure of the Maltese community. It did one important and new thing, however. By abolishing the Senate, it effectually excluded a large part of the priestly and baronial caste. Too proud to engage in the ungentlemanly game of party politics, these traditional leaders of the people retired to sulk in their tents and have been largely replaced by a new caste of English-instructed demagogue. The emergence of the new leaders is the result of that sudden acceleration of English influence which commenced with the reaction against Italian Fascism and received a tremendous boost from the universally closer contact with English, Commonwealth, and American ideas during the Second World War. The immediate result has been something very like a class war, accompanied by the bitter internal stresses which are inevitable if a largely feudal pattern is to remould itself overnight into a modern, classless society.

One Maltese landowner of my acquaintance—a classical scholar like many of his generation—is fond of quoting Isocrates who wrote, some four hundred years before Christ:

> When I was a boy it was considered not only safe but honourable to create an estate, so that almost all men of worth wished to add to their possessions and felt a certain dignified honour in prospering, but now we must apologize for any success in business as if it were an utter violation of the moral law so that today it is worse to seem to prosper than to be an open criminal.

It is fruitless to offer him the obvious comfort that 'there is no new thing under the sun'. He and his kind are convinced that blindness and economic inertia have already pushed Malta too far towards a poor copy of the Welfare State and that nothing but disaster can result.

But the stubborn islanders' sense of clan loyalty persists and in moments of danger or threat to national survival, prelate and peasant, reactionary landowner and Trades Union artisan are miraculously united.

I believe and hope that this unity will survive.

Of course, Malta in the nineteen-twenties was not some sort of survival of a medieval Golden Age—a feudal Utopia in which all was contentment and sunlight.

There was poverty, disease, child-labour, illiteracy, and ignorance. There was a constant shortage of water. Agricultural methods were cruelly inefficient and the poor, meagre soil was dying of over-cultivation. Native art and music were frozen in an Italianate Renaissance mould. Literature was almost devoid of genius, imagination, or originality. Directly or indirectly the mass of the people were absolutely dependent upon the unforeseeable movements of the British Fleet.

But there were compensations. Poverty and disease were palliated by a wide, human charity. Illiteracy protected the people from the evils of irresponsible print and ignorance was not infrequently bliss. The almost complete absence of drunkenness and the high standard of marital fidelity—enforced with an iron hand by Mother Church—eased the burden of want and sorrow. The art and music and literature of the people was in their ancient folklore and in the ritual and ceremonies of their Church. They had Faith, too, in abundance.

II

LEISURE

LEISURE

'Avoid the coffee shops, for in so doing you will avoid the opportunity of both hearing and speaking evil of others. . . . By this I do not mean to say that you should play the Savage and eschew all company. There are many ways of avoiding this and of escaping from the Idleness of the Island, which is very great. The practising of some instrument of music, the study of Books and of Navigation . . . will keep you not to be a friend of Idleness. . . .'

(Marchese Camillo Spreti (1764).
The Manuscript of a Knight of Malta
by Averill Mackenzie-Grieve)

FOR years, Maltese governments, in a laudable search for sources of income other than the Armed Forces, have sought to develop the tourist industry. Their success has been small, for reasons which will appear, and whether any lasting benefits can be expected from highly organized tourism may be doubted.

Tourists, visitors, travellers, expatriates, call them what you will, are as various as humanity itself and usually very nice people; but there is a particular kind—often of Nordic origin—less likeable than most—clothed in unsuitable garments and burned by the unfamiliar sun to the semblance of boiled lobster, avidly photographing the most unlikely objects and secretly wishing themselves comfortably at home in Manchester, Chicago, or Essen; they do not add greatly to the local revenue and carry away highly superficial and garbled impressions. Malta has been fortunate, perhaps, in escaping this sort of tourist. In their stead, she has suffered the temporary expatriates of Garrison Society. Of these, an Englishman masquerading under the of name 'John Wignacourt'[1] has written 'We may be an insular people but the garrison insularity is a caricature'.

Malta's peculiar character as a British fortress and dockyard base has confined the enjoyment of its attractions largely to people

---

[1] *The Odd Man in Malta.*

27

of a highly specialized kind—compulsory rather than voluntary visitors—and it is upon their reports that Malta's reputation has largely had to depend. These people are in the Island because they must be, or, in the case of the females, persuade themselves that they must be, and their interests are limited. Unlike the tourist who is paying for his holiday, they are not resolved to 'enjoy themselves whether they like it or not'.

In the wake of the Garrison community, have come some few visitors of other kinds—friends and relations, amongst whom have been artists and writers, archaeologists and historians; but, in the main, the Garrison has constituted the sum total of Malta's tourists. There has thus been little demand for the public amenities commonly expected by holiday-makers and little choice of interests. Entrée to Service circles has usually been sufficient to ensure an enjoyable time—if somewhat stereotyped and completely lacking in any real contact with the country or its people.

When I was a young officer, we had a popular Gunroom ditty, describing the shoreside existence of the English community in Malta. The printable part of the refrain went:

'Balls, Picnics, and Parties
Picnics, Parties, and Balls'

—and it was a fair description of an aimless but pleasant enough society. Since those days there has been the quiet revolution of the Welfare State and the composition of overseas garrisons has changed sufficiently to evoke Noël Coward's astringent comment (on Singapore) that it '. . . accounts for the disappearance of domestic servants from England'; but the change is superficial. The tempo of existence and the circumscription of interest are little changed.

If, like me, you wish sometimes to escape from the bands of sun-burned Nordic pilgrims or from the vortex of Balls, Picnics, and Parties, there are many things which you may do or see in Malta to 'keep you not to be a friend of Idleness'.

First on the list of places to see I would put St. John's Conventual Church and Co-Cathedral in Valletta.

The main fabric of the church was completed in 1577, under the direction and at the personal expense of the Auvergnois Grand Master La Cassière, as the Mother Church of the Convent and the

Order of Malta, to crown the Grand Master La Vallette's City of Palaces—'*Humilissima Civitas Vallettae*', in its time the least humble of any city of Christendom.

The city and its environs are the work of such immortals as Valperga, Firenzuola, Floriani, Grunemberg, De Mondion, and Tigné; but the original plans were those of Francesco Laparelli, Engineer to Pope Pius V, who flourished from 1521 to 1570, and St. John's is the masterpiece of the Maltese Gerolamo Cassar, student of Michelangelo. His Florentine, mannerist style and his debt to Michelangelo are evident. St. John's is not dissimilar from the Vignola's Church of Gesú, in Rome; an origin shared by another of Cassar's creations in Malta, the Church of St. Augustine at Rabat.

St. John's has been called a 'keep'—not an inapposite term for the stern, Counter-Reformation, military exterior which houses such a riot of beauty and wherein despite a century and a half of spoliation, neglect, and bombardment, so many treasures remain.

The ceiling by Mattia Preti has been called by Sir Osbert Sitwell '. . . one of the finest decorative exploits of Baroque painting'.[1] There are paintings, too, by Caravaggio,[2] Favray, Potenzano, d'Alesio, sculpture by Mazzuoli, silver by Bernini, alabaster by Puget. The visitor cannot hope to do justice to this treasure-house in a day, or a week. If you are here in May or June—months of the Feasts of Pentecost, Corpus Domini, St. Peter and St. Paul, and

---

[1] *Sing High! Sing Low!* 1944.
[2] The famous 'Beheading of St. John' (according to Berenson, one of the finest examples of Caravaggio's work) which had hung in the church for three hundred years was carried, by the Royal Navy, to Italy in 1956 for restoration. I saw it at the *Seicento* Exhibition in Rome, early in 1957, and was disappointed—to my amateur eye the unrestored work was preferable. On its return to Malta it was placed by the Civil Government in their new National Museum in the Auberge de Provence (until lately the British Union Club). The ecclesiastical authorities protested hotly at this —to them—near-sacrilege and the matter was submitted to the Vatican. The case for the Government was that all property of the Sovereign Order, including their churches, passed at the Treaty of Paris to the people of Malta, and hence it is the Civil Government and not the Church who is responsible for the maintenance of such property. The Church, it is argued, is unable to maintain all the national treasures of which it is custodian and, in any case, the conditions in St. John's were harmful to fine old paintings. For the Church, the arguments were less complex—it was a clear case of the seizure of an historic object of devotion and its removal from the site for which it was created. The dispute was finally submitted to the Vatican, who (after a pregnant pause) ordered the return of the masterpiece to the Church and, at a moment which seemed politic to a government which needed all the support it could rally, it was returned. Of such stuff are the sad squabbles of modern Malta.

the Patron St. John—you will see displayed the finest Flemish tapestries that ever came from the loom of Judecos de Vos, after designs by Rubens, Poussin, and Preti, made to the order of the Grand Master Perellos between the years 1697 and 1705.

All this magnificence was not, of course, foreseen by Cassar, though the Grand Master La Cassière doubtless understood where his plan to allocate a chapel to each of the national Langues of the Order would lead. For two hundred years some of the richest and most powerful houses in Europe vied with each other to embellish the Conventual Church of their international brotherhood—a rivalry, it may be agreed, preferable to the avaricious squabbles which were engaging their monarchs.

The chapels on the Gospel side of the Church, facing the High Altar, are those of Germany, Italy, France, Provence, and the Anglo-Bavarian Langue. On the Epistle side, they are those of Leon and Castille, Aragon, Auvergne and of Our Lady of Philermos. Curiously, the only serious damage sustained during two years of almost uninterrupted aerial bombardment by the Italians and Germans in the Second World War was to the two Chapels of Italy and Germany.

The 'odd' Chapel is dedicated to Our Lady of Philermos, whose Ikon had been in the possession of the Order from its earliest times, and for which the Grand Masters and the Knights had a deep devotion. The Ikon itself, reputed to be a contemporary portrait of Our Lady, had been embellished over the centuries with gold and precious stones of immense value. These, together with much other treasure, were impounded by Napoleon; but the Grand Master Von Hompesch—last of the Order's rulers in Malta—was permitted to carry away the Ikon, together with the Hand of St. John. These he sent to the Russian Court where a minority of his Knights took refuge after their expulsion. To the Czar Paul and his successors, the miraculous Ikon became something of a symbol of the regenerated Christendom which they hoped to lead and they, in their turn, re-embellished it even more richly than had the Knights. It became an object of veneration in the Imperial family and, on the fall of the Romanoffs, was taken, with the Hand of St. John, to the Court of Yugoslavia. Rumour has it that they remain intact in the hands of the Yugoslav Communists. Malta, or the Order, may yet recover these historic treasures.

Here, beneath the mosaic pavement, rich with the armorial bearings of the flower of chivalry, rest some four hundred Knights and twenty-six Grand Masters:

> not all of these men were perfect in their lives; many were saintly and some bad; but they have a lesson to teach us. Whether as fallible humans, they failed or succeeded is not for us to judge; it remains that they tried to live by standards which many of us would find impossible and that their main quest was the conquest of Self, which is the only certain salvation for the world which they bequeathed to us. May they rest in peace.[1]

Amongst the treasures of St. John's whose significance is historic or religious, rather than intrinsic, is a bronze crucifix which travelled with the Knights from Jerusalem, to St. Jean d'Acre, to Cyprus, to Rhodes, and thence to Malta. The Archives record that it was anciently believed to have been made from the bronze of the basin in which Our Blessed Lord washed the feet of the Apostles.

There is, too, a wooden image of the Baptist which customarily stood on the poop of the *Capitana*—the flagship of the Order's galley Fleet.

The church is peculiarly rich in sacred relics, some, like many such objects of devotion, of doubtful authenticity and confused history, but most of complete authenticity and thoroughly documented.

Each of the Chapels at one time possessed some relic of its Patron, and it will be noted that the Saints for whom the various nationalities had, in the Middle Ages, a special devotion are not always those who have since grown familiar to us as national symbols.

St. James, for Leon and Castille, is long established. The Epiphany is unfamiliar for Germany. St. George, about whose association with England there has long been doubt ('St. George's Cross' is, in fact, the badge of the Knights Templar) was the patron of Aragon, Catalonia, and Navarre. St. Catharine for Italy is not the modern custom and St. Paul for France, St. Sebastian for Auvergne, St. Michael for Provence all have an unusual ring in modern ears.

Since the Reformation preceded the completion of St. John's and the English Langue was already nearing dissolution when the Order arrived in Malta, there was never an English Chapel and

---

[1] Sir Hannibal Scicluna, Kt., K.G.C.M., *The Church of St. John in Valletta.*

the Chapel of the reconstituted Anglo-Bavarian Langue, of 1781,
has St. Charles Borromeo for Patron.

All the relics were furnished with reliquaries and ostensories of
gold, silver, and precious stones. Few survived the depredations
of Napoleon and many are known to lie in the shifting sandbanks
of Aboukir Bay, in the hold of the French flagship *L'Orient*, sent
to the bottom by Nelson. On several occasions, projects have
been formed to salvage *L'Orient*—a truly rich prize, if modern
salvage methods can ever reach her.[1]

But many precious things did escape through the astuteness of
the Grand Prior—it is not true that the silver gates of the Chapel
of the Blessed Sacrament escaped by being painted black!—and
amongst them is the ostensory by Bernini, made for the right hand
of St. John the Baptist. It is of one hundred and fifty-two pounds
weight in solid silver, and one of Bernini's loveliest creations. A
gold reliquary, studded with precious stones, made for the same
hand, is probably in *L'Orient*. Tradition has it that Napoleon also
collected a ring from the Holy Hand which he placed on his own
finger, remarking that 'it looked better there'.

The Hand has a curious history.

When Constantinople fell to the Turks in 1453, a mass of
Christian treasure was seized by the Sultan. Western Christendom
—thinking their fellow-Christians of the Eastern Schism worse
pagans than the Muslim Turks—for a time made common cause
against the Byzantines and one result of this unholy alliance was a
friendship between the Sultan Bajazet and the Grand Master
d'Aubusson.

Bajazet presented d'Aubusson with the Holy Hand, as well as
with the gold Patriarchal Cross, containing fragments of the True
Cross, revealed to the English St. Helena, mother of the Emperor
Constantine, which is still in St. John's.

The Hand travelled with Von Hompesch to the court of the
Romanoffs and thence, like the Ikon of Our Lady of Philermos,
to the keeping of the Yugoslav Karageorgevich. It is believed by
some to remain in Belgrade and by others to have been returned to
the Patriarchate of Constantinople whence it was taken by Bajazet.

Less thoroughly authenticated—at least as to the identity of the
two martyrs—are the bodies of two Saints Clement.

---

[1] This may be optimistic. Recent research suggests that little of the treasure
remained in *L'Orient*.

One arrived in the Island in 1669, the gift of the Knight Rospigliosi, nephew of Pope Clement IX, and reposes within the altar of the Chapel of St. Charles of the Anglo-Bavarian Langue.

The second was presented to the Grand Master Pinto by Pope Benedict XIV in 1747. Both were received with Royal honours. One—it now seems impossible to say which—is probably the body of St. Clement, Pope and Martyr, third successor of St. Peter and author of the 'Epistle to the Church of Corinth', sometimes attributed to St. Paul.

It was a typically British compromise—the originator was one of Nelson's captains, Alexander Ball, first British Governor (or Commissioner, as he was called)—that the canopied throne of the Grand Master, on the Gospel side of the High Altar, should be emblazoned with the Royal Arms of England to be used on State occasions by the Monarch. And from this seat of honour the proclaimed head of two Protestant Churches may courteously follow the liturgy of Popery.

It seems strange to us, now, that Ball's successor, Sir Thomas Maitland, an oligarch, but a very sound one, who was nicknamed 'King Tom', had some difficulty in persuading the Home Government not to take over St. John's, lock, stock, and barrel, and convert it into a Protestant Cathedral.

Opposite the throne of the Grand Masters, now stands that of the Metropolitan Archbishop—a dignity refused by those Princes even to the Grand Prior of the Convent in his own church, and one which would certainly never have been awarded to the Bishop of Malta whose palace in Valletta was erected, in 1622, against fierce opposition from the Knights. The Grand Master Vasconcellos was, however, over eighty and little disposed to end his days quarrelling with his brother-prelate.

That the Bishops of Malta did have some influence upon the Order may be deduced from the nameless, soft stone tablet which is the only memorial in the crypt of St. John's of the Grand Master Ximenes de Texada—a tyrant for whom the Maltese had no love and whose leading opponent was the Bishop Pellerano.

In the crypt lie those two great leaders to whom all Europe owes so much, L'Isle Adam and La Vallette. Close to his beloved master lies the English Secretary of La Vallette, Oliver Starkey.

St. John's is a kind of tourist's short-cut to Malta. When you have explored it thoroughly you will be better informed than most about the Island's history and about the Sovereign Order, which is and was the greatest single influence on its culture; but there is much else that you should explore in and about Valletta and the Grand Harbour.

Of the splendid buildings which were the Auberges, or Inns, of the Knights and the Palaces of Grand Crosses and Commandeurs, many were lost in the blitz of the Second World War. Notably the Auberges of the Langues of Auvergne and France and whole blocks of such lovely Renaissance buildings as that called 'De Mandolx' at the corner of Strada Forni and Strada Mezzodi (Old Bakery and South Streets).

De Mandolx was one of the Commandeurs who, on attaining the dignity and control of the revenues of a Commandery, were expected to maintain separate establishments and to cease, as we might put it, to be 'victualled in the Wardroom'. These Commanderies were immensely rich properties—quasi-independent enclaves in every country in Europe—which linked the Order with the feudal nobility, and the splendour of some of the Palaces of the Commandeurs was in keeping. Many survive, under a number of disguises, and their names are familiar landmarks: Carafa, Parisio, De La Salle, Verdelin, Bichi (the Royal Naval Hospital now known, due to an English misprint which has been established by usage, as 'Bighi'), Spinola, Vilhena, Cotoner, Scaglia, are some of the better known.

There was never an English Auberge; but a house, still standing at 174, Strada Cristoforo (St. Christopher Street), once the palace of the Englishman Sir James Shelley, was willed by him to be used by the re-established Langue of England, 'When . . .' as was and is the pious hope of so many of his compatriots, 'England should return to the Faith.'

The Auberge of the Anglo-Bavarian Langue which also survives was the Palace of Fra Gaspard Carneiro, Bailiff of Acre, who built it in 1696.

The Auberges of Provence, Italy, Aragon, Castille and Leon also survive. The Auberge of Germany was demolished, with some slight claim of right we must suppose, in 1837 to make way for the Protestant Church of St. Paul, the gift of the Lutheran Queen Adelaide. It is a magnificent building; but quite out of character.

Every building in Valletta was some part of the 'Convent' of

the Sovereign Order; an Inn of the young Knights, a private
Palace, a Treasury, Law Court, Council Chamber, or Church. At
the heart of this fortified monastery and behind the Conventual
Church was the Palace of the Grand Masters, still the official seat
of Government and one of the three official residences of the
British Governor.

In it is a splendid armoury where, despite the thefts of Napoleon
and some other less notable collectors, there are many unique
pieces in an excellent state of preservation. In what was the
Chapter Hall of the Grand Masters and is now called the Hall of
St. Michael and St. George,[1] are the world-famous frescoes of
Matteo Perez d'Alesio, dating from 1601, which have recently been
carefully and expertly restored.

The great State Balls of more spacious days are now infrequent;
but you may be fortunate to attend a Ball given on the occasion
of a Royal visit or for some notable charity, in these inimitable
surroundings where the brilliance of blue and gold, scarlet and
green uniforms, an occasional kilt and the flash of orders and
decorations will recapture for a moment the splendours of vanish-
ing Empire. Here, too, your interest may be caught by the courtly
figures of the Maltese gentry of the Old Guard, resplendent with
the enamelled crosses of the Holy Roman Empire, the Order of
Malta, St. Gregory, and the Holy Sepulchre: their ladies a little
too *soignée* for this careless age and a little too heavily bejewelled
for modern taste; but the jewels are not paste and these people
have known the Palace from childhood, watched Kings, Pre-
sidents, Governors, and Ministers come and go. The Palace is
really theirs. They have 'seen new-rich Empires rise and fall . . .
with Socrates for ancestor and rich Byzantium in their veins. . . .'
You may dismiss them as survivors of a decadent age:

> . . . and yet the triumph of decay
> Outbraves the pride of bouncing fools
> As an old craftsman smiles to hear
> His name respected in the schools
> And sees the rust upon his tools.

[1] The Chapter Hall of the Grand Masters became the 'Hall of St. Michael and St.
George' in 1818, with the institution by Great Britain of the Order of chivalry of that
name. The Order was instituted primarily to honour Crown servants of Britain's new
suzerainty of Malta and the Ionian Islands where, in the words of Sir Thomas
Maitland '. . . only those who are loyal to the British connexion go undecorated'.
The awards of decorations of that Order have since deviated widely from that
purpose.

Nowhere, I think, outside Rome or London in this modern world is there a place like Malta for the living pageantry which brings close home to the ordinary man the changes and chances of history. You will see these same proud, musing, dark-eyed heirs of Greece and Rome at the great ceremonies in the Co-Cathedral (as St. John's Church now is), seated in the stalls of the Sovereign Order while the British Governor, who may be an Orangeman, occupies a dais below the throne of the Grand Master and the Blessed Adrian Fortescue, martyred by an English Queen, gazes curiously down from Preti's frescoes.

Most notable of the surviving Auberges is that of Castille and Leon. It was damaged by bombs, but has been carefully restored and is now the headquarters of the Royal Malta Artillery, the only Maltese regular unit of the British Army, proud of its descent from the Irregulars, the *Cacciatori*, who expelled Napoleon's garrison, and of its battle honours which include Capri, Egypt, and the Battle of Africa.

Another very fine and still unspoiled Auberge is that of Provence. For many years it was the home of the English Union Club; but changing habits, a shift in the centres of population, and of the shape of the Fleet made this similacrum of a London club no longer a paying concern. The Services made a show of resistance to Civil Government pressure for its return, but were, I suspect, somewhat relieved to have the decision to evacuate in favour of the more modern site in the suburb of Sliema, forced upon them. It is now the National Museum, its predecessor having been largely reduced to rubble, though the greater part of the priceless collections which it housed was saved by the devotion of that great patriot Sir Hannibal Scicluna. Malta is particularly rich in the remnants of a unique Neolithic culture and the Museum's treasures of this sort are fascinating.

The Royal Malta Library, originally the Library and Record Office of the Knights, founded by the Bailiff de Tencin in 1760, is yet another treasure-house in Valletta. It houses manuscripts and documents which cannot fail to delight amateur and expert alike. Much of the Archives of the Sovereign Order has been preserved intact, together with thousands of manuscripts of an awesome antiquity and importance. Research students come from every part of the world to burrow in these records and yet fresh discoveries continue to come to light. The show-pieces include a Bull of Pope

Paschal II of the year 1113, letters of Henry VIII, of James Stuart, Charles II, George II, George III, Catherine of Russia, together with the original Act of Donation of the Emperor Charles V and his mother, Joanna of Sicily. It is, however, amongst the less spectacular documents—plans for fortifications, journals, account books, shipping records, regulations for the conduct of fighting ships, penal codes—that the student comes upon treasure trove.

A late Librarian of the Royal Library, Dom Maurus Inguanez, a Benedictine from Monte Cassino and kinsman of the oldest of Maltese noble families has a special interest for Englishmen and his memory deserves their regard. He was the Archivist of the Monastery at Monte Cassino when the Italians entered the Second World War against us, and it was to his keeping that the loyal Curator of Keats's House (Signora Signorelli Cacciatore), in Rome, committed the treasures of the Keats Museum. When the Germans occupied Monte Cassino, Dom Maurus sent the Keats and Shelley relics, disguised as his personal property, back to Rome—under a German guard furnished by the friendly Catholic Commandant— where they remained intact until the British entered the Eternal City.

Although there is some confusion of thought about the 'Hospitaller' character of the Sovereign Order of St. John—their pilgrim hospices were more hostels than hospitals—they did, in fact, always maintain a hospital within their Convents and were amongst the most advanced exponents of medicine and surgery, which their early contacts in the Holy Land with Arabic scholarship had stimulated.

The Hospital in Valletta was—it is now a sad and neglected ruin[1]—one of the wonders of Christendom. The main ward, five hundred feet long, and the ancillary services were so advanced that the Hospital was used, with little amendment, for military casualties of the Gallipoli and Salonika campaigns of the First World War. It was built by the Grand Master La Cassière in 1575. Here the sick were tended by a 'duty watch' of young Knights who served their meals on platters of silver. No man was denied care by reason of race or creed and a wondering English tourist of the time of Charles II reported that '. . . the bedde lynene' was changed once a fortnight.

[1] Now under partial restoration.

Fort St. Elmo, which guards the entrance to the Grand Harbour, and indeed did so very effectively during the Second World War against both air and surface attack, has like the Tower of London the doubtful honour of having housed many a political prisoner: notably the national hero, Don Gaetano Mannarino, who led the 'Priests' Revolt' against the tyrant Ximenes, and one much maligned Grand Master, the munificent La Cassière himself, who was temporarily deposed and imprisoned here by a body of disaffected Knights, led by a mutineer who went by the name of Romegas. He was, in fact, Fra Maturin de L'Escaut of La Cassière's own Langue.

Though the matter belongs properly to a history of the Order it is not uninteresting to note, in passing, that the great Christian victory of Lepanto in 1571, with the design of which the Grand Master Del Monte had much to do and in which the galleys of the Order played a notable part, was followed by a series of internal disorders. Both La Cassière, in 1572, and Verdale in 1582, suffered major insurrections which were hatched within a community no longer facing the immediate threat of Muslim attack.

Opposite the Royal Library in the main street of Valletta—Strada Reale—and facing a dumpy bronze Queen Victoria, upon whose Imperial head one fat pigeon (who vaguely resembles the Empress) keeps perpetual watch, is the Club of the Maltese *élite*, the Casino Maltese, formerly the Treasury of the Order and later that of the Maltese Imperial Government. Entrée, here, is more difficult than to the Service Clubs and will depend, if you are a visitor, upon an introduction to the 'right people'. Once admitted, however, you will find this one of the friendliest, least 'stuffy', most hospitable clubs in the world and, better still, you will be ensured real contact with the Island and its people.

Perhaps, when you have toured St. John's and the Palace, the Museum and the Library you will have had your fill of Carravaggio, Matteo Preti, Giuseppe Cali, Antoine de Favray, Girolamo Cassar, and the rest and, unless you have a special interest in Renaissance art, Baroque decoration, and the history of the Church and her Religious Orders, you may not be much attracted to the lesser known buildings and treasures of Valletta. And it must be recorded that perhaps too much of Malta's splendid heritage is hidden away in dimly lit chapels and cared for by devoted but inexpert hands. The subject is a difficult one for these treasures are rarely just works of art. They are objects of devotion, not infrequently endowed with quasi-miraculous virtues. To display them in modern settings, with the necessary lighting, protected from the smoke of votive lamps and the candles of the devout, would seem to many Maltese, indeed to most other Catholics, to be a sort of sacrilege.

By any standards, the removal of works of art from living churches to secular museums is a questionable proceeding with a distinctly Muscovite odour; but there is the opinion that the proliferation of such aids to devotion is akin to idolatory and that beauty is for the enjoyment of all, whether they be churchgoers or not. I am on the side of the reactionaries. These works—paintings, sculpture, the art of the goldsmiths and the jewellers—were acts of worship in themselves, designed and executed for specific purposes. There is nothing in them which is miraculous, except in so far as *Homo artifex* is a miracle, but they have inspired devotion, contemplation, prayer, brought solace to thousands and been the means of Grace whereby miracles do happen. They should remain in the religious and historic environment for which genius created them.

Valletta's surroundings, the great bastions scarred by war, the Forts of St. Angelo, Ricasoli, St. Elmo, and Manoel commanding the ancient Quarantine Harbour, speak for themselves. No harbour in the world is quite like it. That peculiar play of light and shadow, of theatrically blue sky, and sea the colour of copper sulphate; orange rock bathed in pink haze at dawn and veiled with the 'Heaven's embroidered cloths' at sunset, cannot be put on paper or canvas. Neither is there another anchorage where you may stand upon the high parapet of a Crusader's fortress and look down upon the busy decks of warships and merchantmen of a dozen nations. Hong Kong, Sydney Harbour, the Golden Gate, Plymouth Sound all have their splendour; but the Grand Harbour alone, a mere creek by comparison, seems to have been taken straight from the annals of faerie.

Amongst all the fortifications, of which the youngest is Fort Manoel built in 1723 by the Grand Master Manoel de Vilhena, St. Angelo is the only building not of the Knights, though it was added to by them from time to time. On this site there stood a temple of Tyrian Astarte—Cybele—Juno—the Great Mother whose prophetic cult had so many Christian elements, and Castel

Sant' Angelo was a stronghold under Carthaginians, Romans, Byzantines, Normans, Angevins, and Aragonese. The ancient township which huddles at its feet was long known as Il Borgo and learned Maltese have disputed for years about the origin of the name. The most popular derivation is from the Greek *pyrgos*— 'a port' and certainly this was, anciently, the only port in these parts. An odd parallel to excite the etymologists exists in Rome, where the area called Lungotevere in Sassia which marks the site of an Early Saxon hospice and settlement (Saxon pilgrims were commonplace in the Rome of the seventh century), surviving as the Hospital of Santo Spirito di Sassia, is also called Il Borgo. The area communicates with Rome's Castel Sant' Angelo by a bridge, as did Malta's Borgo with St. Angelo. The learned assure us that *borgo* is from the Saxon *burh*, from which we get 'burgh'. Could the similarity and proximity to Fort St. Angelo have led a pious Maltese generation to call their seaport Il Borgo after the Roman model? Or is it mere coincidence and does the Saxon *burh* descend from the Greek *pyrgos*?

However, the Sovereign Order effectively resolved any confusion by building great, new cities around the ancient port and naming them *Vittoriosa*—for the victory of 1565—*Senglea*—for the Grand Master de la Sengle, and *Cottonera* for the Grand Master Cottoner. All these old cities are now a sad conglomeration of ancient and modern. Lying as they do cheek by jowl with the Dockyard, they were a legitimate target and were literally laid waste. And yet the contours are little changed. By comparison with the stout, stone structure of Maltese traditional building, our English architecture is flimsy and although thousands of dwellings were gutted by fire and blast, few actually collapsed, and those the most modern.

The waterside of Senglea is a little like Venice. Here, too, the high Baroque fronts of dilapidated palaces rise straight from the water's edge, and a young man still sometimes serenades a shy *inamorata* peeping from the lattice of a balconied window, while his *dghajsa*, the ancestor of the gondola, rides gently on the still, evening tide.

Beneath the level of the dignified streets of the city of Valletta— 'built by gentlemen for gentlemen'—there used to exist a curious, troglodyte village called the Mandragg, from the bastard Italian *manderaggio*—'dry dock'. It had been the intention of the Order's engineers to convert a quarry, from which some of the stone for the city had been mined, into a dock for the galleys: a project which was copied in principle by the submariners of the Second World War, who excavated submarine pens very close to what would have been the access to the sea from the Mandragg. It was never completed and the great excavation was hollowed out into caverns and narrow, stepped streets where the very poor dwelt; direct descendants, perhaps, of the emancipated slaves who were accommodated here in the not-so-distant days of slavery.

The Mandragg grew a marvellous reputation, largely, I am convinced, fairy-tales. It was a sort of international *kasbah*, where the most romantic characters, spies, gun-runners and less romantic dope-pedlars, white-slavers, murderers, were reputed to lurk, safe from the police, who would not dare to enter this subterranean nest of bristling villains. You were told that you could only venture down those narrow steps at the foot of Strada San Marco in daylight, and then only in the company of a priest who was known to the inmates.

I once walked around the Mandragg, with a priest, in the little daylight which filtered down from the narrow crevices between the great cliffs of natural rock and the overhang of the palaces at ground-level. It was an August afternoon, and it was cool and pleasantly dim in these caverns of the slaves. The inhabitants seemed singularly friendly and harmless, the only embarrassment being the hordes of small children who clamoured around the old priest and knelt for his blessing, the smallest insisting upon tottering alongside, supporting themselves by clinging to the skirts of his cassock.

The dwellings were spotlessly clean, much cleaner than many of those of the 'surface dwellers' and Maltese women are notoriously house-proud. The only note of squalor was struck by the lavatories which were, for the whole of one rock-hewn lane, outside the front entrances, complete with cisterns and, we were able to observe, very efficient flushing arrangements.

On reporting, with some satisfaction, that I had exploded the myth of Malta's *kasbah*, I was told that, of course, it had been all right in daylight, and with Father Bugeja who enjoyed a reputation little short of canonization amongst the *mandraggari*; but had I gone alone and after dark it would have been a different matter. I never did and I remain unconvinced.

The troglodyte village has now been evacuated and the people have moved into one of those new blocks of flats which look like a packet of matches with a box, here and there, withdrawn a little to serve as balconies. They complain that the difference in levels gives them a poor water-supply: not nearly as good as the Mandragg, and the flats are terribly hot in summer.

2

There are now many breaches in the ancient bastions of Valletta which lead you out into the rather more open country beyond. At one point the great moat has been filled in to within a few feet of the glacis, burying the greater part of a particularly noble angle of the battlement; but you should go out by the old way, through the Porta Reale (Kingsgate) across the moat and towards the suburb of Floriana.

Between Valletta and Floriana is an area called The Granaries where, in underground silos capped by great circular stones and sealed with the Grand Master's seal, the reserve of grain used to be kept against siege or famine. Some few of these silos remain and are in use; but the area has generally been built over or chopped up into flower-beds and shrubberies. Here, too, are the English-style Cenotaph, the Maltese national memorial which commemorates the Eucharistic Congress of 1913 (a very fine figure of Christ by the Maltese sculptor Sciortino)[1] and a graceful R.A.F. memorial of the Second World War.

The Hotel Phoenicia is an attractive modern building, in no way offensive, a hostelry in the modern idiom which compares favourably with anything of its kind in Italy or France and, for its prices, more than favourably with its English counterpart.

Other and even 'more modern' (whatever that may mean!) hotels are proposed; but I regret the passing of those small, family guest-houses with their faded, Edwardian plush, their potted palms, and the highly personal nature of their service.

Facing the Granaries is the building which houses N.A.T.O., the Headquarters Allied Forces, Mediterranean, where Greek and Turk, Englishman and Italian, Frenchman and American meet and work and play together in a harmony undisturbed by international storms; but we must not let this harmony mislead us,

---

[1] Sciortino's most famous work is 'Les Gavroches'—a bronze group to be seen in the little garden of the Upper Barracca. Here there is also a memorial to Lord Strickland—the sculptor's last work, which he disliked.

for sailors are notoriously bad at harbouring ill-will or nursing grudges.

A great part of Floriana, named for the engineer and architect Pietro Floriani, has been rebuilt since the Second World War, and an excellent job has been made of restoring its original appearance while giving it more spacious streets and generally improving its amenities.

Its main landmark is the imposing façade of the Church of St. Publius—first Bishop of Malta, whose father, 'the Chief man of the Island', was healed by St. Paul. He was martyred and is invariably presented in full canonicals, being chewed by a not very enthusiastic lion.

Facing the imposing Baroque church, with its twin towers, is the Maglio or Mall where the young Knights took exercise at the game of pall mall. It is now a very pretty little garden, bright with oleander and Judas trees. It and the graceful spires of St. Publius rising behind it are favourite subjects with artists and picture-postcard men.

Beyond Floriana is the ugly and uninspiring suburb of Hamrun, rapidly becoming an exact copy of an English dockyard town, and beyond it, again, at the head of the Grand Harbour, the Marsa[1]—the 'Marsh'—an area of reclaimed saltings where the Knights used to hunt duck, which is now the centre of much of Malta's sporting and social life.

The Marsa United Services Sports Club enjoys some small subsidy from the Defence Departments; but it is supported mainly by the Garrison and by the great many Maltese who have at one time or another held the Queen's Commission. In origin a Services Club, it is not difficult for visiting civilians to enjoy its amenities.

Here, in what was the country villa of the 'Barons of the Marsh', surrounded by one of Malta's rare expanses of grass, you may enjoy a nostalgic afternoon watching village cricket in surroundings which try hard to reproduce the village green. The illusion is accentuated if you happen to catch a glimpse, above the oleanders, of the spire of the chapel in the cemetery of the Addolorata, which is one of the few perpendicular Gothic structures in the Island. Even the cricketing parson is provided.

---

[1] It was certainly a marsh; but *Marsa* in Arabic also means 'port' and this is the name used for the head of the Grand Harbour which is the commercial port.

Or you may watch polo in an environment evocative of Nani-Tal and *The Maltese Cat*.

Flat racing, enthusiastically, indeed extravagantly, supported by the Maltese farming community, who often put their not inconsiderable capital into horse-flesh, and bet heavily, is varied by trotting. The ponies are tough, little arabs bred from North African stock. If you are a horseman, hacking is pleasant in winter; but not recommended for you or the horse, in summer. The standard of Maltese polo varies with the years, reaching a peak when the Naval Commander-in-Chief, the Governor, or the General Officer Commanding the Garrison is an enthusiast and falling to a poor parody when he is not. It then becomes necessary for ambitious young officers to dispose of their ponies (or their boots) and invest in conjuring sets or underwater fishing equipment.

Dancing by moonlight, amidst fairy-lit sago palms is the correct sequel to the incessant cocktail-parties with which every sort of Maltese society is nowadays beset. Spirits as well as champagne are still very cheap by English standards.

From the Marsa towards the centre of the Island reasonably good roads take you towards the Palace of San Anton, the residence since 1928 of the British Governors. There is, here, a fine Botanical Garden, open to the public and frequent scene of flower shows, fur and feather and agricultural shows, trade exhibitions, and outdoor theatre—put on for charity by one of the amateur dramatic societies or as a 'cultural' venture by the British Council. They vary in merit and popularity in much the same way as the standards of the polo.

The Palace and the garden were created by the Grand Master de Paule—a noted epicurean and (so his opponents, who decried him before the Pope, claimed) a voluptuary.

On the left of the good, straight road which rises gradually towards the ancient capital of 'Mdina or Citta Vecchia is a notable villa which has given its name to the language. It was the personal country retreat of the Knight Franconi; but has, for many years, been Malta's only mental hospital. *Tal Frankuni* is a lunatic—or anyone who behaves like one.

If you are driving a car, or if you are one of those passengers who cannot relax in the hands of a strange driver, there is much that you will have to learn before you can be really comfortable on

Maltese roads. Right of way belongs to the heaviest vehicle. Hand-signals are rare, sketchy, or obscure in intent and light signals are apt to be possessed of an independent life of their own. You must not be dismayed or angry if a heavy truck turns suddenly across your bows. The driver lives down that lane and everybody in Malta knows that he always goes home for a snack at that time. If you are a poor, ignorant foreigner that is not his affair. But, to be quite fair, local drivers are good in their own fashion. Serious accidents are rare, and are most frequently caused by over-confident strangers driving hired cars. A very difficult traffic problem—there are more vehicles per head of the population than in England, in streets and roads still largely intended for horse traffic—is faced by public and police with a cheerful fatalism which somehow gets by. Days on which the traffic is particularly dense and drivers particularly perverse are classified as *Tal Frankuni*, and the long caravan of crawling cars, crammed with three generations, so familiar a mark of the English week-end, is called by the untranslatable Italian *Domenicuzzi*. 'Dirty little Sunday-ites' gets some of the sense.

'Mdina should be seen first at night. Its silhouette, with the fine dome and the graceful towers of St. Paul's Cathedral rising, like an illustration from Hans Andersen, above the battlemented, tapering rock-face, is very beautiful. It is the castle of legend from whose grim gateway El Cid, or Don Quixote, depending on your mood, should emerge at any moment.

A perfect, walled city of the eleventh century, 'Mdina, The Old City, has Norman houses and Spanish churches in a perfect state of preservation, streets even narrower than those of Valletta where the bulbous fretwork of *musrabijeh*, Moorish window-grilles, almost touch overhead. Partly encircled by a moat so wide that it can (and does) accommodate a full-size soccer pitch, and for the rest by unscalable, natural bastions of rock topped by wide, stone parapets, the city was impregnable. Besides its main gateway, it had only one sally-port, called 'The Gate of the Greeks'. Its great wooden doors and the double portcullis have stood open, now, for one hundred and fifty years.

And in the Moorish, Spanish, and Siculo-Norman palaces of Citta Vecchia dwell the same families as dwelt here before Magna Charta was sealed at Runnymede. Their armorial bearings bristle with imperial eagles and royal leopards, fleurs-de-lis and Papal quarterings. One family, indeed, has a not inconsiderable claim to the English Throne by Angevin, Plantagenet, and Stuart connexions. Here in their ancient stronghold they jealously guard what remains of their threadbare privileges and struggle to maintain their historic heirlooms. It is largely due to their efforts that 'Mdina has so long remained an unspoiled museum-piece.

The existing Cathedral of St. Paul (more strictly of St. Peter and St. Paul; but national pride in St. Paul has tended to obscure the Fisherman) dates only from the eighteenth century. It was built in 1702 to a design of Melchiorre Gafà but stands on the site of two earlier churches, the later of which, built by the Normans, was partially destroyed by earthquake and fire in 1693; but the earlier was traditionally the first Christian Church in Europe, founded by St. Paul himself, who almost certainly dwelt hereabouts as the guest of St. Publius, his first convert in the Islands.

Whatever your religious persuasions, I would urge you to hear Mass sung in this very sacred place. It is splendidly done, and you will come to no harm if you meditate upon the indebtedness of Europe to those Maltese peasants who so kindly and hospitably received the ship-wrecked Paul. Had they been of more brutish stock, there might have been no Canterbury, York, or Westminster.

There is much else to see in 'Mdina. Casa Inguanez, Palazzo Santa Sofia, and the Norman House, which has been restored to its fourteenth century state, and is furnished, even down to the drinking-vessels of the men-at-arms, with contemporary gear. The house has, I believe, been donated by its owner to the (English) Venerable Order of St. John of Jerusalem. Since it was never the property of the Sovereign Order, there should be no hard feelings in that quarter. The Roman villa, possibly that of Publius, has not been restored and some of its principal treasure trove was removed to the National Museum; but its ground-plan, mosaics, and sculpture remain *in situ* and much of its contents has been well preserved in the museum on the site. This little Roman museum is well worth a visit. Together with the relics of Publius's villa, it has some Attic ceramics of quite outstanding excellence, a number of Etruscan funerary urns, a portrait-bust of the Emperor Tiberius and another most beautiful bust of Agrippina, daughter of Augustus and grandmother of Nero. The preserved mosaics, too, are of an exceptional delicacy.

Those of us who are misled in our thinking by St. Paul's use of the generic *barbari*—for men who spoke neither Latin nor Greek—will do well to study the lovely head of Agrippina, the wonderful naturalism of the Etruscan figures, and ponder that the people who possessed these things were no barbarians, no savages eking out a poor life on an arid rock, but highly cultured men who knew a great deal about beauty and human dignity.

Agrippina has the face of a gentle, delicate creature. Could her grandson really have been such a monster? The Etruscan work (there are inscriptions, too, as yet undeciphered), so far afield from the supposed centres of this still mysterious culture, is also worthy of a little pondering.

How well the Romans chose their sites. From this eminence, the vista in spring is a foam of purple and green, gold and blue, as the rich colours of the valley seem to lap at the feet of the shadowed hills where the corn and clover end and the dappled rock begins.

No matter how often you take that road towards 'Mdina and climb that last, steep ascent to the gate of the magic city, you will never escape the sense of having travelled from one land to another, from one time to another. The all too crowded streets of Valletta and its environs, the bustle, the uniforms, the packed traffic, the baroque building broken and affronted by frequent ebullitions of Fascist Roman and Welfare Match-box, might belong to a totally different culture from the silent, thinly peopled, clean Norman dignity of The Old City. The air, too, is cleaner and seems somehow brighter. You have, in fact, journeyed in the short space of eight miles from a hotchpotch of the seventeenth and twentieth centuries into an almost perfect survival of the eleventh to fifteenth. It is much in Malta's best interests that this delightful anachronism should survive the assaults of the new paganism.

Towards the western and southern limits of the great outcrop which forms the natural fortress of Citta Vecchia lies the comparatively new town of Rabat. Outside the moat of the walled city, this rambling settlement is probably not much younger in origin; but it consists for the most part of dwellings of the humbler sort— the market and the hucksters' stalls of the Greeks and the Jews who were permitted to enter the citadel, by its single sally-port, only in time of danger. To these have been added a number of recent villas in the style of Italian suburbia, and Rabat is not easy to date. It has, nevertheless, a number of ancient buildings including the sixteenth-century Church of St. Mary of Jesus where the heart of that redoubtable warrior, the Grand Master L'Isle Adam reposes.

The Catacombs may antedate 'Mdina and around them have grown up the usual crop of fables. The Christian Maltese are supposed to have sheltered here from the persecution of the Arabs during the Muslim domination. St. Paul himself is supposed to have dwelt in the Catacombs. In fact, they are simply burial-places of the Roman era. Certainly they have all the indications of Christian burials, too, and of the celebration of the *Agape*; the Love Feast which Christianity borrowed from paganism and with which the Mass was at one time in danger of being confused; but there is little proof that the Catacombs were ever used as dwelling-places or that the Muslim Governors ever indulged in consistent persecution. They were for the greater part of the history of Muslim conquest, notable for their toleration, for their respect for Our Lady (who has a book to herself in the Qur'ān) and the 'Prophet Jesu'. Like the Romans, they also entertained the strongest prejudices against disturbing the dead.

Do not venture alone into the Catacombs of Rabat. It is as easy to get lost there as it is in the tombs of Rome where Bosio, the great historiographer of the Knights of Malta, was lost in 1593.

Another very venerable building in Rabat is the Dominican Monastery, a fastness and a miniature town in itself whose immense walls enclose a self-sufficient community which has withstood as many sieges as the fortified city.

If you are a friend of the Dominicans you may be fortunate enough to be a guest at their annual *Festa*, when the strict rules of the Order are relaxed and you will dine with them in their refectory, where Dominicans have dined upon fish from their own ponds, meats refrigerated in Sicilian snow, fruit from their orangeries and orchards, and wine from their own vineyards for six hundred years.

They were here before the Knights of St. John. They have seen Grand Masters, Inquisitors, Archbishops, Grand Priors come and go. They were here, in their battlemented convent, defying Sultans and Barons, when their own unhappy Savonarola challenged the Franciscans to ordeal by fire in distant Florence. They expect to be here, teaching, caring for the poor and the sick and comforting the aged, long after our navies have melted away.

There is much in the monastic life to commend itself to a sailor, much that is familiar; the discipline, the ordered day with the bells marking the hours and the duties, the comradeship and the sense of community, the long, quiet days at sea cut off from the world of noise and the scramble of competition when a man may meditate—or pray.

Near the great monastery is the famous chapel built upon the site of the subterranean grotto which housed a miraculous likeness of Our Lady during the Arab period. The story goes that a church in this vicinity was sacked and burned by corsairs in the eighth century; but its most prized possession, the sculpture of Our Lady with the Infant, was rescued and hidden in a cleft of the rock. Three hundred years later—which would have been after the expulsion of the Moors by Roger of Sicily—a sportsman in search of game lost one of his dogs and, clambering about the rocks after him, he came upon a cavern from which a brilliant light emanated. Here he found the long-lost image and here was erected the church which has been a centre of pilgrimage and devotion ever since.

The grotto remains, immediately beneath the chancel. For several hours in the day it is open to the public who may enter it by a winding stairway, and when the grotto is closed, the sacred image is visible from the church through the circular grille which now encloses the original mouth of the cave.

The story of the finding of the image, the sacking of the church, and the building of the new church, is told in a series of charmingly natural mosaics decorating the grotto. The image itself, a bas-relief in marble, is very lovely.

The story is common enough. I think that there are a dozen such stories told of Spanish shrines. Its accuracy matters little as long as Our Lady of Rabat continues to hear the invocations of the Faithful.

From Rabat, many roads lead to sites of recognized tourist appeal and, better still, to some beautiful little backwaters of no possible notoriety.

To the south, on a prominent spur of the plateau called *Tal Virtu*, stand two quaint structures. On the extreme point of the spur, commanding an uninterrupted view of as much as a third of Malta and the sea beyond, is a castellated 'grange', rather in the style of the wooden forts inhabited by lead soldiers, surrounded by gnarled pines, windswept and grotesque. It is a private villa, much favoured as a temporary home by senior Naval officers and built, it is inaccurately said, by the benefactor who also built the unusual, oblate-domed church which stands beside it. Toy castle and bare dome present a strange silhouette, the dome looking like an astronomer's observatory and sometimes pointed out as such. The castellated villa is less than a century old, having been built in 1900 but it is not without its (completely apocryphal) legend.

Near the church, stands a stereotyped statue of Christ the King. The fabric of the church is split from dome to foundation, and the story runs that the builder of the castle and of the church, having led a life as sinful as most of us, and in the doing of it amassed a considerable fortune, offered the building and the statue which was to crown its dome, for his sins.

The church completed, the story goes on, the statue was hoisted on to the dome. Immediately, a shock like an earthquake was felt and, for full measure, a clap of thunder accompanied the shock. The statue was cast to earth and the stone of the church split throughout its height. The offering had been rejected and the unconsecrated church stands deserted and decaying as an awful warning to us all.

The church is, in fact, much older than the house. The statue never reached the dome and the cracked fabric is almost certainly the result of poor foundations and an earthquake—minor quakes are comparatively common in the Island which lies on the fringe of the Vesuvius formation.

I repeat the story simply as an example of the inherent local temptation to regale the willing ears of the English with yet another Maltese superstition. It is not long since I heard this particular fable being retailed, with suitable frills, by an ex-tenant of the Toy Castle to an appreciative audience in a London Club.

In this area called *Tal Virtu* there has been built since the Second World War, a very fine Teachers' Training College. Designed by a Maltese architect, it is modern in style, light and airy, yet dignified and blending perfectly with its environment and repeating the essentials of native architecture. I wish that more modern buildings were like it. The project is the child of the English Province of the Order of the Sacred Heart. If those excellent nuns can transmit a small part of their traditions and their erudition to a new generation of Maltese Government school teachers, the future is bright for Malta's children.

3

From Rabat to the Castle of Verdala is a pleasant walk past fields and little farmhouses, towards the thickly wooded valley of Buskett—'The Wood'—Malta's only large area of woodland. The castle is named for its builder, the Grand Master Loubenx de Verdale and dates from 1585. Verdale or Verdala died a Cardinal, in Rome; but the honour did not cure his broken heart. He had been impeached by his Knights and arraigned before the Holy Office for luxurious living, misappropriation of the Order's funds and conduct verging upon heresy. All the charges were dismissed; but the wound of the revolt was too deep and the broken old man died soon after his public vindication.

Verdala is an imposing structure, with castellated battlements, looking as if it has been transported from the Welsh Marches and seeming somewhat embarrassed by its Mediterranean surroundings. With the Magisterial Palace in Valletta and San Anton it completes the three official residences of the British Governor, though it is used but sparingly in these stringent days when even Governors hesitate to maintain the state and retinue which such dwellings demand. Surrounded by pines, cypress, pepper trees, holmoaks, and olives, the castle looks down the valley of Buskett (*Boschetto*) upon acres of fine oranges, lemons, pomegranates, dates, tangerines, apples, plums, persimmons, loquats and, in the wild hedges, even those very English symbols, oak, ash and thorn.

A stream, in winter a torrent, winds through this wooded retreat towards the lower valley Tal Inkwisitur and thence to the sea.

The gardens of Buskett are open to visitors at all seasons and the inevitable 'Chalet' called 'The Road House' has lately been built for the comfort and sustenance of the public who will, doubtless, add to the amenities by littering the quiet avenues with bottles and cigarette packets;[1] but the lower valley is little frequented save on the occasion of the great national holiday of *Imnarja* (*Luminaria*—the Feast of St. Peter and St. Paul). There is an agricultural show and a fatstock competition, and, in the evening, a strange singing contest when men compete at the

[1] It was worse than I expected. There is a Juke Box.

immemorial game of the *ghanja*. These are rhyming verses, extemporized on the spot and chanted to the traditional, ululating lilt which closely resembles the *flamenco* singing of Andalusia. There is a very similar tradition in Sardinia, though not, I think, in Sicily where the more tuneful airs of Naples have ousted the aboriginal Punic cadence. The *ghanja* are not attractive to Northern ears, yet they have a haunting spine-chilling quality which is not easily forgotten and the facility with which interminable rhyming couplets are extemporized is amazing. I remember one of these contests between a Florianese rejoicing in the ancient Maltese name of Buhagiar and a Gozitan called Jones. Buhagiar had flaming red hair and Jones looked more than a little Semitic. The Welsh voice won, however.

You should come here early one autumn morning and walk in the orange groves while the heavy dew is still silvering the spiders' webs. Do not pick any of the oranges nearest the main road. They are very bitter, despite their roseate splendour and need a deal of sugar, even for marmalade. If you want fresh, sweet oranges, seek out one of the friendly gardeners who will (officially!) sell them to you for a song. The gardeners do not speak much English; but you may meet one of the permanent officials of Malta's Department of Agriculture. English and Italian trained, they are practical farmers and horticulturalists, devoted to their uphill task and liking nothing better than to recite to you the whole tale of husbandry in the Islands: the soil, the pests, the ecology of every crop that is raised or that it is hoped to raise. These few dedicated characters have achieved prodigies in an arid, unrewarding climate against the odds of a stubborn, conservative peasantry, a progressively inadequate water-supply, and an uncertain and grossly inadequate public purse.

There are many ancient references which suggest that, long ago, Malta was quite thickly wooded and that the area of Buskett was much more extensive than it now is. An early code of penal laws covers the preservation of game and refers specifically to the 'forest' of Buskett where hares were hunted. An unfortunate serf caught with a hare was required to eat the animal, raw, until 'skin, bones, and fur' had been consumed; perhaps a more humane penalty than the hanging or transportation for life inflicted at a much later date upon English poachers—or is it?

It is possible to imagine a connexion between this curious

penalty and the custom of inserting in marriage contracts a clause
to the effect that the husband undertook to take his wife, annually,
to the Feast of *Imnarja*, to 'buy her a piece of jewellery and to feed
her upon Sweetmeats and Rabbit stew'. Contracts of marriage
actually contained this clause as late as the early part of this
century.

The disappearance of trees would have been a natural result of a
spreading population and—as in the Greek Islands and in Cyprus
and Corfu—of the omnivorous goat.

If you wander a little off the main paths of Buskett, you will
come upon little glades bright with grass and wild flowers, or
carpeted with pine needles, which might belong many hundreds
of miles north of these sun-drenched islands.

You may smell the pleasant tang of wood smoke across the
heavy scent of the pines and you will have come upon the primitive Pottery, where the Department of Agriculture produces and
fires its own ceramics. The old potter can still mould by hand an
infinity of pleasing shapes, decorated with traditional designs as
old as Nineveh. If he likes the look of you, he may mould you a
musbieh, the earthenware lamp of Punic pattern exactly as it is
found in the Phoenician tombs which are constantly being
turned up by plough and bulldozer.

These little tallow- or oil-lamps were commonly used in their
thousands to illuminate the outlines of churches and public
buildings on Feast Days. Their winking orange flames were much
to be preferred to the dead stare of the electric circuits which have
generally replaced them.

From Buskett a road winds over the hilltop to the south,
petering out into little better than a mule-track and then recover-
ing itself and becoming again a good, metalled road as it descends
into the valley called Tal Inkwisitur, from the Palace of the
Inquisitor which stands at its head. A building partly of the
twelfth and partly the seventeenth century, tucked into the lee of a
cliff, it looks from a distance more like a creeper-covered Georgian
country house than the dreaded haunt of restless spirits which
legend has made of it. The title 'Inquisitor' has special overtones
in the English mind—Torquemada, the Pit and the Pendulum,
the Iron Virgin, and the burning of St. Joan. In fact, the Inquisitors in Malta seem to have been singularly docile and un-
frightening personalities. The Holy Office was established long

before the arrival of the Sovereign Order; but there are no records of terrifying trials for heresy. A manuscript of the sixteenth century contains the report of an 'Inquisition' carried out into the condition of all the parishes in Malta. It is a valuable record, but contains no recommendations more lethal than '. . . the doors of the Sacristy of the chapel at San Martin have poor hinges which should be renewed. . . .', '. . . the Parish Priest at this place is too old for his arduous duties and he should be replaced by a younger man.'[1]

There are, it is true, records of acrimonious disputes between Bishops and Inquisitors, Grand Masters and Grand Priors and the Holy Office—mostly on matters of jurisdiction and precedence; but in general the Inquisitor seems to have been no match for sabre-rattling Grand Masters who were often Cardinal Princes and Bishops who were the proud successors of St. Publius. At least one Inquisitor, Fabio Chigi, who became Pope Alexander VII, having served as Malta's seventeenth Director of the Holy Office from 1634 to 1639, retained a lifelong attachment for the Island. Shortly before his death he donated an antipendium and four chasubles to St. John's with his arms of Chigi-Rovere embroidered in silk.

The Palace of the Inquisitor is Government property and has occasionally been leased by English tenants whose imagination—salted by a little wishful thinking—has conjured up the ghost of a Maltese Torquemada who never existed.

If, instead of shaping your course west and south from the Dominican Monastery at Rabat, you had turned west and north from the main gate of 'Mdina, passing the Roman villa on your right, the road which corkscrews down the lip of the valley of Imtarfa would have led you to a stretch of delightful, unspoiled country.

Malta lies in the sea like the deck of a sinking aircraft carrier, with the side to the south-west high out of the water, sloping towards the north and east, with the deck awash at several points. To the west, with the exception of the mouths of some water-courses and of the main valleys which traverse the Island at three points, the cliffs are sheer and high and the beaches narrow. And the west coast is but thinly populated, the overgrown fishing village called Zurrieq—'Blue', from the famous Blue Grotto

[1] MS. of the 'Inquisition of Mons. Duzzina—1571' in the Royal Malta Library.

which lies at the foot of its cliff—being the only considerable township on this coast. There are thus wide areas of rugged, open country, thinly cultivated fields and rocky, heath-covered hill-sides, amongst which little, isolated farms and hamlets, connected only by rough tracks, remain so far secure from the doubtful blessings of progress and the noise of dedicated holiday-makers.

On your right, about a mile out of 'Mdina, a steep hill descends into the bed of the *wied*, or riverbed, to the artificial lake, called after its English creator Chadwick Lakes. A very pleasant spot, and Malta's nearest approach to a true river. Here the *wied* has been dammed and a rare head of water fills what must surely have been, at some distant date—perhaps before the subsidence which separated the Islands from Sicily—a great and deep river. There are willows here and the wooded bank at the lower end of the lake is a favourite haunt of the Yellow Wagtail. I have counted as many as a dozen of these lovely birds during the migration seasons of spring and autumn.

Below the dam, the river gradually dwindles from a healthy torrent in February to a trickle, connecting a series of rock-pools by late April. At this time, the pools are black with tadpoles and I wonder what becomes of all the frogs and how many of the little creatures survive the fierce heat of summer.

Under the damp rocks of the eroded banks there live families of Skinks—those distinctly prehistoric little monsters who may grow to as much as a foot in length and change the colour of their shining armour from a warm orange-grey to almost black, though not as rapidly as their cousins the chameleons. Maltese boys hunt the skink, trapping him with a noose of dry grass, having enticed him from his hide with a fly or some such bait. They say that he makes an intelligent pet. Beyond the turning off the main road which leads down to the lakes, and to the west, the road descends into a plain which might, in the remote age of Maltese rivers, itself have been a lake. It is very marshy in the rainy season and very fertile. In the spring, Water Mint, Kingcups and Rushes, Crack Willow and Water Marigolds grow in and about the streamlets by the roadside and the surrounding hills are full of the voices of warblers and larks.

This road will take you to Imtahlep: a curious name and difficult to pronounce, for the central 'H' is a true aspirate, which means literally 'The Milking'. Here is all the suggestion of a lost continent, as if you were travelling up-stream, along the banks of a great river, opening here and there into wide lakes. The valley should continue towards some mountain-peak; but the rock has collapsed here and slid, with the rest of the range, into the sea, forever cutting the bridge which led to Africa: the Atlas and lost Atlantis.

The cliffs fall straight towards the sea for a hundred feet and then spread out into curved plinths of cultivation, like the rice paddy of the Indonesian hills for another three hundred feet. Then the land rises again, slowly, towards twin outcrops like Sheba's Breasts in *King Solomon's Mines* or the Jungfrau and it is, I think, from this unusual formation that the place gets its name. Beyond the Breasts is another cliff, this time dropping straight into the sea, two hundred feet below. Here, safe amongst inaccessible crags from the guns of *soi-disant* sportsmen and the thefts of egg-collectors, the seabirds breed and a rare colony of jackdaws is known.

The whole of this area is particularly rich in bird life. The woodchat shrike seems specially common. For this we may be grateful to a notice, much weathered but still legible, which forbids the shooting and trapping of birds within this, the property of the Barons de Piro d'Amico Inguanez, scions of the House of Anjou whose worn escutcheon, with its Imperial quarterings, surmounts the stone gateway giving access by a steep and narrow cliff pathway to the hamlet which clings precariously to the rock-face and, beyond it, to the land of 'The Milking'.

The people of this remote hamlet are great husbandmen. In byres hollowed out of the rock and in natural caverns which have been little altered, they keep a sizeable herd of Kerry cows, and their innumerable pigs, chickens, and goats all seem thoroughly healthy.

A Government elementary school has lately been built upon a flat eminence at the head of this strange and lovely valley. It is not a beautiful building and the farmers' and peasants' children who will use it have their fill of scenery; but we must not grudge them the best things in their own land.

While you remain upon this western edge of the Islands, the megaliths of Hagar Qim and Mnajdra, and that lonely survival of the lost continent, the islet of Filfla, with the much-publicized Blue Grotto of Wied iz-Zurrieq should command your attention.

Hagar Qim is approached through the village of Qrendi. If there is not yet a by-pass, you must negotiate one of the narrowest village streets in Malta and, to ensure that your skill is tested to the extreme, it has a right-angle bend in the centre. I once drove a Service bus through Qrendi, full of sight-seeing sailors. We stuck.

I remain convinced that the bus would have been there to this day—or at least the irreducible portion of its chassis—but for the 'pully-hauly' efforts of my passengers who, I do believe, literally bent that bus round the corner.

These Maltese villages must have been ideal for the conceal-ment of malefactors or the discomfiture of slave-hunting corsairs. Indeed, I think they were constructed to that end, like the Arab towns of Tunis and Algeria or the little seaports of Sicily and Calabria. Every village has, too, its relatively gigantic church, with few windows at eye-level, and those heavily barred. The walls of all these churches are immensely thick and the doors would withstand a battering-ram or a cannon-shot. The roofs are ideal vantage-points from which to bespatter a too-daring Moor with boiling oil or molten lead. Happily, there has been no street-fighting in these villages since Canon, later Bishop, Caruana led his gallant rabble of ill-armed peasants victoriously against the trained troops of Napoleon.

The megaliths at Hagar Qim and Mnajdra have been excavated, restored, re-excavated, and described by experts too often to need any repetition here of the scores of controversial theories which they have inspired. They remain a puzzle. Loosely dated as Neolithic, they are more complex than Stonehenge and show clear evidence of the true arch and the unsupported dome. Their pit-marked decoration, the Oracle chambers, sanctuaries, and sacrificial altars have been held to belong to a much more ad-vanced culture than is apparent from contemporary remains of what are supposed to have been similar civilizations.

Pay little attention to the 'official' guide. He is a local farmer, a worthy old gentleman who is not really a guide at all; but supple-ments the Government retainer which he receives for guarding the temples by reciting a patter which he must have picked up from a very old guidebook—published, as many of them were, without benefit of history or archaeology.

He will show you signs that the temples were first destroyed by

fire and then overwhelmed by a flood—The Flood, of which he
quotes the exact date. Sodom and Gomorrah and Noah's Ark
clearly play cartwheels in his head. He will also display hand-axes
and arrow-heads which I am sure he manufactures himself, from
prototypes in the Museum.[1]

The more notable finds: seven figures known as 'The Fat
Women of Qrendi', steatopygous Earth Mothers of a fertility
cult, decorated pottery, and some objects in obsidian, are in the
Museum at Valletta.

Both temples are wonderfully sited, Hagar Qim on a hilltop and
Mnajdra some little distance below it, in a slight declivity nearer
the cliff-top and the sea. Both are of a similar cult, though Mnajdra
has been supposed to be more recent and is somewhat better
preserved. The voice of the Oracle can still be made to function
in Mnajdra.

Little is to be learned from the names of these megaliths, except
confirmation of their antiquity. Hagar Qim means, in an archaic
Maltese, nearer to the original Aramaic by several thousands of
years than the modern language, 'The Ancient Stones', and
Mnajdra is from a root which means 'Herd' or 'Herding'. The
tops of the unexcavated pillars, protruding from the soil, would
certainly have resembled a herd of sheep or goats, which suggests
that the temples were deserted and buried when the first Semitic-
speakers came to the Islands in, perhaps, 2000 B.C.

Those temples are amongst the better preserved examples of a
great number of similar, supposedly Neolithic remains, temples,
tombs, standing stones and what, in the north, we should call
'Hut Circles' with which Malta and Gozo are literally crowded.
There is a definitely Celtic air about these remains. And their
local-names, too, have a Celtic flavour: 'The Chieftain's Stone;'
'The Giants'; 'The Giant's Tower', none giving any clue to their
origins, since local tradition, as in the Celtic lands, has it that all
are the work of a race of giants, Polyphemus or Hercules.[2]

The most famous and the best specimens of successive cultures
are the temples at Hal Tarxien and Safflieni which may well be
Early Minoan at their most recent. They are, so far, the sole
examples of an occupation continuing well into historic times and
have yielded some examples of a quite unique sculpture.

[1] He is no longer there. He used to infuriate me; but now I miss him.
[2] English folklore derives Stonehenge from a race of giants who carried the great
stones from Africa.

It sometimes seems that there are almost as many pagan temples in the Islands as there are Christian churches—and more may yet come to light—so that we can only assume a prehistoric Malta, thickly inhabited by a civilized people, the centre of a fertility cult which embraced a large part of the Mediterranean.

As you stand on the hillside by the temple of Mnajdra, the little rock of Filfla sits, solitary in a silver sea, remnant of a great expanse of hill and valley which once stretched unbroken towards what was to be Carthage, the Atlas, and the great lakes of the Sahara.

Filfla has long been used by the Navy and by the Air Force, as a gunnery and bombing target. How many tons of high explosive have been cast at this unfortunate little island it would be difficult to assess. The rock remains surprisingly unimpaired, except for the litter of metal which defaces its surface and for the occasional, unexploded missile, much sought after by the fishermen of Zurrieq who—rumour has it—use cordite and nitro-glycerine in their Festa fireworks, which are certainly notable for the magnitude of their explosions. Imagination is staggered at the thought of unexploded nuclear warheads being retrieved for use at the annual honouring of St. Sebastian or St. Catherine, though if we must make bigger and better bangs, it may be that the fishermen of Zurrieq put them to the best use.

Filfla has the ruins of a little chapel, dedicated to Our Lady, Star of the Sea, and is otherwise noted for a unique blue-black lizard with a forked tail, and as the breeding-ground of a peculiar variety of Mediterranean Shearwater. These comic birds nest in the crevices and rabbit burrows, seemingly undeterred by high explosives. Their numbers have much reduced of recent years, the intensity of bombardment having more than balanced the protection from human attack which it formerly afforded them. They spend the long daylight hours fishing and return at sunset to feed their young, setting up an unmusical and deafening squawking. They cannot walk or hop with comfort, as their undercarriage is set far back and they must shuffle over the rocks, with fish-stuffed beak, towards their noisy offspring. Even with the depleted numbers of today's colony, it is marvellous that any parent can distinguish its own family. A few storm petrels also nest here.

You must retrace your steps, through Qrendi village, and inland, if you are further to explore the north and east of the main Island. It seems strange to be talking of turning 'inland' upon an

Island around which it is possible to sail in a day; but this is one of Malta's charms.

Nowhere of greater altitude than eight hundred feet above sea-level and a bare nineteen miles across at its broadest part, there is, nevertheless, a compelling illusion of height and distance. There is a peculiar radiance in the light and a sense of age in the deep shadowed rocks. The low, rugged hills which are the bones of the Earth Mother and the quiet valleys of her eternal fertility, seem perfectly to imitate the mountain and countryside of a vaster scene.

4

From east to west, the island is crossed by a series of miniature mountain ranges: the geologists call them 'faults' and the Maltese call them *qala* or *montagna*. The major ridges are those of Bingemma, Wardija, Bajda and Marfa. The names of three of these ridges are self-evident. Wardija means 'flowery' and it is true that the ridge, which is comparatively well watered by natural springs, is notable for its profusion of wild flowers and the unusually green colour of its hillside. Bajda means 'white'—and also 'egg'—and this ridge could qualify for either description by colour or shape. Marfa means 'spoon'—an apt description of the topography in this area.

But Bingemma is more difficult. The steep scarps hereabouts are honeycombed with rock-tombs, which have yielded evidence of pre-Christian burials dating from two to three thousand years before Christ. Tradition has it that the people who used the burial-caves were 'the Jews', and attempts have been made to derive the name from an Aramaic root meaning 'Sons of Benjamin'; but the theory is far fetched and possibly stems from a Maltese habit of describing their pre-Christian ancestors as 'Jews' —anyone who was not a Christian being either a Roman or a Jew. These rock-tombs are almost certainly Punic and earlier.

This ridge of Bingemma is a natural defensive line and was fortified from early times. English maps mark the fortifications as the 'Victoria Lines'. The forts of the nineteenth century are now largely abandoned and the wild fig and the carob, the prickly pear and the milky sea squill, caper bushes and heath and thyme are slowly but inexorably taking over. They will not survive, these great concrete structures, as long as Hagar Qim.

From many points on the main roads, you will see on the horizon a great stone beehive which, if you are familiar with the Buddhist lands, is clearly a *dagoba*—it is a trick of the land contours which brings the horizon level with the base of the dome of Mosta Church.

If you turn to your right at the foot of the battlements of 'Mdina, just before you reach the last steep incline into that city, passing the airfield of Ta'Qali (which, with the Naval Air Stations at Hal Far and the Civil Airport of Luqa, occupy an immense proportion of the tiny Islands), you will come by way of a wide, ugly new bridge, to the outskirts of the rambling market town of Mosta.

The new bridge crosses the Wied il Kbir—'The Great Watercourse', which higher up is Chadwick Lakes.

Formerly, the graceful but dangerous little bridge, now reserved for foot and horse traffic, was the only link between two major roads. If you met a flat cart drawn by a determined mule in the middle of that bridge, there was no alternative but to back and the parapet is low and the bed of the Wied some fifty feet below you. At one end of the old bridge is a forlorn little chapel of St. Paul the Hermit, bearing a marble tablet which announces, as do many of these disused country chapels:

Non gode l'immunita ecclesiastica.
'No right of Sanctuary'

Mosta dome is justly famous. Designed by the Architect Grognet de Vassée—famous for his theories about the 'Atlantean' origin of the Maltese Islands and people—in what he described as 'Atlantean' style,[1] its pseudo-Corinthian façade is surmounted by the third largest unsupported dome in Europe.

The cost of this very splendid building was defrayed entirely by the peasant farmers and the *pitkali*—the farmers' middlemen—of Mosta. All the inhabitants gave their labour, too, over a period of thirty years. The structure was commenced in 1832, the new walls being erected around the original parish church which was then demolished and brought out, stone by stone, through the doorways of the magnificent new temple. The work was not finally completed until 1863. In the sacristy is an unexploded Italian

---

[1] It is suspiciously similar to the Pantheon of the Emperor Hadrian.

five hundred pound bomb (now safe!) which penetrated the dome and reached the crypt, doing no more damage than a neat perforation to indicate its course. The people of Mosta, not unreasonably, attributed the survival of their beloved dome to the intervention of Our Lady.

Mosta Church is a favourite with tourists; but if a self-styled sacristan offers to display the mummified corpse of his grandmother in the crypt, where intra-mural burial was necessarily resorted to until recently, I hope that you will tell him that he is a disgusting old man and threaten to report him to the Curia.

From Mosta I would recommend that you drive to the village of Naxxar which stands on the hill called San Pawl Tat-Targa— 'St. Paul of the Steps'. A rich valley full of vineyards lies spread like a green quilt between the hills of Bingemma and Wardija. On the left of the steep, winding road, some four hundred yards from the hilltop are some of the finest examples of one of the world's archaeological puzzles—the Maltese Cart Tracks.

In a number of areas, throughout the Islands, there are systems of deep tracks, not unlike the chariot-ruts in the streets of Pompeii. They vary in their complexity and in their degree of preservation; but all are of uniform gauge and have what looks like a highly developed system of points, sidings, and by-passes.

It is impossible now to guess in what direction they may have been designed to run. Large sections have been obliterated by cultivation and what look like small sections of the system sometimes turn out to be recent trenches, excavated for the cultivation of grape-vines. At one point, near the cliffs of Dingli, the main track runs clean over the rock's edge.

At 'St. Paul of the Steps' the well-preserved example is a little to the west of the hill called *Telgha Ta' Alla u Ommu*—'The hill of God and His Mother'—from a wayside shrine of Our Lady.

The road may have obliterated part of this example, which exhibits the most fascinating pattern of point systems for several hundred yards, runs down into the valley, and peters out where it meets ancient cultivation.

There are said to be vestiges of similar, complementary tracks in Sicily and on the Tunisian coast.

Theories are legion about the origin of these rockhewn 'railways'. It is said that the tracks are those of carts or sledges used to transport the sparse soil from the lower levels and from

the valleys to the eroded hilltops. Or they are the tracks of
vehicles used to carry the great stones, quarried elsewhere, for the
Neolithic, Cretan, and Punic temples. None of these theories is
particularly convincing. At few points in the Archipelago is there
any water at or near the hilltops and while it is true that terracing
and the recovery of eroded soil has gone on for thousands of years,
these tracks would only have carried soil, in general, to the most
unrewarding, unwatered, and windswept locations. The soil-
transport theory also presupposes that the tracks are no older
than the age of settlement and cultivation—say 5000 B.C. I do not
think the geologists can tell us quite how old they are; they but
are, I think, a good deal older than that.

As far as can now be judged, the tracks ran straight across hill
and valley, though seeming to keep to the sides of the hills, like
the ancient paths of the English downland, and avoiding the
lower levels where possible.

In places, the tracks are puckered and folded to conform to the
irregularities of the rock-surface. They seem to have been softened
by great heat and then to have cooled and set in the new curves.
This, in itself, seems evidence that they are older than some vast
but unrecorded volcanic disturbance.

The temple-building theory seems equally untenable. Certainly
the tracks do occur near some of the megaliths (e.g. at Hal Far
where there are several dolmens and a trilithon) but they are quite
absent from other sites where the building task was clearly greater
and where acres of naked rock are innocent of any vestige of a
'cart-track'.

It has also been suggested that the apparent tracks are simply
cultivation 'pots'—with which they may certainly be confused in
places—and that their uniform width apart is merely the convenient work-space which a man would need between rows of
grapes or some similar crop; but 5000 B.C. seems, again, to be the
limit for such a purpose and the 'points' and 'sidings' would have
no reason. A further conjecture combines the soil and the 'pot'
theories, perhaps suggesting some purpose in the sidings; but
dates again seem to dispose of this.

One more theory advances the existence of a primitive irrigation
system which trapped the brief, heavy rains and led the water
towards the cultivated areas. Were it not for the age factor and the
volcanic puckering, this theory would not seem too far fetched.

But why, then, always in consistent pairs and why leading so often straight into water-courses or over sheer edge of cliffs?

Some connexion with the Atlantis theories of Grognet de Vassée has also been mooted. De Vassée held that Malta was the vestige of an Atlantean continent—a continuation of the Atlas range—inhabited by a highly civilized people who had not, nevertheless, discovered the use of wheeled vehicles. These people—and the lost continent—were engulfed by the Flood of Noah and Deucalion, leaving the Berbers, the Maltese, and the pre-Latin Etruscan Italians as their surviving descendants. All Vassée's theories have long since been discredited; but there may have been some seeds of truth in them.

The peasant is quite explicit—the tracks are just what they are called—Cart Tracks. What carts? He does not know. When were they made? '*Eluf ta' Snin*'—'Thousands of years ago.' By whom? '*Min jaf?*' 'Who knows'?

It was that great Maltese scholar, Sir Themistocles Zammit, who first propounded the theory that the tracks marked the route of the regular, seasonal migration of a nomadic, food-gathering people during the vast passage of time between the appearance of man and the volcanic cataclysm, perhaps some thousands of years after the end of the last Ice Age, which broke the land-bridge between Africa and Europe and overwhelmed Vassée's Atlantis.

If these people were Neanderthalers (no confirmed trace of them is recorded in Malta; but there is ample record of a large colony in Gibraltar), their food-gathering migration could have covered a period from, perhaps, 500,000 to 70,000 B.C. If they were the more highly cultured, Cro-Magnon men, their migrations could have lasted from 70,000 to 10,000 B.C.

The wheel was not widely known before 2000 B.C. (the American cultures—Atlanteans too?—were ignorant of it until A.D. 1000) and even where it was known, for example, in the form of the potter's wheel, its use for transportation seems to have spread but slowly. The men of Ur of the Chaldees had standardized the span of their chariot wheels so that they might run on tramlines in the city streets by 3000 B.C.; but the Egyptians were still using sleds or sledges until much later.

We do not know whether Neanderthal man used a sledge. He had fire, used tools of a sort, and buried his dead with some apparent expectation of a resurrection; but he was a slow-witted fellow and while his sledges may have left their tracks in the Maltese rock—and they had four hundred thousand years in which to do it, for Neanderthaler hardly changed his habits at all —we cannot be sure.

We do know that the sledge was in common use by 10,000 B.C. and may have been in use much earlier. We also know, with a fair chance of certainty, that man spread into Europe along the North African littoral. First, in his seasonal migrations which lasted for hundreds of thousands of years; thereafter, he may have been cut off by the collapse of the land-bridges or he may have changed his route, because the temperate climate of the African shores began to change and food was harder to find, becoming a permanent settler in southern and Central Europe.

There is abundant evidence that a man of some culture lived upon what is now the Dogger Bank, in company with the mammoth, the sabre-toothed tiger, and the pigmy elephant.

The bones discovered in the cave of Ghar Dalam—the 'Cave of Darkness'—in Malta are those of a variety of creatures, including the pigmy elephant, contemporary with man, who could not possibly have reached the Maltese Islands by sea. There was also a single human jawbone—possibly Neanderthal. This evidence is conclusive enough, I think, that the land-bridge existed long after the appearance of man.

Many American Indians were using the sledge well into historic times and the Tierra del Fuegans still use it.

The American sledge was drawn by a horse; but who drew it before the horse appeared in America, with the first Europeans? It was a platform structure lashed to four stout poles and its dimensions were naturally limited by the horse- or man-power which could be brought to bear upon its maximum load.

And here, I believe, is the solution to the Cart Tracks.[1]

Having once manhandled (for draught-animals are improbable before 6000 B.C.) his cumbrous, rickety fleet of transports across the land-bridge northwards to a country of good summer gleaning and then southward again to the temperate African coast in winter, what more natural—even for the blundering Neanderthaler and

---

[1] The solution does not differ materially from that of Sir T. Zammit, and a paper submitted in 1954 to the Society of Antiquarians by Instructor Captain Gracie, R.N., is not inconsistent with it.

certainly for the intelligent Cro-Magnon—than to follow the same
well-worn track, chosen not for ease of terrain but for freedom
from the salt marshes of the low shore or the valley thickets which
sheltered the sabre-toothed tiger, year after year? And there were
many thousands of such years. The leg of a platform sledge, with
its cargo of skins, rude weapons and tools, old men and women,
babies, a robust chieftain, would break. The convoy would be
delayed, while the following vehicles were dragged and shoved
ahead of the casualty. In time, the points and sidings would
develop—accidentally, like most of this early man's discoveries.

Experience, too, would limit the height and breadth of the
sledge. Shafts were developed and the space of the sledge's legs
would be dictated by the pulling breadth of a squat, broad man's
shoulders. And this, as it happens, is the gauge of the tracks.

So, for countless years, these tracks were the highway upon
which the first men made their way into Europe. Then came the
upheaval which smashed the land-bridges and submerged these
rocks which were to re-emerge still bearing these puzzling
memorials to a vanished race.

This is what I like to think; but since no pundit has confirmed
this, or any other theory, beyond argument, you may care to
contemplate the tracks and let your own imagination go coursing
down the vast corridors of time.

5

At the foot of the hill called 'God and His Mother', the road
forks to left and right. To the left, a narrow, very English sort of
lane flanked by pine trees brings you out into the village of Bu
'Arrad, which used to be called Burmarrad; but since this means
'The place of sickness', the offending 'M' is often dropped. By
some extraordinary process, the English have managed to turn
the name into 'Burmah Road'. Despite his known affection for
Malta, there is no record of any peculiar connexion between this
village and Earl Mountbatten!

Here, you are on the main coast road—Malta's *Corniche*—
which runs, almost continuously by the seashore, from Valletta to
Marfa. To your right is the bay of Salini, the 'Salt Pans', where the
recovery of sea-salt had until lately been a Government monopoly
since the time of the Grand Masters.

As you might expect, the salt flats attract wild duck in the migration seasons, and if you are lucky enough to pick a day when there are no guns about, you may see mallard, teal, shoveller, and widgeon. Near Salini, too, I once counted twenty whiskered terns.

To your left is the growing resort of St. Paul's Bay. Until lately, a mere fishing village with one or two summer villas, it has spread out and along the shores of the bay in a not unattractive ribbon of Italian-style seaside villas, of the quaintly conceived shapes to which modern Italy is addicted.[1]

Here is the famous St. Paul's Island, separated from the mainland by a narrow and always turbulent strait, the 'place where two seas met' . . . upon which *euroclydon* blew the Apostle and his shipmates. Here, too, is Ghajn Razul—'The Spring of the Prophet'—where St. Paul is supposed to have slaked his salt-caked lips and not far away, the spot where the serpent came out of the fire of dry sticks. *Euroclydon* still blows—though it is now the *gregale*—and it is not hard to imagine the shipwreck, as the long, blue, white-toothed rollers come galloping into the bay and break upon the jagged point of Selmun.

On the ridge of Wardija, overlooking St. Paul's Bay and the village of Bu 'Arrad is the isolated hamlet of Wardija. The most pleasant approach to it (though the road is not good) is by a steep incline which rises to the left of the main coast road, just where a little hump-backed bridge crosses a water-course and where, amongst a clump of pines, there used to be a rare specimen of a silver birch.

Wardija lives up to its name. In the spring and autumn there is a profusion of wild flowers and the purple clover and the yellow mustard grows high in its fertile, little fields. The village used to comprise a tiny church, some scattered farmers' *razzett*—'she-beens' is the sense of the word—and a *palazz*. The country-folk invariably promote any house much bigger than a cottage to a 'palace'. They like to talk of 'our palace'.

Of recent years Wardija has become popular with Maltese of means and with British and American expatriates. It has mains electricity and ample water; but fortunately, development has been tasteful and, despite one of those monstrous ammunition dumps surrounded by barbed-wire which so commonly deface the

---

[1] Another claim to fame for this bay, is that Lord Charles Beresford used to take the last German Kaiser picnicking here.

Maltese countryside[1] it has not quite lost its rural charm. One
building of note, apart from the *palazz*, which is very like an
English country house, is a miniature Scottish castle, with snuffer
towers, emerging above the tops of the pine trees on the wooded
hillside; but one of the towers has collapsed, exposing a flimsy and
spurious interior. I wish the owner would repair it.

If you drive along the ridge of Wardija and turn right where
you come to yet another ugly ammunition depot with its inevitable barbed-wire, you will come down into the valley of San
Martin, one of the most fertile and most intensely cultivated areas
in Malta. Its charm has also been sadly mutilated by some supremely ugly civil defence works; but time and the wild heath will
deal with these.

On the right, as you descend towards the rich valley of Pwales,
which connects St. Paul's Bay on the east to Ghajn Tuffieha—
'The Well of Apples'—on the west, is a grotto which reproduces,
in miniature, the shrine of Our Lady at Lourdes. A great centre
for local pilgrims, the charming little shrine has already grown a
crop of devout legends. The owners of this land maintain the
shrine and have some difficulty in dissuading the devout from
decorating its cavern walls with the crutches and walking-sticks
of minor miracles. No authenticated miracle has ever been claimed
and there is no surer way of embarrassing the Church than to
encourage pious hearsay. But I wish the pilgrims would not
inscribe their names on the pillars of the gateway! Though I am
sure that Our Lady does not mind, the announcement that
CENSU SPITERI LOVES ANNI GATT is not a necessary incentive to
devotion, and the bald record of P. F. C. HENRY O. HIPPENBACKER
U.S.A.A.F. seems also a little unnecessary.

The tiny Chapel of San Martin, which is also maintained by the
owners of the estate, is unimposing as architecture; but it dates
from 1383 and has a Siculo-Norman nave. It is one of a diminish-
ing number of these little country chapels which used to serve the
farming community. It still has regular Masses; but in Malta, as in
England, the days of the country houses with their chapels and
their chaplains are passing. In a worthy desire to protect the
peasant from the 'absentee landlord' rents are pegged at a ridiculous level (in this particular case, sentiment as well as the law has

---

[1] It is fair to add that, since the kind of ammunition stored in these dumps
would be quite valueless in a modern war, the Armament Supply people are making
an effort to evacuate and obliterate these barbed-wire eyesores.

contrived to keep the rents at the level of 1804), and, whereas a few years ago, a country priest would have been glad of a living worth thirty pounds a year, that income would no longer keep him on bread and water. With easier transport, the country-folk travel to Mass in the bigger centres and the country chapels are fit only for some ageing priest with a meagre competence to end his days in the clean air, within sound of the laughter of the peasant children.

Opposite the grotto, there rises a flat-topped hill called Il Qala. Here there are a number of bell-shaped excavations, arranged in a circle about one central pothole, which may be Punic tombs. At other points (notably about Bingemma) similar excavations have turned out to be 'beehive' tombs—a series of cells, communicating by narrow shafts at several levels. The San Martin excavations have never, I think, been properly examined and they may turn out to be merely grain-storage pits.

It is a great place for birds, this valley. The rarer warblers, shrikes, doves, kingfishers, the hoopoe, and the golden oriole are not uncommon. The kingfisher is, in fact, called *Tajra ta' San Martin*, though perhaps because it appears in mid-November about the time of the Feast of St. Martin.

The English commonly complain that 'there are no birds in Malta' and, a little inconsistently, that 'The Maltese shoot everything that flies'. The latter statement is only too sadly true. Worse, they trap anything that sings or has a bright coat and put it in a cage.

Nevertheless, if you are fond of all God's small creatures that fly and creep, swim and crawl, Malta has plenty to offer you. Because the bird-life is shy and confined to the remoter parts of the Islands, there is more reward in the detection and identification even of species which are common by English standards, and in the discovery of their haunts and local habits.

Roberts in his *Birds of Malta* lists three hundred and nineteen species of which, he says, one hundred and twenty-five may be met with fairly regularly. He claims that only about ten are permanent residents. I think that this is probably a conservative estimate.

It has long been believed that the dislike of land-birds for a long sea-passage causes them to select points, in their migration, with the shortest sea-routes and that Malta thus receives a concentration of migrants. Roberts, quoting Moreau and Gibb, however, claims that there is no regular concentration, the apparently widely representative numbers of migrants being due merely to a favourable site from which to observe a series of broad front migrations.

It has been computed that, in the course of a season, some fifteen thousand birds could pass close to any observer in the Mediterranean area. Malta's share then, is by no means generous and apparent variations in the frequency of occurrence may well be accounted for by weather conditions and, above all, by the accuracy of reports and the maintenance of records. In this latter respect, Malta is ill-served. The first catalogue was compiled by Schembri in 1843 and a series of later observations by Wright, Despott, Gibb, de Lucca, and Roberts have added to the list. Much, it seems to me as an amateur, remains to be studied in the field of Maltese ornithology; but technical accuracy and the scientific approach aside, there is a world of fun for any newcomer with but an elementary knowledge of bird-life.

Even the sparrow exhibits a typically Maltese internationalism. He is usually called 'the Roof Bird' and, as the House Sparrow, is about the only feathered creature which survives and multiplies in the urban areas. With his polished chestnut gorget and his distinct eye stripe he seems, in Malta's bright light, to be a gayer fellow than his English cousin.

There is also the Tree Sparrow, who lacks the eye stripe but has an inverted comma for neck decoration; the Italian Sparrow, *Passer italiae*, with his white arm bands; the Spaniard, *Passer hispaniolensis*, with his speckled waistcoat, and the Rock Sparrow with a golden smudge on his shirt-front. It is claimed, too, that there is a Maltese sub-species of the Spaniard, *Passer hispaniolensis melitae*; but the morals of the sparrow are notoriously loose and, with the exception of the distinctive Rock Sparrow, with his charming name of *Petronia*, I doubt whether any of the species can claim purity of race. They are, to be sure, a pest to the farmer and steal vast quantities of his hard-won corn. I cannot blame the farmer who goes after sparrows with a gun.

At San Martin there is one very tall aurecaria pine which is the home of hundreds of tree sparrows. I have counted four hundred and eighty of their untidy, composite nests—like blocks of council flats—in this one tree. Allowing the conservative figures of two survivors per nest and three or four matings per year,

a minimum of three thousand tough little corn thieves emerges
from this colony annually; but their twitterings at dawn and sunset and their admirable, indefatigable industry are somehow
endearing. The sparrows yield their fortress to no other winged
thing but the tourist starlings who pass twice yearly on their way
to and from Trafalgar Square and occupy the pine for a few
weeks. I have seen these pert rascals put a sparrowhawk to flight
and chase him—by orderly flights and squadrons, each attack
wave being relieved in succession—far out to sea.

As well as the sparrows, many other species are native to Malta.
By all accounts the resident warblers are increasing. The members
of this family are legion and many of them hard to distinguish.
The Wood, Icterine, and Melodious Warblers all sport bright
yellow waistcoats, have similar songs, and frequent the thick
foliage of the wild locust or carob trees. The Sub-Alpine Warbler
can be mistaken for a robin, though he wears his crimson plumage
much higher towards the neck and has wings and back of a darker
brown. The Blackcap Warbler is the *Kappanera*—a smart, grey
fellow with a distinct skull-cap. He is bolder than many of his
family and often ventures into the gardens of the big town.

Sardinian, Garden, Spectacled, Yellow-browed, Chiff-Chaff,
and Reed Warbler are all common and breed in Malta.

Some indication of the local habits of most Maltese birds can
be gleaned from their Maltese names. Few of the warblers are
distinguished, almost all being *Bufula*—'The Beany One', or
Ghasfur-il-Harub—'The Carob Bird'.

Two words are used for the names of birds: *Tajra*, literally 'the
flying thing' which is also applied to a child's kite and to an aircraft, and *Ghasfur*, invariably applied to the passerines. The Golden
Oriole is *Tajra Safra*—the 'Yellow Bird', and *Ghasfur-il-Bejt* is the
'Roof Bird' or House Sparrow.

For the expert ornithologist there may be some advantage in
examining the native bird-names. The prefix *Bu* signifying 'having
to do with' or sometimes simply 'of', is a sure sign of antiquity in
personal- and place-names. *Buhagiar*—'having to-do-with stone'
—is a stonemason. *Butiggieg*—'having-to-do-with chickens'—is a
chicken farmer. These old surnames appear, unlatinized, in the
earliest written records and may well indicate, in a bird-name,
that the species is native or has commonly appeared as a migrant
for a very long time. Other names, which are obviously of foreign

origin, ought to indicate rarity or recent appearance. In general, these rules seem to work.

The Stonechat has been recorded as a permanent resident ever since such matters have commanded attention and his name is an onomatopoeic repetition of his call: *Buzafzaf*. The Woodchat Shrike, another resident, is *Bugiddiem*—'The Biter'.

The Nightingale, on the other hand, is rare and only very occasionally breeds in Malta. He is *Rosinjol*, from the French. The Robin is not rare; but his visits are brief and irregular. He is *Pittiross* from the Italian for 'Redbreast'.

Other names describe the bird's appearance by association and may, for that reason, be even simpler to date. The Black-eared Wheatear is *Dumnikan*—'Dominican'. The Dominicans appeared in Malta in the thirteenth century. The Ring Ousel is *Tas-sidrija-Bajda*—'White Waistcoat', and the Alpine Swift, 'White Belly'; so that we may be entitled to guess that the Swift made his appearance before the introduction of the waistcoat as an article of costume.

The Black-winged Stilt is *Fra Servent*, or 'Serving Brother' and his relative, the Oyster Catcher, *Kavalier*—both relating to the kind of cloak or surcoat worn by members of the Sovereign Order of St. John. The Oyster Catcher is and, by all accounts, has always been more common in the Islands than the Stilt, so perhaps he was first identified in the sixteenth century and the 'Serving Brother' shortly afterwards.

Not all Maltese bird-names have as pleasant an association as the Stilt or the Wheatear. The Short-eared Owl—a resident—is called *Omm is-subien*, which may be translated as 'Mother of Boys' and one may romanticize with thoughts of a remote connexion with the goddess Athene—wise warrior and protector of men, whose symbol was the owl; but unfortunately, classical imaginings are damped by the fact that *subien* also means 'lice' and the owl certainly suffers from her share of feather lice.

There is still much to be learned about Malta's birds. The older records, such as they are, note many species as rare migrants which more recent investigators claim as residents. Others are now common which are classified as rare by the older authorities.

The Great Grey Shrike is noted by Despott and Wright as a rarity and a migrant; but for three seasons running, I watched a pair of these predators mate, nest and rear their young, though it is true that I never saw the young after they left the nest, in the same clump of carob trees at San Martin.

The Kingfisher, too, is stated by Despott and others to be only an occasional visitor; but each November, for several years, one or two of these lovely little fishermen have appeared at San Martin and stayed until January.

It is the streams which water this valley and flow down to the plain of Pwales which attract the Kingfisher. The streams have plenty of frogs and freshwater crabs and there are many ponds and water-tanks in which golden carp abound. The ponds have all plenty of leafy cover around them. One late autumn afternoon, I surprised the blue and gold visitor stealing fish from a fountain inside the enclosed patio of the *palazz*.

It is a great shame that no official action seems possible to reduce the indiscriminate slaughter by gun and trap which goes on. We must grant the farmer his right to destroy the birds that ruin his crops, amongst which are many which we would count as fair game for the pot in England, like the quail, snipe, dove, and plover, all of whom pass over in their hundreds on migration. The starling, too, and the duck are fair game; but it is sad to see yellowhammer, bee-eater, golden oriole, redstart, robin, calandra lark, martins, swallows, hawfinch, greenfinch, song thrush, and blue rock thrush all fall victim to the not always accurate gun or the cage in a Valletta shop. Hawks, too, are shot on the charge that they take young chickens; yet they seem to survive. The sparrowhawk, harrier, falcon, and kestrel are constantly to be seen sailing and hovering over the bare hills at all seasons.

There is, it is true, a local ordinance which lists the protected birds, but I have never heard of a prosecution under it and, in any case, I wonder how many would-be sportsmen can identify a short-toed lark (which is protected) at fifty yards, or distinguish him from the calandra lark (which is not protected).

Nevertheless, we English must not be too self-righteous in the matter. Lark pie was a favourite English dish, and we massacre young rooks in their beds, cage the linnet, and breed pheasants for the sole purpose of blowing them to pieces. Any bird-lover will offer you an appalling list of the English species which have been exterminated through the efforts of marksmen, egg-collectors, and breeders of cage-birds.

The road which passes the Grotto of Our Lady of Lourdes

meanders down the valley towards the fertile plain, watered by the springs which rise from a bed of blue clay at the mid-level of the ridge of Wardija. It is a Roman road, as was lately discovered when a season of exceptional rains washed the top surface down to a series of those typical great paving-stones over which the Legions carried the *Pax Romana* from the Crimea to North Berwick. This same road runs over the hill towards Ghajn Tuffieha and has, on the left, just before you come within sight of the fine sandy sweep of the bay, a complex of Roman baths with the remnants of fine mosaic pavements, an altar to Ceres, and a well-preserved water-system fed from cisterns which were connected to spring-water. For many years the baths lay exposed to the depredations of souvenir-hunters and the mosaic pavements had been used by the soldiery as a dump for bully-beef cans. It has lately been cleaned up and enclosed, a worthy undertaking which, nevertheless, makes it more difficult of access to the well intentioned.

The valley of Pwales divides the ridge of Wardija from that of Bajda. Sloping gently upwards from east to west, its eastern mouth is the wide rocky bay of St. Paul where the ridge falls away into the sea, with the little Islands of Selmun and Selmunett to mark the submarine continuation of the *montagna*. To the west, the valley ends at the cliffs of 'The Well of Apples', a fine stretch of sand enclosed by weird rock-formations, dear to the Royal Marine Commandos who find it an excellent training-ground for their rock-climbing gymnastics. It is an all too popular bathing-resort to which the sun-happy English community flocks in its hundreds.

On each side of the valley, the rugged cliffs are full of caves; many of them inhabited. These cave-dwellings are dry and warm in winter and cool in summer. They house whole families whose amenities are primitive but efficient, and their robust health puts the town-dwellers to shame.

On the point of Selmun is the castle of that name, built by the Countess Catharina Scappi in the sixteenth century and still inhabited by her kin.

From Ghajn Tuffieha to Marfa, on the Gozo Channel, the west coast is rugged and forbidding. A small triangle of country hereabouts is innocent of negotiable road, thinly peopled, and largely unspoiled. Here you will see the traditional 'flat cart', an all-purpose affair of transverse slats which transports anything from a load of clover to all the children. Harnessed to one of the large, hardy breed of mules peculiar to Malta, the unusually high wheels carry the flat cart over rock-strewn tracks which no other vehicle could survive. Here, too, the *faldetta* and the *ghonnella* are still worn. The former is a black, stiffened hood which was once the walking-out version of the unstiffened, blue and white, spotted head veil and skirt combined, called *ghonella*.

Both head-dresses have almost disappeared from the towns and larger villages. They are old fashioned and have suffered from the silly fables told of their origin, such as that which alleges that the *faldetta* was assumed by order of the Church, to be worn for a hundred years as a badge of shame to mark the immoderate and immodest conduct of the women with Napoleon's soldiery.

The black silk hood, with its stiffened frame, is, indeed, a very ancient piece of costume throughout the Mediterranean, with variants in Corfu, in Crete, and in Sardinia. It appears, too, in bas-relief on a Carthaginian tomb and a Frenchman, André Maurois, has disposed of the Napoleonic legend, thus:

Certains guides racontent sur l'origine de la 'faldetta', de sinistres histoires: c'est le Pape qui avait assigné, pour cent ans, cette coiffure aux femmes de Malte, comme penitence pour la faiblesse de la ville et sa redition à Bonaparte en 1798—'Pour cent ans?' Dites vous—'Mais il y a deja plus de cent ans.' La verité est beaucoup plus simple. La faldetta existait bien avant Bonaparte. A la Bibliothèque de Malte, le chevalier Scicluna m'a montré des estampes du seizième siècle où, dejà, ce voile figure. Cette explication historique comme tant d'autres n'est qu'une legende.

We should, before leaving this district, notice the church of the small market town of Mgarr. It has been called 'The Egg Church' because it was built with funds raised exclusively from contributions in kind of one egg in every ten laid by the devout hens of Mgarr. Certainly, the dome, whether by design or not, which is distinctly graceful, has the lineaments of the sharper end of an inverted egg.

Another story is told of Mgarr: that it is here that the intermittent appearances of golden sovereigns in the Valletta markets have their origin. Some fifty years ago, some bold fellows held up and robbed a cashier of the Dockyard (this much is true, and the exercise was successfully repeated in 1950). They were detected and punished: but their golden gains were never recovered and some of the rascals were known to be natives of Mgarr.

But the Maltese peasant is a great hoarder of precious metal. He has small faith (and who can blame him?) in paper money or in nickel coinage; but he will carefully abstract any old silver florins from a handful of change and some of the women still wear their savings around their necks in the shape of a *barbazzal* or *dudu*, literally 'worm', of gold made in the dying technique called by the Neapolitans '*Grand Spinat*'. The Maltese have centuries of experience of debased coinage and are instinctively aware of the trickery which we now call inflation.

Beyond the Bay of St. Paul to the north is the Bay of Mistra, from which an excellent road climbs dizzily towards the little township of Mellieha, whose name is exactly the same, in Punic, as Salini—'the Saltings'.

This is a very old settlement, claiming, like so many coastal areas, a personal connexion with St. Paul and the first Apostles. The imposing and very lovely Church of Mellieha stands upon a headland looking down upon the wide curve of Mellieha Bay and the saltings of Ghadira. Characteristically fortress-like and grim rather than graceful, it is, nevertheless, stimulating, with its great dome rising from terraced foundations where the rock has been cut into vertical faces and reinforced with stone walls. At the base of the greater church, tucked into a terrace, rather like a baby bird sheltering beneath its mother, is the famous Chapel of Our Lady of Mellieha which boasts a portrait of the Mother of God reputed to have been painted by St. Luke. This is, I fear, a devout and harmless fable, the probable fact, since the picture is no older than the thirteenth century, being that it is the work of a Florentine known as San Luca.

. Like the men of Mosta, the villagers of Mellieha built their own church, in this case, upon the crest of the high promontory, above the roof-level of the older, thirteenth-century shrine of Our Lady.

The designer was not an architect but a master-mason, one Busuttil, himself a Mellieha man, and the work was an undertaking of national wonder and interest in the early part of this century. It even stirred the interest of the English garrison who sent their military bands to play in the village square while the work was being done. A curious sidelight of the church project and the interest which it aroused amongst officers of the Garrison, was a friendship between a British officer and a local peasant who was famous for his gigantic stature and his marksmanship. They used to go after quail and plover together and, in February of the year 1902, in which the church was completed, an article appeared in *The Field*, describing how the Maltese Nimrod had brought down a hundred and fifty-eight birds in one afternoon, missing no single shot. Nimrod is still remembered as *Salvu ta'l'abjad*—'Salvatore the White One' (he was a baker by trade). Besides his marksmanship he was noted as a phenomenal fisherman whose hauls with a cast-net were historic.

At this time, too, they will tell you, there lived in Mellieha 'the most beautiful woman in the World'. She was called *Il Warda Bajda*—'The White Rose', and foreign artists used to clamour to be allowed to paint her portrait; but this would have been sinful vanity and 'The White Rose' was good as well as beautiful. So her famous beauty remains only a legend. Her granddaughters are pretty, but unremarkable.

Tales like these you will hear in any village, in the wine-shop, as the peasant farmers sit over their rough wine and their bread and oil.

Mellieha Bay is as popular, in summer, as Ghajn Tuffieha, and it has grown a crop of beach-shanties or 'chalets' and the stalls of purveyors of ice cream, cola drinks, bubble gum, and other horrors of civilization; but it is good to see the ordinary Maltese family disporting themselves on the sand, in costumes which would have been thought so immodest a generation ago as to earn a police summons.

In the old days, *Lapsi*—The Feast of the Ascension—was the only time for families to go bathing and to play at swings. Exposure to the sun and air was thought dangerous, as a habit, as well as immodest and, as did our own Victorian forebears, everybody wore far too many clothes.

I remember the pilgrimages to the sea at *Lapsi*, when you would see ladies of extreme modesty bobbing up and down in shallow water in long shifts which ballooned and floated to the surface, all oblivious of the fact that the translucent waters of the Mediterranean concealed no part of their charms from the passing eye. In those days, only the mad English spent hours toasting themselves upon rock or sand and being run in by the police for exposing their broiled midriffs.

But only a few people, and those, too, the mad English, venture far from the towns and villages after the first rains and the damp chill of autumn. Then Mellieha Bay is deserted. The sand is cleansed by the fierce seas of the *gregale* of its ice-cream cartons and paper-bags. Masses of green weed are piled up and the clean, white bones of the cuttle fish and small pink shells are brought in to decorate the sand with every wave.

Maltese beaches are not notable for their sea-shells and the rock-pools are only rich in marine life at a few points where a constant swell keeps them fresh. The tides are negligible, so that the creatures of the sea live always below the surface. But it is not necessary to go very deep to discover the fairyland of a marine garden. On this eastern coast, particularly, the rock shelves gently at many points out into the deep water like the head of a mushroom (perhaps it is this formation which inspired the theory that Malta is mushroom-shaped and mounted upon a stem which will some day snap) and the slopes of these shelves are full of life and colour. The weeds are golden and green, and little fish, silver and blue, and transparent, ghostly shrimps swim in and out of the magic forest. A little deeper, the anemones flaunt their fatal beauty against rocks which are red, green, gold, and purple. There is the Plumose Anemone which shades from a delicate salmon-pink to the smooth white of old porcelain, and the Opelet like a green and lilac plant. The Strawberry Anemone, too, looks good enough to eat as it sits in its bed of coral.

There are fantastic Fanworms, which operate just like those paper fans in a cardboard tube, and Sponges and those strange animals called 'Sea Mats' which are so beautiful in the sea and so ugly in the air.

The bright orange, slimy coat which covers some of the rocks is a colony of tiny creatures called ascidians. The Common Crab scuttles busily about near the shore-line; but the Edible Crab is to be found only in the deeper crevices. There are other edible crabs too, in the deeper submarine caves: the Spider, with his heavy camouflage of algæ and the Sponge Crab, so called because he wears a sponge on his back to deceive his enemies. The Hermit Crab is also a resident, living in the stolen shell of a whelk or a periwinkle.

Shrimps abound and Prawns also. Limpets are eaten; but Maltese Mussels are reputed to be poisonous.

Both red and yellow starfish are common. The Yellow or Sand Starfish grows to as much as a foot across. The wonderful Sea Horse also grows to an unusual size in these warm and nourishing waters, as does that monstrous slug the Sea Hare.

8. Water Seller: nineteenth century

9. 'Mdina: the walled Norman capital

10. Marsamxett from the bastions

13. Wied iz-Zurrieq

14. The Fleur-de-lys
Fountain, Floriana

There is an infinity of sea-creatures, sufficient, if you wish to make a study of them, to occupy a lifetime. As with the birds the local-names have an interest of their own. The Freshwater Crab, a gallant fellow who stands on his hind legs and menaces you with his claws, rather than retreating like his seagoing cousin, is called *Grang tal'ilma*; *ilma* being taken to mean fresh water. Sea water is simply *bahar*—'Sea'. The Common Shore Crab is the 'Harbour Crab', the Spider Crab simply 'Spider' and the Angular Crab, with his long-stalked eyes, *Zakak*, a name also applied to the White Wagtail, but I fail to see any connexion. The gay, red and blue Swimming Crab, with his legs like a pair of oars, is 'the Butterfly'.

Another form of the Spider Crab with four horns is known as *Ghagusa*, a name also used for old women possessed of the Evil Eye, which we may take as 'Witch'. The Sponge Crab, with his specially adapted extra legs for holding his camouflage in place, is *Kapott*—'Cloak'. The Common Lobster is known, but is uncommon in Maltese waters. The Spiny Rock Lobster or Crawfish is called *Awwista*, which we may take as a corruption of *Langouste*. The Flat Lobster is *Cikala Hamra*, or Red Cicala and the Mantis Prawn, who does 'pray' like a Mantis, is *Cikala Bajda*—'White Cicala'. This is curious because the Cicala or Cicada, proper, is not called by this name but by the onomatopoeic *Werzieq*.

The minute Porcelain Crab, barely a quarter of an inch across, with his high-set eyes, despite his humble proportions has managed to impress his personality. He is called *Mewt*—'Death's Head'.

Malta's land isopod, the Wood-louse, a relative of the lobster, rejoices in the suggestive title of 'Earth Pig'. When I was a child in the West Country, we used to call them 'Sow-pigs'.

If you intend to explore the sea-bottom in mask and breathing-system—and a spring-gun if you must—I should warn you that there are both short and long-armed octopods in plenty, and while it is true that they are cowardly creatures, they will fight back, as you would, if you step on their faces. There are also Sting Rays and an evil relative of the Lion Fish, with a baleful, red-eyed glare and an armament of spines. He is one of the few naturally truculent fishes, and a wound from one of his spines is instantly poisonous and can be serious.

You must also be wary of the Sea Egg, Urchin or *Rizzi*. He looks like the purple husk of a chestnut; but he is very much alive and his spines, which are equipped with thousands of tiny mouths, will train automatically towards an approaching shadow. If you should collect any of these spines in your hand or foot, the local cure is a poultice of hot onion, drastic but effective. In places, the sea-bed is carpeted with those sluggish animals, the Sea Cucumber or *Bêche de Mer*, a favourite weapon with small boys, being a sort of natural water-pistol which ejects a stream of liquid with considerable force if squeezed lightly about the middle. A delicacy in the Pacific, I have not heard of the Sea Cucumber being eaten in Malta or Sicily.

You will not meet many of the bigger fish in shallow water and the Shark and the Barracuda are mercifully rare. Once only in living memory is a man believed to have been taken by a shark and that is by no means certain.

Sharks do come into the Mediterranean and the Suez Canal has been blamed, for they are supposed to follow ships through, from the Red Sea; but in the Central Mediterranean they seem to prefer the waters around northern Sicily. Shark steak is a popular delicacy in Messina.

Dolphins, those friendly mammals who seem unable to resist human company, make frequent expeditions into the harbours. Sometimes, one is gaffed by a boatman close inshore and there is a flurry of excitement as the poor beast is dispatched.

Tunny fishing has long been a national industry, though not a flourishing one, because the capital has never been available to develop a fishing fleet on the vast scale of the Sicilian tunny fleet. The lights of the Sicilian tunny boats returning from their grounds, north of Lampedusa, look like a N.A.T.O. Task Force on exercises. They are not allowed to land their fish in Malta and the only practical result of an attempt to protect the local industry is that tunny is an expensive luxury.

In much the same way as they announce that 'there are no birds in Malta', the English often aver that there are only three kinds of fish: *Dendici*, *Lampuki*, and Red Mullet. They are not wholly to blame, for generations of Service cooks have been trained to believe that these are the only sort of fish the Englishman will eat. I once attempted to feed a ship's company on *Kavalli*. Most of it went down the 'gash' shute. A month later we put on the same fish, only this time we described it as Mackerel, which is what it is. They ate it and came back for more.

Of the mackerel family, alone, there are dozens of examples to be found in Maltese waters. The *Kavall*, or Spanish Mackerel is, perhaps, the most common. It is an attractive fish, with the characteristic mackerel markings, which soon fade, when it is landed, from the brilliant gold and silver and green and blue to a duller silver and dark grey. The *Lampuka* is a coryphene, sometimes described in English as a dolphin; but it is not the mammal *Delphinius*. It has also been called the *Dorade*, thus confusing it with the Gilt Head, so common in the Atlantic, particularly around Bermuda. The *Lampuka*, with its delicate grey shading along the dorsal fin and its bright yellow belly is attractive under water; but it fades to a dull grey in air and is unexciting in taste like so many of the warm-water fish of the inshore rocks.

The Pilot Fish, called *Fanfru*, is another common member of the mackerel family. The Remora, or Sucker, is not so common but he follows Shark, Tunny, and Swordfish and is often brought up in the tunny nets. As a general guide to marketing, a fish with an obvious Maltese name is likely to be an inshore type and will not be as tasty as those with Italian names; but the rule is not always easy to apply. The Remora is called *Pixxi Tmun*, not easily recognized as *Pesce Timone*—'Rudder Fish'.

Pliny says that the Remora was responsible for the loss of a naval action in which so many of the suckers attached themselves to the keels of the losing side as to make their ships unmanœuvrable! It is also said that the Remora has been used, on a lead, to trap larger fish with its sucker device.

Largest of all edible Maltese fish is, of course, the Tunny. Fish ten feet in length and of a thousand pounds weight are not uncommon. The migration of the Tunny has long been a matter of study. Aristotle had a theory that the fish originated in the Atlantic, entered the Mediterranean along the North African coast, into the Black Sea and back to the Atlantic by way of the southern European shore. More recent observations establish that the Atlantic Tunny remains in his own ocean and that the Mediterranean fish lives in deep water in the winter, surfaces in summer, and makes for shallower waters where the female spawns. In August, the young Tunny, known as 'shiners', are caught in quantity. In November the fish take again to the deep water.

Close relatives of the tunny are the Albacore or *Alonga* and the striped-bellied Bonito or *Kubrita*. The plain Bonito is also a common catch from August to November. He rejoices in a variety of local-names—*Tumbrell*, *Mazzita*, *Tombitombi*, and *Zgamirru*, all describing the same fish.

The Belted Bonito, a fierce hunter who chases the flying fish, is called *Plantu* or *Palamit*, both corruptions, I think, of his Latin name *Polamys Sardis*. He is not very good eating and is sometimes supposed to be actually poisonous.

Two fish, with Italianate names of which I know no English equivalent, the *Acciola* and *Cervjola*, are excellent eating. Both are long, thin fish with a brown back and a silver belly.

A very beautiful fish, with mackerel markings in green, blue, and silver is the Imperial Horse Mackerel but it is a rare visitor to inshore waters.

The *Tonna Bajda* or White Tunny is the 'Dolphin' of heraldry, with a noble and learned-seeming brow.

The Black Perch is another rare visitor, known as 'The Foreigner' or the 'Turkish Lampuka'. It is not good eating, though preferable to its cousin, the Castor Oil Fish which is used only as a medicine.

The Boar or Cuckoo Fish is fairly common and serves to enliven the duller patches of sea-bottom with his small, flat, red, yellow, and silver striped body.

Amongst the fish familiar to English housewives, excellent eating, and commonly seen in the Maltese markets, is the John Dory, with his famous thumb-mark of St. Peter. His official title is *Zeus Faber*, and critics who care to see a connexion between early representations of St. Peter and the Roman Jupiter or Greek Zeus may also wish to ascribe the association with St. Peter to a similar syncretism.

In Maltese, he is called *Moxt*, which means 'comb' (and is also a term of abuse, on the principle of rhyming slang) and, direct from the Italian, *Pixxi San Pietru*. Lanfranco says that John Dory is a corruption of *Jaune d'oree* and adds that he is a fraud, since Lake Gennesaret is fresh and the John Dory is essentially a salt-water denizen. Lanfranco[1] has also pointed out that *Zeus Pungio*, a close relative, is even commoner in Malta than *Zeus Faber*; but has never formerly been distinguished, despite the distinctive spine behind the eye and the much fainter thumb-mark.

[1] Guido Lanfranco, F.R.E.S., F.Z.S., F.B.S.E., Malta's outstanding and inde-fatigable naturalist to whom I am indebted for such of my technical references as are accurate.

Turtles are caught quite often around Malta and Gozo and I have heard that they used, at one time, to lay eggs on the remote, sandy beaches. You will see them from time to time in the fish market and they are, by English standards, cheap.

The red meat of the Sea Egg or *Rizzi* is a local delicacy. You must split the hard carapace down the centre. If it has a monk in the centre—a tiny organism that certainly resembles a cowled monk—it is a male and no good. The female, however, secretes a sac of minute red eggs, about sufficient to cover your little finger-nail. Two or three dozen *Rizzi* will yield enough meat to cover a slice of bread. It tastes like red caviare.

You will see old men gleaning the rock-pools for sea eggs and for the deposit of coarse sea-salt which dries on the higher levels of the rocky shore. With this and a thick slice of the sticky, wholemeal Maltese bread, they will contrive a meal. The salt is rich in ammoniates which the commercial processing removes, and who can complain about red caviare? The old beachcombers who affect this diet will assure you that it keeps them free from colds, rheumatism, and indigestion. I expect they are right.

The empty dried shell of a sea egg is a marvellous thing. Hold it up to the light, and there emerges a complex pattern of lacy perforation and low relief, the prevailing motif of which is, strangely, a Maltese cross. It would not surprise me to learn that the first lace-maker to produce the traditional design (which is dying, like the industry itself, in favour of more 'popular' shapes) copied it from the husk of an echinoderm.

Maltese beaches and cliffs present an accurate cross-section of the rock-pattern of the Archipelago, a layer of sand or soft limestone, then a harder, more brittle layer, another darker stratum and, finally, layers of hard, grey stone, fretted and eroded so that you might, in many places, mistake it for coral. In the limestone which is really a mass of fossil *Globigerina*, are countless other fossils: dumb memorials to an age of reptiles and sufficient evidence that what is now high cliff once lay at the bottom of an ocean. Auger shells are everywhere; but commonest of all are the trilobites, so common, indeed, that you might believe the Islands to consist exclusively of the embalmed bodies of these ancestors of the Sea Urchin.

Were it not for the fossils, the rocks of Malta would present a drab and uniform texture at and near sea-level. But on the hillsides and the uplands they are infinitely coloured and shaded, and have a definite seasonal change, though at first sight they seem barren and naked.

They are, in fact, clothed in tiny lichens, liverworts, and mosses, all of which have a distinct seasonal cycle. Six of the Maltese lichens are unknown to science in any other part of the world, as are some one hundred of the native fungi. Of these latter, many are edible; but I do not recommend any amateur to eat his personal selection, for many are also deadly.

Here and there, at scattered points, the rocks have a crystalline formation and what looks like fluorspar and 'potato stone' may be detected.

The best and most secluded beaches are difficult of access, save from the sea. And this is a mixed blessing, for on English high days and holidays and invariably at the week-ends, a fleet of Flag officers' and captains' barges and motor-boats, of R.A.F. and R.A.S.C. water transport, converges upon these popular 'English' beaches. It is the Union Club and the Marsa gone afloat. If you would escape them, avoid the seashore on Sundays, in summer.

The English have their own names for their favourite beaches— Anchor Bay—Island Bay—Paradise Bay—Slug Bay. Not all the native names are preferable. One is Ras-il-Fenek—'The Rabbit's Head' (where there is an intriguing fossil in the overhanging cliff which could be a pterodactyl); but Gnejna—'The Garden of God', Fomm-ir-Rih—'Mouth of the Wind', and Wied iz-Zurrieq—'The Blue Gorge' are surely preferable.

We have an unlovely habit of avoiding the embarrassment of failing to get our tongues round foreign names by renaming places. On the China Coast there is a lovely bay, popular with picnickers, called in Cantonese 'The Weeping Lover', from a curious rock-formation. Our charts show it as 'Gin Drinker's Bay'.

6

Inland from the Sandy Crescent of Mellieha Bay lies the valley of Ghadira—'The Pool'. In summer a series of arid sand-pits surrounded by feathery tamarisks, rising gradually towards fields of corn and pumpkins, this is a string of freshwater ponds from autumn to spring, fringed by rushes and the marshy ground beloved of the wading-birds. Here, on a sandspit not fifty yards from the main road you may see dozens of Plover, Ringed,

Little Ringed, and Kentish (called 'the English Plover'), and on
the ponds themselves there will be mallard, teal, pochard,
shoveller and widgeon as well as coot and moorhen. The shooting
hereabouts is rented by a Maltese gentleman of sensibility and the
waders escape indiscriminate massacre. I am sure that wild birds,
migrants as well as residents, quickly learn and transmit to their
progeny a knowledge of the sites which are safer than others. How
else is it that the waders have taken so soon to frequenting the
airfields which were formerly under cultivation and well shot
over? They flock, on a rainy day, to the wet tarmac and the short
grass of the Naval Air Station, perhaps deceived a little by the
similarity of the shining concrete to wet sand; they hurry about
amongst the puddles with great confidence, seeming fully aware
that they are safe from guns. At Hal Far, you will see redshank,
greenshank, stint, dotterel, golden and grey plover, and lapwing,
standing about as unperturbed as they would on an English
mud-flat.

If you will, take the road from Mellieha Bay, up through a
miniature mountain-pass towards Marfa; but do not yet press on
to the extreme·northern limits of the main island. Turn right at
the crest of the hill, towards a headland—the handle of the Marfa
'spoon'—called Armier. To the north and south there are some
lovely, small beaches, unfrequented on most week-days and
almost always in winter, and the vista of the bay to the south and
the Comino Channel, with Comino and her little consort Cominotto (Kemuna and Kemnett in Maltese) and Gozo to the north,
is superb.

The cliffs which enclose the Mellieha Bay are very strange.
For a distance of a mile or more they are split, quite neatly and
uniformly, along their whole length, as if cleft by the axe of some
angry Titan. The separated sections hang outwards as if they
would at any moment fold over like a slice of fruit-cake. And like
this, they have hesitated for countless ages. In the deep chasms so
formed, inaccessible to any but the most expert rock-climber, the
sea-birds and the sand martins wheel and roost in unaccustomed
security and the persecuted rock thrush finds sanctuary. His
splendid plumage has been his undoing; orange-scarlet breast,
slate-blue head and white rump too often enliven the shop-fronts
of the Sliema bird-fanciers.

The headland of Armier is thinly cultivated to the south, but rich in a large part of its northern slopes. At one time, however, the whole area seems to have been under cultivation, for there are low, dry stone walls or their scattered remnants everywhere in the little peninsular, and many of the cromlechs which the peasant farmer erects against sun and rain and uses as hides for his constant war on the birds.

Wheatears abound here in the autumn. They seem to have no fear of motor-cars and are undisturbed by the movement of humans inside them. Throw some crumbs out and sit quietly in your car and they will alight on the bonnet—very gay little fellows with their warm peach waistcoats, grey jackets and caps, and firmly marked black and white tails.

At Armier I saw a solitary rook. The sweet, thin song of the warblers in the stubble and heath ceased abruptly as the shadow of this rare and lonely intruder passed overhead. I think they must have taken him for a hawk.

After dark, and sometimes in the brief twilight, you will see rabbits here. The Maltese rabbit (*Oryctologus cuniculus*) is shy and rare. He is shot at sight, for if he were allowed to subsist on any considerable scale the Island's food-supplies would soon disappear, so much of the staple crops being literally rabbit-food. He is an attractive little beast, smaller and having more the colour of a hare than his English cousin, he is called *Fenek* which happens, also, to be the Arabic name of the African desert fox. In places, notably on St. Paul's Island, around the airfields, and in the deserted forts, he survives in noticeable strength.

Inevitably, Maltese wild mammals are nowadays few. The hedgehog (*Erinaceus europaeus*) seems to thrive. In high summer they take to the roads, perhaps in search of water, and are slaughtered in dozens by passing cars. At least two species of bats (*Vespertilionidae*) flourish. One is the small, ugly black fellow whom nobody loves and another the golden brown, silken coated creature with large, round ears who can endear himself even to the anxious female who believes that bats are all determined to entangle themselves in her hair.

At sunset, the bats emerge in their hundreds from the eaves of old houses and the fissures in the high bastions. A crack in the stonework scarcely wide enough to admit a finger suffices for access and exit to and from a space which you would think could not hold more than two or three of the little animals.

The brown rat is all too common and displays all his usual skill and initiative at robbing hen-roosts and rolling the eggs out of nesting-boxes. The house mouse is also widespread.

The stoat (*Mustela erminia*) is commoner than you would suppose from the paucity of his natural prey and his cousin, the ferret, is bred in Gozo. The common shrew is also a native. There are many semi-wild cats—for the most part domestic escapes, much cross-bred—but they also exhibit a frequent atavism to the true Mediterranean cat: that slim, graceful animal whom the Egyptians worshipped under the appropriate name of *Pasht* and whose portrait so often occurs on stele and obelisk. There is no wild animal of the dog family, though some of the country beasts which the peasants keep as watch-dogs are but faintly domesticated. The Maltese Poodle, a little ball of white fur with boot-button eyes, may be of very ancient origin. The Grand Master Pinto, who flourished from 1741 to 1773, kept them and they were an established breed in his time.

The commonest, and perhaps the only, native dog is the miniature Greyhound, somewhat like the English Whippet, called *Tal Fenek*—the 'Rabbit Dog', and much prized by the farmers who have carefully bred them for centuries. He, too, is an ancient Mediterranean type whose likeness is common on Egyptian monuments. The god Anubis wears his head. It is possible that, as a pure breed, this dog survives only in Malta and Sicily. He has recently achieved notoriety and popularity in Italy, due to the interest of a Sicilian noblewoman (the late Donna Agata Paterno di Carcaci) who bred the animals in her kennels near Catania.

Not native at all—the Englishman amongst domestic animals— is the Beagle Hound, common in all the country districts, and still very true to type. They are descended from a pack imported during the last century by an English officer whose determination to import the British way of life led to the short-lived maintenance of a Drag Hunt.

Amongst the native domestic stock are the Maltese Black Fowl, a fine layer and good table bird, and the inevitable Maltese Goat. The fabulous Shoat or Geep is in fact, a Barbary Sheep: a forlorn-looking beast who certainly looks undecided whether to be a sheep or a goat. During the Second World War, the goat population virtually disappeared, even the most decrepit Billy being an attractive candidate for the pot. Saanens and Nubians have since been imported and the bewildered Shoat who never knew whether to produce wool or milk, and was not very good at either, is disappearing.

The goat has for many years been the basis of innumerable anti-Maltese jokes, usually in the worst of taste, amongst the Garrison, and it is true that the driving of herds of goats through populated areas and the delivery of milk by the simple means of milking the animal at the doorstep was not a salubrious practice. The height of low comedy was reached when, in an attempt to make the process more hygienic, the animals were compelled to wear brassières when on their rounds. The goat has now been exiled from the towns and the sale and pasteurization of goats' milk centralized under Government control. The danger, which used to be very real, of contracting undulant fever is now at an end, and if you can get used to the sweet tang of goats' milk it is very good for you being much richer in protein, I am told, than cows' milk.

Malta might have enjoyed a more enviable reputation as a health resort in the past, had it not been for the undulant fever which was so unhappily, and unjustly, labelled 'Malta fever' in the early years of this century.

English travellers of the last century, with the unlucky exception of Byron, a fairly unreliable reporter by any standards, speak highly of the climate, the people, and the amenities. 'It would be difficult to find a more cheerful, lively little tract of industry and content . . . where luxury and convenience can more readily be obtained. . . .' wrote Tallack in his *Malta under the Phoenicians, Knights and English* in 1861. And in 1880, an Anglican cleric, the Reverend Mr. Godwin, found that the Maltese scene 'left its mark upon his memory when the vividness of fairer scenes had faded away . . . and sunsets', he wrote, 'steal over these waters and the glowing gold of which an artist may well despair of imitating'. And then, quite suddenly it seems, we begin to read of Malta fever and a terrifying vision of an island overrun with disease is somehow created.

The fact is that undulant fever is and was endemic in the goat (as tuberculosis is and was in the cow) and was not uncommon in every land where goats' milk was standard. On the other hand, goats' milk was, I believe correctly, supposed to be good for patients convalescing from any kind of fever.

For a long time, sailors admitted to the Naval Hospital at Bighi, possibly suffering from mild fevers of various origins, were put on a diet of goats' milk. They died, with unaccountable regularity, and there grew up a legend of this terrible and peculiarly Maltese fever, of unknown origin. It remained for a Maltese, Sir 'Temi' Zammit, to suggest a connexion between the fatal fever and the milk diet. Subsequent research proved his guess to be correct, but the legend of 'Malta' fever persisted. Its eradication from the Island has not been easy. The Maltese did, and still do, occasionally suffer from the fever but it seems to have been less often fatal in their case since they undoubtedly enjoyed some measure of immunity, as the English do to tuberculosis, and a peasant farmer is naturally reluctant to destroy the infected animals upon which his livelihood may depend, on the sole direction of a civil servant who talks of a disease which means little to him. But the Government milk undertaking is heavily subsidized and it usually pays the goat-owner to retain its approval.

Cows have always been kept, but more as draught-animals or as a badge of status than for profit, but they are now becoming much more general, and considerable herds can be seen in parts of both Malta and Gozo.

The native Maltese cow is a rangy beast with a khaki coat and long, wide horns who can subsist on a diet almost as meagre and as undiscriminating as the goat's; but Friesians, Jerseys, Shorthorns, Ayrshires, and other foreign breeds have been imported in increasing numbers of recent years.

The Guinea Pig, called *Fenek tal Indi* or Indian Rabbit, is bred for the table. He tastes, as one would expect, like sucking-pig, another delicacy enjoyed by the peasant, but infrequently eaten by the urban type, from whom the farmer and the middleman would exact a suitably extravagant price. The native pig is the Maltese White now much interbred with imported stock. Like the Irishman, the Maltese peasant is a great pig-fancier and he manages to collect a fairly handsome profit on his pork. Local prejudice against frozen or chilled meat persists, and the prices paid for fresh, locally killed meat are higher than are usual in England.

It is often assumed that, like the other Mediterranean peoples, the Maltese are not great meat-eaters, and it is true that their basic diet is 'fried and farinaceous'—pasta, oil and fruit, and vegetables—but their habits have been changing for two or more generations. In 1880 the Reverend Mr. Godwin[1] reports that 'Only two-fifths of the meat eaten on the Island is consumed by the Maltese, the remainder being required by the English population. . . .' Since the Maltese have never outnumbered the Garrison by less than twenty to one, that allocation left little enough meat for the natives. Nowadays, despite the rigid frequency of fast days and days of abstinence, the average Maltese family has adopted the 'Sunday joint' regimen of the Garrison and, in consequence, I think, eats too much.

Pigeons are also bred for the table rather than as show-birds, though there are pigeon-fanciers and some farmers keep a few Fantails because they are pleasant to have about. The Turtle Dove, which breeds amongst the remote cliffs of Dingli and Gozo and is also a migrant visitor, in force, is commonly trapped and domesticated. They will cross-breed with domestic pigeons and make charming pets.

Guinea Fowls and Turkeys are bred for the English Christmas and the American N.A.T.O. 'Thanksgiving'. Their names suggest that they are recent arrivals in the island. *Galina*, which is Spanish for 'Hen' (whence, too, the English West Country 'Gleenie') is used for the Guinea Fowl[2] and *Dundjan* from the French, for 'Turkey'. There is a remote connexion between Malta and the appearance of the turkey in England. It was a Captain Strickland, kinsman of the Anglo-Maltese family of that name and one of the Genoese Sebastian Cabot's Captains, who imported the first turkeys from New England. His branch of the Stricklands are the only family to have a turkey in their armorial bearings.

It would be quite wrong to accept the commonly received opinion that the Maltese, as a people, are cruel to animals. It is true that they do not understand the exaggerated English cultus of the horse and the dog and English people are often shocked to be told that the crop-eared meat-fed animals to be seen in some villages are fighting-dogs; but cock-fighting (which survives in England) is unknown and neither bear-baiting nor fox-hunting has ever been understood or practised by the Maltese.

It is, rather, a matter of priorities. A frugal people has never been willing to lavish upon animals the care and attention which, they feel, is due first to children, and the Maltese is sometimes

---

[1] G. N. Godwin, *A Guide to the Maltese Islands*, Malta, 1880.
[2] The Guinea Fowl is also called *Farauna*.

careless rather than deliberately cruel. Nevertheless, he is capable
of extravagant affection for a pet animal and is sincerely attached
to his horse, his mule, and his shooting dog.

7

Few of us can bring ourselves to love a snake; but the Maltese
abhorrence of this often beautiful creature is almost pathological.
To him, the Serpent is truly the embodiment of evil and although
none of the native snakes is venomous, thanks, they say, to St.
Paul, all are slain at sight. There are, it is true, indications in
folklore that a cult of snake worship once existed in the Islands;
but this vestige of paganism may increase rather than diminish
the inherent dislike.

The delicate, golden Leopard Snake which seldom exceeds
eighteen inches in length is called *Lifagh* and the variants of the
Dark Green Snake, which grows to as much as four feet on occasion and varies from a lovely silken green to an enamelled black
—are all *Serp*.

The Leopard Snake eats mice and will drink milk, so that he can
become a useful and attractive house guest.

The story of St. Paul and the Viper has given rise to as many
legends as the apocryphal Irish exploits of St. Patrick.

Guido Lanfranco, the naturalist, once embarked in print (very
bravely, I think, for there are valiant spirits who will have no
tampering with their own reading of Holy Writ) upon a learned
discussion about the Viper of St. Paul. He reminded his readers
that Holy Writ had never stated that St. Paul had banished all
'vipers', or venomous snakes, from Malta, pointing out that the
name *Lifagh* had always been applied indiscriminately not only to
Coluber Leopardinus; but to every species other than the *Serp* and
that Holy Writ, in the vernacular, gave no clue as to the actual
species of snake involved.

The discussion waxed warm and ended in a splendid confusion.
If there were no vipers in Malta, and never had been, then Malta
was not the island of the shipwreck and the ancient claim of
Meleda, in the Adriatic, could be revived. If, on the other hand,
St. Paul's viper was an imported example, brought in in a cargo of,
say, fruit or timber, how did the natives recognize it? And how
did they know it was venomous? No conclusion which robbed the
national Apostle of his miracle was to be countenanced, though

we may suspect that neither St. Paul nor the Roman shipmen, nor
the kindly Maltese, were any of them naturalists. The Leopard
Snake does not look very unlike a viper and (despite their insist-
ence that St. Paul banished the venomous snakes) I believe that
few Maltese (or Englishmen) would deliberately pick one up.
Surely we shall not be far wrong to assume that the people believed that all snakes were venomous: and the Saint may have
thought so, too.

One of the many dependent legends which have been attached
to St. Paul has to do with the fossil sharks' teeth, found in abundance in the limestone fossil deposits, called 'St. Paul's Tongues'.
They were made into amulets against poisoning and applied, in
powdered form, to wounds.

Malta has several other reptiles. Commonest is the beautiful
green Sand Lizard. The blue-black, fork-tailed variety, peculiar
to Filfla, has already been noted. I do not know his ancestry, nor
can I imagine any reason why he should have selected this strange
colour. His forked tail is, I suspect, a mere freak of osmosis. The
Green Lizard grows to six inches and more, and is particularly
bold, or careless, so that you may often catch him by the tail, which
he promptly sheds, leaving a most unpleasant still wriggling object
in your fingers. The lack of a tail does not appear to discommode
him though it clearly has a purpose, for he soon grows a new one.
He can be trained to come at a call, but you must first discover the
exact, fine-pitched whistle to which his reptilian ear is best
attuned. The wrong note seems to give him actual pain and will
put him to immediate flight. I do not know whether he or the
Wall (or Turkish) Gecko is the most adept insect shot. Both are
expert at rapid detection and cunning stalking of their prey. The
Gecko, who rejoices in the strangely appropriate name of *Wizgha*
has the advantage, like his close relative the Chameleon, of a
readily adaptable colour scheme. He is not an attractive creature,
with his squat, spatulate body, evil prehistoric head and pre-
hensile toes. The dwellers amongst lime-washed walls are white
as albinos, the only colour about them being their glittering,
questing eyes. Others who live amongst the darker rocks are
almost black. They will sit for hours, immobile and melting into
their background, and when an insect comes within range their
swift movement is always slightly repulsive. Yet they, too, can be
domesticated and will take an insect from your hand.

The Ocellated Skink is another greatly unloved survivor from the age of dragons. He, too, has a wide choice of snaky surcoats. Only the laminated plates of his underbelly remain pale in colour. He seems most active in summer, when he lurks wherever a little shade and some residual moisture can be found. In the winter, I have the impression that he goes into a sort of hibernation, for he then becomes sluggish and tractable and will suffer you to pick him up without apparent resentment. A sudden glimpse of his serpentine head and the fore-part of his fat body, peering from the mouth of some small cavern can give you a mild shock, for he looks like the fore-end of a snake which would, in proportion, be many feet in length. He is called *Xahmit L'art* which means 'The Earth's Fat One' and his boiled cadaver has medicinal properties, they say, for the treatment of inflammation of the eyes.

Frogs are to be found wherever the winter torrents leave traces of moisture and they flourish in and about every pond, reservoir, or patch of damp soil. The Maltese native is the Painted Frog.

Maltese lepidoptera also offer a study which could fill a lifetime. The habits, migrations, and ecology of the butterflies and moths can be closely related to bird-life, for it seems that Infinite Wisdom has provided a sort of flight refueling system for the migrating birds whose airborne larder flies on the same routes and at the same seasons as its devourers.

At least ten of Malta's commonest butterflies are migrants. Most are readily recognized by the Englishman: the gardener's great enemy, the Cabbage White (both Great and Small) migrate as well as being indigenous. They can be met far out to sea, in vast clouds, sometimes falling exhausted into the waves and covering great areas with their poor, dying wings.

The Clouded Yellow and her variants is commoner here than in southern England. She is a splendid creature in an orange and green cloak; but her husband, as is often the way with insects, is a drab little fellow and there are variants of the species which are hard to distinguish from the Whites.

The Bath White is rare and since she travels usually in the company of a cloud of Whites, only the expert eye is likely to detect her. The Red Admiral and the Painted Lady are indigenous and prolific, as well as arriving in large numbers as migrants. The Long-Tailed Blue and his smaller cousin are regular visitors, though I have never seen more than one or two at a time.

By all accounts, the Skipper family has become more common of late though this may be more apparent than true, since the informed study of Malta's small creatures is recent and much of our information is due to Guido Lanfranco, a naturalist of European fame whom, however, you will need to seek out: for he is a man of vast humility and as shy and retiring as one of his own rarities. His personal collections of lepidoptera are unique. The father of Maltese entymology was Count Alfred Caruana Gatto.

Apart from the migrants, there are at least eleven species of resident butterfly, and, amongst them, pride of place must go to the lovely Swallow-tail, beloved rarity of the English schoolboy. She is called *Farfett tal Fejgel* or *tal Busbies*, Rue or Fennel Butterfly, on both of which wild plants her larvae feed.

Farfett is the name of any fluttering thing. *Farfett il-Lejl*— 'Night Flutterer', is a Bat; and a Dragonfly is 'The Water Flutterer'. The country-folk make no distinction between a butterfly and a moth, unless it be a Hawk Moth, whose family has a name of its own.

The Swallow-tail, like many other species who breed in the long, warm Maltese summer, has four broods annually compared with two in England, and presumably because she is less rare, is less persecuted. Her lovely gold and brown wings, with crimson peacock's tail eye and blue fringed underwing may be seen throughout the summer, and not infrequently on a mild winter's day wherever there are flowers, wild fennel, or scented rue.

The Whites are also native and as unpopular as their English relations. They breed, not only on all plants of the cabbage family and cultivated stocks, but also on the Wild Caper bushes: dull plants, with round, fleshy leaves, until they unfurl the splendid banner of their waxen flower with its violet and golden heart.

The Sulphur Yellow Cleopatra looks very like the English Brimstone. It hibernates and breeds only once a year.

Meadow Brown, Speckled Wood, Wall Brown are all common, frequenting the sort of country, or the nearest approach to that sort of country, which their names indicate. But none of these seems yet to have decided upon a colour scheme, and it is difficult to distinguish the one from the other. The Small Heath is not particular about diet or breeding-ground, and you are as likely to meet her on a petrol-pump in Sliema as on a hillside in Gozo.

The Common Blue, whose tiny wife goes about disguised as a

Brown Argus, is more common than in most parts of Britain. The small Copper has a range of colours by which it is possible to judge his age.

For the expert, there is always the exciting hunt for rarities. *Eumenis Semele* has only been seen twice between 1910 and 1939 and *Polygonia Egea* has appeared once. *Danaus Chrysippus* was seen in 1923 and, again, in 1952.

Doubtless because of their distinctive, hovering flight, the Hawk Moths have a special name. All are called *Bahrija*, a word whose derivation defeats me, though it is evidently from the same root as 'sea' and 'sailor'. If it were to mean 'Female Sailor', which I am fairly sure it does not, there is a lively temptation to associate the species with the Women's Royal Naval Service and the Silver Striped Hawk which frequents the vineyards, and is called *Bahrija ta'Dwieli* might be supposed to represent a 'Wren' with vine leaves in her hair.

Commonest of the Hawks is the busy, darting Humming-bird Hawk Moth whose wing beats are so rapid that he seems airborne by magic, or like some tiny brown and gold satellite. He remains quite stationary at the mouth of some trumpet-shaped blossom, plunging his grotesquely long proboscis into the hidden store of nectar.

The Striped Hawk Moth is called the Pumpkin Hawk, and the Spurge and Convolvulus Hawks have translations of the English name.

Largest of the Hawk Moths listed by Lanfranco is the Death's Head Hawk, another English schoolboy's treasure. His caterpillar, like that of all the larger members of the family, is a fearsome horned beast in green armour with a disconcerting trick of suddenly snapping his thick body into strange contortions.

If you leave your unscreened windows open, in the country after the lamps are lit, you will have ample scope to study the winged insects who will land on the tablecloth in their hundreds; but the best time to study the moths (with an ultra-violet lamp if you can contrive one) is at dusk when they seem to navigate towards their favourite flowers on a beam of scent. The Hawks are particularly sensitive to sweet smells and seem, too, to prefer the white flowers which remain open after dark.

The Grasshopper family is well represented in Malta and the dreaded locust is not uncommon. Large members of his tribe are called *Giurati*, or *Jurat*, the name given to the elected Maltese Councillors, who were also the Judges, on the Semitic and Punic pattern. With their bulbous, inquiring eyes, their well-filled paunches, and the long gown of their wing-cases, they represent the peasant's mental picture of Authority—they also consume the leafy crops.

Cicalas or Cicadas live in any patch of bush or tall grass and fill the summer air with their strident fiddling. I believe that this mass piping serves an essential purpose in the life-cycle of the tubby little beetle. First a single Cicada will call, haltingly, as if lost and lonely. Then another, then two or three and finally the whole tribe will answer. At first, it is possible to distinguish individual voices, but as the key is picked up, the whirring notes merge into a single, not unpleasant, mildly soporific tune, rising gradually to a crescendo and then tailing off and ceasing abruptly, with perhaps a single dunce still scraping away alone. He seems suddenly to realize that he is out of step and falls at last into an embarrassed silence.

I believe that the whole performance is a kind of marriage dance.

The Maltese name for the Cicada is a very exact reproduction of the song—*Werzieq* or, as we should write it in English *Wair-zeeah*; but the abrupt, suppressed cough of the termination, which so perfectly reproduces the ending of the Cicada chorus, is a sound which we do not use and have great difficulty in copying.

The Honey-bee is domesticated but also occurs wild. The production of honey used to be a flourishing industry, and there is still a good deal bottled for the market in Gozo and Comino as well as at Mellieha and Wardija. All Maltese honey has a distinctive flavour of the Wild Thyme (*Thymus capitatus*) with whose scent the summer hill-sides are heavy. But the countrymen claim to be able to distinguish between Gozo and Comino honey.

Amongst the solitary bees is the big, round, blue Carpenter who makes his home in an excavated tunnel of soft or rotten wood, therein devising a complex of tiny cubicles for his family. If you tap the bole of his tree he will respond with an infuriated buzzing which is magnified by the echo in his tunnel. If, by chance, you should knock against the low branch of a carob which houses the Carpenter, it is momentarily alarming to be greeted by the deep voice of this ogre artisan of the insect world.

The Praying Mantis is common. A weirdly beautiful, ghostlike creature with pale green, transparent body, huge luminous eyes and the lifted hands, not praying but predatory, and armed with razor-sharp, saw-toothed swords. The revolting domestic habits of the female are widely known; surely the most perverted of insects, but the empty integument of a consumed spouse has a strange beauty, too.

There are three species of the Mantis native to Malta: *Mantis religiosa*, the common green to ochre form, seen in its adult state from July to September and known as 'Satan's Mare'; *Revitana baltica*, an uncommon orange form with clearly marked wings, and *Ameles abjecta*, a much smaller form in which the female has only rudimentary wings and both sexes have an upward curving body.

There are both Blue and Scarlet Dragonflies, to be seen diving and hovering over any pond or fountain, and so anxious to deposit their eggs on the surface of the pond that they sometimes spin in. Only the very large goldfish will attempt to swallow them, and their progeny, the Dragonfly larvae, terrorize the smaller inhabitants of the pond.

Malta has no fireflies (the Tourist Bureau might consider importing them) but the Glow-worm bravely displays her sodium lamp in the crevices of the dry stone walls, particularly in the region of a pond or spring.

A pond is a great joy, anywhere; but in Malta, in the long, arid summer it is a veritable oasis of the mind. The golden and silver Carp grow to a great size and are particularly fond of small slices of raw Jerusalem artichokes which they seem able to smell from a distance.

In the old Maltese country houses there are always ponds where you may sit and drowse away an eternal afternoon, quietly content with the ceaseless panorama of life and colour. The Geraniums, scarlet and pink and white, overhang the water, making cool caverns of shadow where the golden fish 'dawdle away their watery noon' and the surface is disturbed only by the erratic wake of the Water Boatmen and the occasional 'plop' as a more wakeful fish takes a too daring midge. The Dragonflies dive and dart, and the gold and blue Swallowtails, and the bees alight to feed or rest on the scarlet and white of the flowers.

The men who built these old houses understood all about leisure and how it should be employed. Sitting and being still are arts which we busy English have much neglected—greatly to the peril of our souls and of those whom we infect with our restlessness.

Wasps are not a nuisance; though you need to be wary of their nests which vary in size from the small conical structure, attached to any convenient twig or stone, of the drab grey colour of its background, and housing perhaps a dozen intrepid defenders, to the hanging Babylon which you may come upon between the unopened, inner and outer shutters of a country window, with hundreds of citizens.

Very like a wasp is the black and yellow Mud Dauber who builds a home like a tiny, mud sand martin's nest and hunts spiders, in whose body it lays its eggs.

Malta has her share, too, of the less pleasant insects. There is a native Scorpion who will give you an unpleasant nip and a nasty swelling. He varies in colour from a splendid, metallic purple to black, and sometimes a rather horrible white. Birds know that he is dangerous and will dance round him, making rapid stabs at his waving pincers and then retreating; but, once he is disarmed, they will swallow the scorpion without apparent harm.

There are Mosquitoes, but none of the malaria carriers, the Red Cockroach (known rather more pleasantly in the West Indies as the Sugar Beetle), Earwigs (which do not get into your ears), Weevils, the Death Watch Beetle, and the Centipede. They are a murderous crew on the whole. The Centipede eats young cockroaches, the Spider eats the flies and the Scorpion eats spiders.

There are also Ants and Termites. The Termites make their nests wherever there is a slight deposit of soil amongst the rocks. They seem to know that arable land is perilous. They break up the soil into a very fine tilth, of infinite, microscopic nodules of uniform size and erect an earth-work like a miniature Avebury about the central chamber which houses their queen who according to some authorities is at once the source of their immortality and their supreme intelligence. Their normal diet is grass seed; but they will attack fabrics if you are careless enough to let them into your wardrobes or your boxes.

8

Malta is rich in wild flowers. Even in the intense heat of summer when the hot south winds seem to bring with them the breath of the African deserts, over one hundred native flowers can be found and patches of wild greenery survive in the shade of the clumps of carob, fig, olive, and holmoak.

The fragrant Fennel is high and delicately feathered and the Caper is in full flower. Many familiar English names are there—Nightshade, Thyme, Henbane and Fleabane, St. John's Wort, Vervain, Heliotrope, Bindweed, Penny Royal, Purslane, Pimpernel, Speedwell, Ragwort, and Golden Samphire. Nearer the sea are the Horned Poppy, Sea Lavender, Sea Pancratium, Sea Rocket, Horehound, and Larkspur.

There are three species of Maltese Golden Thistle; a wild, spiky asparagus with clusters of golden flowers; buckthorn and blackberry, which often seem to conspire together to make an impassable barrier behind which the small, wild creatures may shelter.

The Maltese Centaury is peculiar to the Islands and it is claimed that the Land Caltrops grows only upon the bastions about the Grand Harbour, nourished by the blood of the heroes of the Turkish Siege. For this reason its fruit has the form of the Cross of the Sovereign Order of Malta.

The Squirting Cucumber, which explodes in a shower of rather unpleasant moisture at a touch, is another summer plant of the rocks and walls, as is the Nicotiana called 'Wall Tobacco' by the Maltese.

Every country hillside is unattractively bedecked, in the hot months, with the squat, dead leaves, and the protruding turnipy bulb of the Squill whose fleshy leaves appear in the spring, dying off before the rich heads of purplish blossom appear in the early autumn. The root of the Sea Squill is poisonous; even the goats leave it alone.

Ferns are rare in Malta, with the single exception of the lovely little Maiden Hair Fern which braves the heat in every well-head and every damp crevice of shadowed rock. Its local name is 'Well Parsley'.

All wild flowers are *Haxix Hazin*—'Bad Greenstuff', but one of the farmer's chief enemies is the 'English Weed', Yellow Wood Sorrel or *Oxalis cernua*; so called, they will tell you, because 'it spreads all over the earth'. Yet, it is a beautiful weed with its trefoil leaf to remind us of the Blessed Trinity and its bloodstains for the sufferings of Our Saviour. Its golden flower is sometimes flecked with scarlet, and of a deep orange where the chemistry of

the soil is richer. It is also supposed to have been introduced by an
English lady early in the last century.

Malta has two Springs—the first in September when the warm,
first rain touches the parched soil and, miraculously, arid dust
becomes a pale, green carpet overnight. First to flower at this time
are the lovely little Dwarf Narcissus and the miniscule Wild
Crocus, some yellow (the Meadow Saffron), some blue. Every
rock-puddle where a little clay clings to the parched stone seems
to leap into triumphant multi-coloured life. The Common
Narcissus and the Wood Anemone which the Maltese, too, call
'Windflower', Buttercups, Kingcups, Daisies, and the Blue
Pimpernel (commoner than the Scarlet) all spring up amongst the
fresh, clean shoots of the Fennel and Wood Sorrel.

Just before the first flowers of the Sorrel appear, the spears of
the Monk's Cowl Orchis push their way up to the light, to be
followed soon by the opening of the cowl, a marvel of waxy
perfection and delicate shading of bronze lines upon a background
of cream and green.

From December to February ('Fill-Dyke' is also the sense of the
Maltese country-name for this month) the wind, which is the
enemy of all life in this crouching land of storm and sun, and the
hailstones reduce everything almost to the bleak semblance of an
English winter. But in March, the roadsides and the fields blossom
again into an explosion of colour so violent, and so brief, that it is
possible to live in Malta and be so 'town bound' as to miss it
altogether.

The grey and golden hill-sides are dappled with the fresh green
of the wild grasses and sprinkled with the purple and blue and red
of the wild flowers. Even the bare rocks change colour and the
monotonous stone walls, still clean from their winter washing,
wear wreaths of fresh Honeysuckle and Ivy and Bindweed. The
fields are brilliant with the purple Clover *Hedysarium Coronarium*,
called *Silla*, and the cactus *Opuntia*—Prickly Pear, puts out new
growth, shading its tattered, grey trunks with green.

The local names for wild flowers are often apt and descriptive
but often, too, obscure by allusion to some ancient myth or piece
of country-lore. Many are identical or similar to the English
names and perhaps there is a remote, common origin; Windflower, Kid's Tail, St. John's Flower, Old Man's Beard, Wild Tea,
are examples.

It is possible, as with the birds, that established native flora can
be distinguished, by its local name, from the immigrant or the
recent import. Here, too, the prefix *Bu* seems to be a mark of antiquity. Such names simply describe the nature of the plant, as with
Bloom Rape which is called the 'Parasite' or 'Sucker'; but the
Sorrel, called the 'English Weed' is supposed to be an English
importation, the allusion to its tough persistence being, I think, an
afterthought.

Some native names are very charming. The Wild Erica, which
hides from the wind by clinging close to the rock is called 'Sweet-
heart of the Rocks'. The Wild Arum is 'Holy Mary's Pitcher'.
Others are not as pretty as the English names; 'Love Lies Bleeding'
is 'Smoke on the Ground'.

Apart from the many species which an Englishman would
classify as weeds, there are many cultivated imports which have
established themselves and now grow wild, slowly reverting to
their origins. The Geranium and the pompous-sounding Pelargo-
nium will grow anywhere and are called *Sardinel*.

Pomegranate and Bougainvillea, Oleander, Rose, Fig, Walnut,
Tamarisk, Almond, and the Japanese Medlar (*Mespilus japonica*,
all flourish as escapes from cultivation and jostle each other for
survival in the richer, watered valleys which have not yet been
sacked by picnic-parties or military exercises.

Crops also betray their origins by their names. Of the two
forms of Artichoke one is called *Qaqocc* and the other *Arcicok*:
both evident attempts to pronounce 'Artichoke'; but the former
has long been established and the latter is recent. And, lest we feel
tempted to laugh at the peasant's clumsy tongue, it is well to
remember that the English 'Jerusalem Artichoke' has no connexion of any kind with Jerusalem; but is merely a clumsy English
rendering of the Italian *Gira Sole*.

The Maltese Artichoke is a rewarding crop, as both root and
flower develop and the ripened sunflower seeds are used as
animal-feed.

Tomatoes, which are grown in profusion, are *Tuffieh*, literally
'Apple' in Gozo, and *T'Adam*, the 'Fruit of Adam' in Malta.
There would seem to be a direct connexion, here, with *Pomme
d'Amour*—'Love Apple'.

In referring to potatoes, you must be careful, for *Patata* also
means that part of the anatomy upon which it is customary to

sit. The Maltese Potato is one of the Island's few noticeable exports.

Two and, on irrigable land, sometimes three potato crops a year are grown so that there is a luxury demand for the out-of-season 'new' Maltese variety. Foreign varieties acclimatize well and are said to develop some immunity to the common diseases, so that there is also a considerable demand for seed-potatoes for export.

Carrots and most other root-crops do well, too. The local Turnip is the Kohl Rabbi, called *Gidra tal Foss*—'Moat Turnip'. The early thinnings make an excellent salad, raw, with oil and black pepper. The Pumpkin family does well. I have never seen the English Vegetable Marrow in Malta; but the dwarf variety, called *Qara Bali*, grows splendidly. Cooked in butter, with a suggestion of garlic, they have a fine flavour which is never met in the tasteless giants which win prizes at English shows. The Maltese giant of the pumpkin tribe is the *Qara Ahmar*—'Red Pumpkin'. You will see these immense pumpkins drying on the walls and rooftops like great parks of Cinderella's coaches. The outer skin hardens in the sun to the consistency of pottery and the rich, nourishing, red pulp retains its moisture and its flavour almost indefinitely. The Red Pumpkin is the base of the Maltese brand of Minestrone, a thick, vegetable soup full of stored sunshine.

A matter for constant surprise in so arid-seeming a land, like the prolific frog, is the prevalence of snails.

All the English varieties will infest your garden; the Roman and the Common Snail and those attractive striped Grove Snails whose coloured shells vary from black and yellow to ivory and claret.

It is the Common Snail that is esteemed as a delicacy in Malta, though I believe the Romans and Italians used to eat the Grove Snail, now supposed, perhaps from their bright colours, to be poisonous in Malta. The annual gathering of snails is still a kind of national game, like the English blackberry season, or the search for horse-chestnuts to make 'conkers'. You will see Mother, Father, and all the children clambering over the rocky hill-sides filling little baskets with the fat snails who have just been tempted from their summer hides by the mists and the heavy evening dews of that late summer season called *Gharixa ta' Santa Marija*—'Our Lady's Cloak'—when Our Lady takes pity on the sun-baked earth and on parched humanity by casting her cloak over the fierce face

of the sun. The snails must be taken at just that moment when they
emerge to feed upon the first green of the misty season. Their
flavour is best at the end of their long summer fast. If you eat
them later, when they have gorged themselves upon the seedling
shoots of the new grasses, they are said to be too strong and you
may suffer the pangs of a too concentrated ingestion of chlorophyl.
Should you be so unwise, the cure is *Ilma Zaghr*, a concoction of
orange blossom and herbs which is, I assure you, infallible against
less innocent excesses than the eating of snails at the wrong season.

You must soak your snails in salted water for three days, wash
them thoroughly in fresh water and simmer gently for three hours
in a liquor of water, red wine, pepper, and salt. With them you
should serve a green sauce of capers, garlic, and mixed herbs.

Snails are confidently reputed to be a sovereign remedy against
coughs, colds, and infections of the liver; a conviction which
survived in the English countryside until recent times. In Victorian England snails were sold, beaten up in milk, as a cough cure.
On the whole, I prefer the Maltese recipe.

A version of the game of 'Conkers' is played by Maltese boys,
with snail-shells. The shells are not mounted on string, but are
projected at each other with forefinger and thumb, as in marbles.
Considerable skill is needed to bring the least vulnerable part of
your shell into violent collision with the more thinly armoured
side of your target.

9

The Maltese farmer does not love trees, neither is he very expert
in their cultivation and care. He tolerates the carob, which gives
valuable animal-feed and he cultivates oranges, figs, lemons and
olives, pomegranates, almonds, and an occasional apple or medlar.
The persimmon is a recent import from Sicily and does well in
irrigated and sheltered locations. Many ornamental shrubs grow
excellently and the oleander is thoroughly established; but ornamental shrubs are confined almost exclusively to walled private
gardens, a few public parks, and some newly planted roadsides.
Grape-vines do well and there are several very drinkable types of
wine; but despite Government protection, the wine industry is
half-hearted. The peasant farmer still produces his own raw and
rather potent brew and the reputation of Maltese wine has suffered
from the sale, in waterfront wine-shops, of a sort of Red Biddy

—raw wine, fortified with cheap spirit, which has been elevated by Garrison officialdom to the status of a mysterious infuriator called 'Ambeet' (a mispronunciation of the Maltese word for 'wine', which is *Imbid*) against which the troops are sternly warned and which they promptly investigate.

The farmer's paying crops are roots, tomatoes, green vegetables, marrows, pumpkins, and melons, with occasional small production of luxury crops like strawberries and peaches. Trees, he believes, take life and moisture out of the soil, and long-term stratagems to conserve soil or increase the precipitation of dew leave him unimpressed. He will cultivate flowers for profit. Gladioli, dahlias, daffodils, narcissi, carnations, friesias, ornamental poppies, all grow with ease and profusion and are flown to the continental markets (and to Covent Garden) with a handsome profit. Maltese roses have long been famous. There is also a flourishing Government-sponsored seed-production industry which exports flower-seed after a toughening process of one or two Maltese seasons; but it is the farmer's wife who cultivates those little pots of multi-coloured geraniums and sweet-smelling basil for pleasure. The basil has magic properties and, with the bull's horns which decorate so many peasant-dwellings, serves as a specific against wandering spirits and the Evil Eye.

For the peasant farmer, the same enemies are everywhere: winter gales, only partially broken by the low stone walls and the hedges of cactus and canes; drought, exhausted soil, and his own stubborn, outmoded methods. With few exceptions, the Maltese intelligentsia has no love, no interest for the soil, and the peasant has been left very much to his own devices since the time of Hannibal. He wants quick results and has no time for experimentation. Like all men of the soil, he distrusts new ideas. If his crop is poor it will, anyway, yield him some return. The new methods may fail, and the ingrained habits of centuries surrender reluctantly to changed circumstances.

During the siege of the Second World War the peasant farmer, rightly a reserved occupation when every other male in the community was in uniform somewhere, came into his own and astronomical prices were obtainable for his produce. There were, of course, controls; but an open market which is not, be it noted, quite the same as a black market, was impossible to suppress. Many families who had never possessed more than a few trinkets and a bag of silver coins, by way of capital, hidden beneath a loose stone in the upper room, found themselves with a sizeable fortune at the end of the war.

Some bolder spirits invested in modern equipment: harvesters, tractors, powered tools, pumps, or better stock; but many preferred to go on treading out the corn with a cow, yoked to a mule, on a threshing-floor of beaten earth, separating the chaff with flails and the agency of the wind; with wooden hand-ploughs fashioned from a conveniently bent branch and shod with untempered metal; with the universal broad, digging hoe (south of Rome, men dig towards the body; in the north away from it, though there are interesting exceptions in the Celtic parts of Britain where a type of mattock called a 'bidduck', exactly resembles the Maltese *mghazzaq*). For pumping power they used the blindfolded mule, tethered to the cross-beam of a rotary pump as old as the Pharaohs.

The innovators reaped an immediate profit on their investments in the post-war years, and many of them, with their sons and daughters, are now flourishing citizens of Australia, Canada, and the U.S.A. The young men are leaving the land anyway, and it is fashionable to see nothing but tragedy in the lives of the stubborn old survivors, still clinging to their outworn, back-breaking labour, a dying race in bondage to a dying soil. Yet their lives are not all bleak misery and they have virtues which their children will lack.

Their homes are admirably adapted to their way of life, and if there is an absence of hygiene and labour saving, there are compensations. We more highly mechanized specimens of our species invariably seek an escape to something resembling these simplicities whenever our too complex lives allow us.

The typical peasant home will have but two or three rooms, a stable or byre and an open courtyard with a well, pump, or, for the lucky dwellers near spring-water, a tap. Each house is a miniature fort, surrounded by a high wall and with one square turret having doorway and windows facing inwards towards the courtyard. Access is by a single, wide gateway into the yard which houses much the same orderly disorder as you will see in any farm-yard—the flat cart, the hand-ploughs, tools, a donkey, and a solitary prized cow, chickens wandering at will in and out of the living-rooms, and an assortment of dogs; perhaps a kid, the pet of the younger children, and pigeons cooing in the stone dovecote in the eaves of the turret.

The lower rooms, only, are used every day; but in the Maltese climate life can be lived very much in the open and the rooms are needed only for sleeping. In summer, the older children may sleep in the open, too; and very pleasant it is to lie on the rooftop while the universe wheels overhead and the moonlight lies silver on the fields and the distant sea, and the only sound is a little wind that rustles the leaves of the fig trees, or the stirring of a pigeon in her nest.

The upper room is the 'best' room; reserved, like the Edwardian front room with its lace curtains and its aspidistra in a brass pot, for social occasions. In it are the family's most valued possessions. A portrait of the Patron Saint, the Holy Father, The Queen, the Wedding Group—very stiff, with Pappa (who, even now, rarely wears shoes) in white tie and black jacket and Mamma, now bent and gnarled like an old carob tree, a delicate little thing with big, rather frightened eyes, all lace and frills. A highly coloured group, too, taken in Sydney or Melbourne, of the son in Australia and his large, blonde Australian bride. Always there is a Crucifix and a statuette of Our Lady before which an oil lamp burns continually.

Since it is in this room that birth and death also come to the family, there is a vast, brass bedstead, with spotless linen and a good deal of lace which has been handed down for generations. In a great locked coffer the bride's heirlooms, which came with her dowry, are kept. Not infrequently these great coffers contain articles to delight the antiquary, for they are great hoarders of gold and jewels, these peasant women.

The bed is reserved for births, sickness, and death and, ironed and neatly folded in the coffer, like a bride's trousseau, are the fine linen grave-clothes in which these people will go, independent and proud, to their last rest.

There is no kitchen as we would understand it, much of the cooking being done outside the house upon a stone barbecue (not at all unlike the fashionable objects which rich Americans erect in their gardens) and, although electricity is available almost every-where in the Island, the fuel is generally charcoal assisted with paraffin. There is also an ancient version of the town-dweller's gas-ring, a kind of pottery tripod which is placed over a charcoal fire. Great heat can be generated over a short period by fanning the charcoal with a palm leaf and you may warm or boil a pot of water or soup rapidly, make coffee, or heat a flat-iron.

Sanitation is a cross between the commode and the earth closet, and the Maltese equivalent of the 'Family Eight Holer' is a gigantic pottery receptacle not unlike a Greek amphora, much fancied by English visitors for decorating their drawing-rooms, to the delight of their native domestics.

Bathrooms are unknown, still, to most of the country-folk, for, as one old peasant woman put it, 'What a waste of space just to wash oneself!'

A poor sort of life you might think: fun for a short time, like playing at gipsies; but you must remember that these people have not been softened by the town. They wake with the dawn and are about in the fields or on the hill-sides all day. Their normal fare is simple—a loaf (they all eat a great deal of bread), some tomatoes, oil, anchovies, a handful of olives, eaten in the fields in the shade of a tree or wall. In the evenings they will eat a plate of *Minestra* and then sit for a while at their doorways, gossiping, and are abed soon after sunset. But there are feast days, christenings, weddings—and there are plenty of these in a community of large, closely intermarried families—when the traditional sweetmeats, the *timpana*, a large, round dish of macaroni, eggs, chicken liver, and mincemeat; kid, sucking-pig, rabbit stew, fruit, nuts; fierce local wine and brandy are consumed with an appetite sharpened by anticipation and abstinence.

The children run wild, for compulsory education is difficult to enforce and school hours in the summer are short. They make themselves useful at an early age, herding the goats, milking the cow, harnessing the mule, fetching and carrying for Mother, and helping with the succession of babies who appear with healthy regularity. These people are not poor, they rarely lack anything of the essentials. Clothing, except on high days and holidays and for church-going, is not important. They are not less healthy or less comfortable for going barefoot or, at the most, wearing sandals. They have a fund of common sense and country-lore which is no bad substitute for book-learning and modern medicine. They have a great sense of independence and idolize their children, for whom they will make every sacrifice. The notion of a Society for the Prevention of Cruelty to Children is beyond their comprehension and they are beginning to see the need for education. They have heard, vaguely, of the Welfare State and suspect it. The older generation of peasant farmers would be deeply shamed if they felt that anyone but themselves contributed to the maintenance of their families; but they are a dying race.

Some of the sons may stay with the land. They will build new rooms on to the little fortresses of their fathers, have kitchens and bathrooms; perhaps gas and electricity, washing-machines and refrigerator, and farm with mechanized devices. Their children will go regularly to school, wear shoes and ride motor-bicycles, and crave television and the cinema. They will laugh at their grandmother's superstitions and Our Lady's lamp will go out from lack of oil. They will certainly not be happier and they will not be at all nice to know.

Others will leave the soil and go in search of the will-o'-the-wisp of high wages and short working weeks and they will be discontented, insolent, thoroughly unpleasant people.

10

From the crest of the ridge of Marfa the road slopes gradually down to the sea and the Comino Channel. This is a barren land with but one natural water-course of any size. Yet, with infinite toil, some crop-bearing land has been won from the rock and the windborne salt. The land is dotted with small reservoirs, fed with brackish water pumped by windmills from the filtered sea, which is not far below the rock-surface.

On a misty day the Gozo Channel has something of the look of a Scottish loch. To the east the islands of Comino and Cominotto seem to enclose the waters of the strait and, to the west, low cloud melts into the steep, sharp headland of San Dimitri and the sheer, four hundred and fifty foot cliffs of Ta'Cenc. It is a dangerous channel, full of cross-currents and sudden squalls. You should nurse no illusions about the placid Mediterranean if you sail small boats in these waters, and do not, unless you are a very accomplished swimmer, try to swim to Gozo.

A Lieutenant-Governor—that great lover of Malta, Sir Harry Luke—has done it and so have other experts; but it is an exercise best avoided by amateurs.

The narrow, shallow strait which separates Comino from Cominotto is a favourite picnic spot. The bottom is clear, white sand and there are submarine caverns, lit by green and silver, refracted sunlight, through which you may dive from one rock-face to another.

Comino harbours a particularly vicious sort of 'hot-footed fly' who conceals his nasty, nipping habits beneath the semblance of a common house-fly. He particularly likes delicate, Nordic skins; but, like the mosquito and the sandfly, he will leave you alone as soon as you are acclimatized and have a little sun stored in your body. The tiny island has a fort, built by the Grand Master Wignacourt in 1610, a church, and a fishing village. It produces a particularly fine kind of honey and has a *festa* all to itself as well as its legendary personality.

It is history that the Jewish mystic, Samuel Abu Lafia of Saragossa, was exiled here in the year 1288. He was the founder of 'The Practical Kaballa', a movement aimed at uniting Christianity, Judaism, and Islam. He attempted to convert Pope Nicholas III to his ideas and, in Sicily, proclaimed himself Messiah. The Rabbi Solomon Ibn Adret of Barcelona described him as 'dangerous', and he was expelled in turn from Spain, Italy, and Sicily. In Comino he wrote a great part of his *Book of the Sign* and is remembered in local legend only as a close relative of the Evil One.

There is no regular ferry service to Comino and, since the island is leased to a private owner, you should obtain permission to land (a formality too often set aside by members of the British Services); but it is not difficult to hire a *luzzu*—one of those sailing-boats straight from the *Odyssey*—at Marfa. The *Senjur* of Comino will probably be too surprised at your seeking his leave to land to say 'No.'[1]

Except in the worst of the winter storms, there is a regular steamer service to Gozo; both from the Grand Harbour and from Marfa. You may take a car across in a little steamer that looks, in mid-channel, like an ocean liner, for here, too, there is the illusion of height and distance, which makes the voyage to Gozo seem like a journey into a new land.

In some senses Gozo is indeed a different country. The Maltese of Gozo is very different from that spoken in Valletta, and it is not only a difference of accent, though that is so pronounced as to make the same word sound as different as English is from

---

[1] I understand that the island has now been leased for tourist development. I am sorry.

Dutch. It is a difference, too, more than of a dialect, for the vocabulary retains hundreds of words which have fallen into disuse in the main island. A good rule of thumb for the philologist is to assume that the farther you are from Valletta, the purer the spoken tongue and the nearer to the original Aramaic. To the men of the main island, smaller, quicker, more urbanized, volatile, and less reliable, the Gozitan bears much the same relation as the Highland Scot to the cockney. He is bigger, slower, tougher, dour, and—so the Maltese say—less generous. Yet, if you admire any of his possessions, he will make you a present of it and be offended if you refuse the gift. Maltese stories against the Gozitan bear a close resemblance to the traditional stories of the Aberdonian, and the Gozitans have a primitive kind of bagpipe, made from a pig's bladder and called 'a belly'.

In Gozo many of the old traditions and the old way of life survive. The *faldetta* and the *ghonnella* are still worn. The country carts, the *dghajsas*, and the fishing-boats are still gaily coloured and the *ghanja*—those country songs like the *flamenco* of Andalusia— are still composed and sung to a guitar accompaniment. Lace, once a major industry and a valuable export from all over the Islands, is still made by hand. Little girls (and little boys, too, for it keeps them out of mischief) move their chubby fingers cunningly amongst the bobbins of the lace cushion under the tuition of old dames, sightless with age.

Much like the main island in general contour, Gozo is greener, has deeper valleys and steeper cliffs, and its curious and sketchy road-system—in plan like the bones of a fish—protects it from over-much invasion.

The tiny harbour at Mgarr, where you will land, has a miniature breakwater and a village that straggles uphill towards a graceful Gothic church, not at all unlike a fishing village on the Cornish coast. The road to Rabat, or Victoria, the little dependency's capital, is as good as most in the main island, and Rabat itself is a miniature 'Mdina, though for the most part of somewhat later date. The citadel dates from the fourteenth century.

Gozo has suffered its share of vandalism. In 1848 the Fortress of the Grand Master Garzes, built in 1601, was demolished by military engineers to make a road. In the Second World War a very ancient watch-tower was bulldozed to make an air strip.

The same Neolithic people who erected the great temples in

Malta were busy in Gozo. The megalithic temple of Gigantija is better preserved than Hagar Qim, and the inhabitants of the near-by village of Xaghra still come upon decorated pots whose ochre designs are intact.

Gozo—rather than Malta, where classical allusions are few—shares with Sicily the tradition of having figured in the voyages of Ulysses. It is thought to have been the home of Polyphemus, as well as of Calypso, though it can hardly have harboured both. Certainly, the rock-formations and the megaliths recall the Cyclops, perhaps more vividly than the 'Ciclopi' which the Sicilians will show you at Aci Trezza. The area called Kala Dweira is particularly rich in impressive rock-scenery. In Gozo, generally, the layers of harder limestone are nearer the surface, and its heights have resisted erosion longer than those of the main island. Hence the deeper valleys and the more precipitous cliffs to the west and north. The shoreline of Gozo is not unlike Adrian Cowell's description of Roirama:

> Everything was of stone, piled and carved as if a million demonic rock artists had contrived the decoration of a Titan's torture chamber . . . huge formations eroded in the shape of a thumbscrew, a dying camel, a tortoise about to be beheaded and a pig. . . . No medieval priest of the Devil can have had a site more suited to black magic . . . surrounded by gargoyles many times the size and far more ugly than those of Notre Dame.

This coastline, too, is a giant's playground and there are huge fossils in the rocks of a truly gigantic sea-urchin, looking like the discarded quoits of some Cyclopean sport. The vast rock doorway at Dweira has a perfectly squared lintel, standing three hundred feet above the level of a constantly angry sea that seems to batter resentfully at the base of the great pillars.

The big, salt pool, called 'the Inland Sea', is fed by the outer ocean through a narrow rock-tunnel and forms a perfect natural haven for the fishermen's craft. It is reputed to have been used as a hiding-place by a fabulous pirate called Hassan (he also has caves named after him in the cliffs at Kalafrana, in Malta), and it is true that in stormy and misty weather the rock-entrance could be missed and the pirate craft seem to disappear, as if into some marine Aladdin's cave.

The pillar of rock called 'the General's Rock' used to be connected to the cliffside by a cable-car and the collection of a rare fungus, which grows only here, was a flourishing industry. The fungus was used as late as the First World War in the treatment of haemorrhages. Admiral (then Captain) Dillon, a not very reliable authority who seems to have believed everything he was told about Malta, writing in 1814, says the fungus was 'eaten as a delicacy by the Grand Masters'.[1]

On the northern shore of Gozo is the fabled Cave of Calypso, overlooking a bay of golden sand called Ramleh (which means 'sandy'). It is a charming cave in which any tired sailorman might be forgiven for lingering in the company of a Gozitan nymph.

The Romans, with their unerring eye for a site, built a villa here and a mole, the remnants of which are still clearly visible.

Gozo remains, as yet, a little land of simple people with an un-spoiled Faith. Their show-piece is the lately completed Church of Ta 'Pinu near the village of Gharb, dedicated to Our Lady. For many years a shrine stood here to which the fisherfolk and the farmers used to bring their troubles, their hopes, and their fears, asking the Mother of God to intercede for them, and so many were the graces vouchsafed to those who prayed here that the place became especially sacred in the mind of every Gozitan. The new church—not quite like any other church in the Islands, with a separate campanile—is their offering of faith and gratitude. Its bare interior is already festooned with votive offerings, evidence of graces and little miracles that no Gozitan questions. One thing is clear: these people are sure that their prayers are heard, and who are we to say that they are not?

The Maltese remain indefatigable builders of churches. From the time of the megaliths they have lavished all their skill, their art, and their imagination upon the building of temples and this is, I think, one of the hardest things for a foreigner to understand. It is true that he, too, used to build some magnificent churches, and occasionally he still does. And Stonehenge was a temple; but, why, he wonders, in so poor, so sparsely populated an area as Ta 'Pinu, should so much toil, so much treasure, have been expended upon a church which would not disgrace a cathedral town? Why, with so many churches already and people living in caves, are new churches still being built? The answers come more readily to the Catholic mind; but even the Catholic Englishman

---

[1] *Dillon's Narrative 1802-1839.* Navy Records Society. Omits the Malta Section of the original which was lent me by Professor Michael Lewis.

has his doubts, for he, too, has been nurtured in a post-Reformation environment.

Above all, let us remember that every church in Malta is filled to overflowing five or six times on Sundays and Days of Obligation and you will never, at any hour, find one empty of its group of pilgrims, penitents, and devotees.

To suggest that the Faith of the Maltese differs in any essential from the Catholic Faith in Italy, Spain, Ireland, England, India, the Philippines, or Japan would simply not be true; but there are differences of custom and background, and they are not always readily understood even by English Catholics. Non-Catholics of all shades, alas, not only misunderstand but too often misrepresent.

The Church was established here before St. Peter had reached Rome, and so fierce is the Maltese pride in the antiquity of their Faith that they sometimes deserve the charge of being more papist than the Pope. A minor change in the liturgy, in the rules for Fasting and Abstinence, or even their own Archbishop's disapproval of long-established, pious practice, is sometimes received with only a grudging obedience.

There has been no Reformation. Indeed, at the moment in history when the Northern Europeans were busily dismembering Christendom, the Maltese under the rule of the Sovereign Order were being, as it were, reinoculated with that ideal and were pouring out their blood and their sweat in its defence. The Counter-Reformation, diverting the genius of the Renaissance from its pagan course, added a fresh impetus to Maltese Faith.

English influence, but more, perhaps, the general materialism of the times, has done something to undermine the citadel of the Church amongst the young people of the towns; but in the main their attachment to their Faith is synonymous with their nationality and many a Maltese would deny that sooner than deny his Church.

The thought of God as a living, breathing presence, of the Mother of God and of the Saints as close, personal friends who may be talked to at any odd moment, and who will answer, is no longer natural to most minds, and this is why so many visitors fail to see that another Maltese church is not just another edifice to be entered when social convention or fashion dictates. To the Maltese it is a second, and a true home. Its treasures are God's; but the baron and the barrister, the peasant and the artisan share them with Him and will defend them with their lives. Few, I think, would understand Paul Claudel's mystic invocation.

Salut, grande Nuit de la Foi,
infallible Cité
Astronomique
C'est la Nuit et non pas le brouillard
Qui est la patrie d'un Catholique.

The country of Maltese Faith is neither a city of night nor a dim borderland of theological fog. It is a simple, sunlit land, like the rock which has bred it.

It is fair comment that the Maltese are 'too much at home' in church. To the visitor, their behaviour is casual, noisy, almost disrespectful. It is, in fact, the behaviour of children, happy in the company of beloved parents. These people came here as infants in arms and have spent much of their lives here ever since. The altar, the dim faces of the Saints, the pictures, the silver and that single shaft of sunlight which seems always to strike the tabernacle are as familiar as the furnishings of their homes and the faces of their mothers. There is little awe or terror in their faith. Even the Holy Souls immersed in the flames of a medieval Purgatory are invariably depicted by Maltese sculptors with broad smiles, because (they will tell you) the Souls have heard the message of Divine Mercy. And the events of the Gospels might have happened yesterday. So much of the life and colour, even the language, of the Gospels is part of the Maltese scene as these people know it. A child in a manger, goat-herds on a starlit hill-side, journeys on donkey-back, the triumphant palms, the wine-jars at the wedding-feast, the sturdy Fisherman, the Tax-Gatherer for a foreign ruler and that ruler himself, bewildered and despairing of the 'natives'. None is a character or incident, as they are for us, of a tale from a distant, foreign land. All are factual, everyday Maltese people and events. And the churches, the houses which the people have raised with their hands to the glory of God and for their own comfort, have been for centuries their main symbols of national Faith and pride and, not infrequently, more than symbols, but also fortresses in which they have taken refuge from their enemies.

About the Maltese priesthood there has always been something of the Byzantine tradition of ethnarchy (this the British have

wisely recognized, in sad contrast to their attitude in Cyprus) and
from similar causes. Under a succession of foreign dominations
it was natural for the people to look to their priests and their
bishops for leadership. Under the Sovereign Order, themselves a
Religious Community, the only native Maltese who could aspire
to membership of the ruling caste were the priesthood who could
be, and often were, elected to the powerful chair of the Grand
Prior of the Church. The British have never quite forgotten that,
so far as legal and constitutional considerations went, they owed
their Sovereignty of Malta to a national revolt against the French
led by a priest, Canon, later Bishop, Caruana, supported by a
notary, Emmanuele Vitale and a merchant, Vincenzo Borg.

It is not unusual for liberal-minded foreigners to jump to the
conclusion that the position of the Church in Malta is a relic of
medievalism and feudal oppression. The truth is far otherwise.
The priests are of the people and have invariably led popular
movements against oppression or repressive foreign domination.
Don Gaetano Mannarino, who led the almost successful revolt
against the Grand Master Ximenes in 1775, is a national hero.
More recently, the priesthood has been in the forefront of most
movements for social and economic reform.

It is, nevertheless, true that many Maltese priests are poorly
equipped to resist the virus of twentieth-century materialism and
the subtleties of anti-Catholic intrigue. They tend to rely too
much on an authority and a discipline which is too easily mis-
represented; but the danger is realized and, in the meantime, the
Maltese continue to build churches and their land remains one of
the few where prayer and the practice of Religion are part of
everyday life.

11

For a period of three months, from 25 November 1831, Malta
and its Dependencies possessed another island—now marked on
the charts as 'Graham's Reef', from the name of the British officer
who hoisted the Union Jack upon a volcanic island which bobbed
up overnight between Sicily and the African coast. Being nothing
but a loose pile of scoriae, it was rapidly eroded and reduced to
a shoal.

Malta is still mildly volcanic and earth tremors of varying
intensity coincide with the periodical misconduct of the Aetna,

Stromboli, Vesuvius family. There is no doubt that noticeable
subsidences have occurred within historical times, and some
authorities have it that the whole archipelago is slowly but per-
ceptibly sliding into the sea. There are maps of the eighteenth
century which show rocks and islets around the coast, above sea-
level, which are now within the ten-fathom line. One in particular
—distinctive from its rectangular outline—appears on a map of
1775 off Delimara Point. It is still there, but now lies at a depth
of several feet.

12

There is a deal more to be known and told about Malta. I have
said nothing of the villages and market towns to the south and
east of the Grand Harbour, of the coast between Marsa Scala and
Benghajsa, where a Carthaginian called Hannibal Berqa (Barca)
lies buried and where the Conqueror of Spain and Italy may have
been born—of Siggiewi—which the English call 'Siggy Wiggy'—
Imkabba, Kirkop, Attard, Lija and Balzan, Gudja, Axiak, Zejtun
and Zabbar; of Birzebugga—'The Well of Olives'—where there
is a temple of Tyrian Astoreth, of Migra Ferha—'The Good
Tidings', Tal Ghazzenin—'The Idlers', Rdum il Bies—'The Sea
Hawk's Nest': all have their legend and their history and their
own charm.

If you are a historian, an archaeologist, a naturalist, a biblio-
phile, a philologist, or a connoisseur of architecture and the arts,
you will find endless enjoyment within the narrow confines of this
rich little rock, and if you are, as I am, a mere dabbler in these deep
matters, your pleasure will be the greater.

If you enjoy swimming and hunting fish, riding, polo, horse-
racing, tennis, cricket (and even Rugby football in the short
winter season); if you enjoy 'balls, picnics, and parties', Malta can
offer you all these, and Garrison society, if you have not had a
surfeit of it, can be vastly entertaining.

If, on the other hand, you want merely to sit in the shade and
think, there are a thousand less pleasant and more costly places in
which to do it.

For me, the memory of 'Yells, bells, and smells' will always
call—the yells of the vendors of exotic sweetmeats and strange
commerce, the bells of a people at prayer, and the smells of
roasting coffee and jasmine in a shadowed patio.

III

THE KNIGHTS

THE KNIGHTS

'Sir Clement West . . . moved about preceded by a Mace
Bearer, carrying a golden mace, or Staff of Command with
the Royal Arms of England . . . in this guise he presented
himself in the Palace of the Sovereign Prince of Malta . . .'
(*The Book of Deliberations of the English Langue of the
Sovereign Order of Malta.*)

I T is not possible to visit Malta, even for a matter of hours,
without hearing about 'the Knights'. They built these bastions
—that church—this palace—this was their shipyard—their
galleys anchored here—their slaves were locked up there. A great
deal of fact and even more fiction is retailed about them; but who
and what they were, and why, are questions to which a wide range
of garbled answers is current.

The tourist pamphlets often reproduce the bare bones of the
history of the Sovereign Military Order of St. John of Jerusalem,
Rhodes, and Malta—a chronology and a list of names of Grand
Masters and Knights, strange and foreign to the English eye (for
even familiar names are commonly disguised beneath a Latinized
or French version—as '*A forte scudo*' for Fortescue) and a catalogue, perhaps, of battles and buildings; but such chronologies
have not served to inform even the Maltese themselves very
clearly about what the Sovereign Order was and is—a tourist
notice in *The Times* lately referred to Malta's connexion with the
Knights Templars, who were suppressed two centuries before the
Order came to Malta, and who were never in Malta at any time.

The guide-book will tell you that the Order of St. John, sometimes called the Hospitallers, is the oldest surviving Order of
Chivalry, founded in the Holy Land in the eleventh century by
a monk of the Benedictine Rule, as a nursing fraternity, becoming
militant and military by the twelfth century, and a sovereign
aristocratic republic by the early fourteenth, inheriting the riches
of the suppressed Templars in that century and owning lands and

whole provinces in every European country; numbering amongst its brethren Popes and Emperors who were honoured to be of its company.

What the guide-book will not tell you is how deep an imprint little more than two and a half centuries of the Order's rule has left upon Malta and how much of the unique, cosmopolitan, feudal, and religious structure of the Island's culture is owed to the Knights. Neither will it be plain how close are England's—and all Europe's—historical contacts with the Order.

The great Conventual Church of St. John, the Auberges or 'Inns', the Magisterial Palace, the Palaces of San Anton and Verdala, the lovely city of Valletta are show-pieces of which the Maltese are justly proud; but the visitor, bewildered by such a wealth of Baroque survival will not know that the games the children play in the streets, the food they eat, the phrases the Maltese barrister uses in the courts, the weights and measures in the market are all of Knightly origin. Neither will he readily understand that the vision of the Blessed Gerard, the Benedictine Founder of the Order, has survived and is, in essence, more potent today than it was when Richard Cœur de Lion tilted at Saladin.

The writing of post-Reformation English history has served to obscure, for the Englishman, the close association between his country and the Order of St. John. Indeed, for most people, the title is automatically attached to the Venerable Order whose splendid work is most widely seen in the guise of the St. John Ambulance Brigade. A Protestant copy of the Sovereign Order (though it numbers Buddhists as well as Catholics amongst its members), the Venerable Order nevertheless does strive to keep alive the ancient link and has, incidentally, at its headquarters in Clerkenwell, one of the finest collections of 'Melitensia' extant. The Order in England was first pillaged and then suppressed at the Reformation—many of the Knights suffering martyrdom at the hands of Henry and Elizabeth I. A French attempt to effect a *rapprochement* between Catholic root and Protestant branch failed—for the sufficiently good reason that an international religious Order, owing spiritual allegiance to the Holy Father, could not easily embrace a natural offspring whose loyalties were essentially national. The same difficulty exists with similar offspring in the Lutheran countries; but some sort of understanding with the Sovereign Order, whose headquarters are now in Rome, at the Palazzo Malta, is not impossible and practical co-operation, on an international level, is always a fact.

The ideals of the Knights, as they took shape in the Holy Land of the Crusades, suffered a change, during the first two centuries, from the simple, hospitaller vision of the Blessed Gerard to a more militant concept of Christendom and its preservation, in much the same way as the Crusades themselves reacted at first to the proselytizing zeal of Islam and, later, to every schism or heresy which threatened the unity of Christendom.

The Crusades failed—as all attempts to unite Europe and the Christian West have failed—because of national jealousies and because the sense of spiritual unity was not (and is not) strong enough to override those jealousies. But the spirit of the Crusades, together with Gerard's vision, survived in the Order which was the first international Christian society of a military character and which has outlived all others. It was founded upon a voluntary surrender of individual liberty and national loyalty to a supra-national ideal. It embodied, too, the concept of chivalry, of *noblesse oblige*, carried to an extreme of Christian idealism in the strict rule which demanded sixteen quarterings of nobility from every postulant—a proof which some Royal Houses would find difficult. The greater, it was argued, the claim to nobility, the greater the obligation to spurn no task, however menial or distasteful, in the service of the pilgrim, the poor, the sick, and the aged.

The pomp of noble quarterings was the measure of the obligation to follow the Divine example: *Dominus Jesus, postquam coenavit cum discipulis suis, lavit pedes eorum et ait illis: Scitis quid fecerim vobis, ego Dominus et Magister? Exemplum dedi vobis, ut et Vos ita facietis.*

The ideal was, perhaps, too high. It was asking a great deal of the young men of rich and powerful families to surrender homes, brides, power, ambition, to a life of monasticism and Christian virtue, of prayer and contemplation. It was asking a great deal more of them to keep their vows in a military community, immersed in the changes and chances, the plunder and the pride of battle in a distant land full of strange temptation. Small wonder that many fell short of the ideal, the more marvellous that so many so nearly achieved it.

Like the Templars, the Hospitallers were much influenced by the enemies upon whose borders they lived and fought. For monasticism itself there was plenty of Oriental precedent, and the Christian anchorite, hiding from the world, had his Judaic predecessors. To the people of Palestine, there was nothing strange about a monastery, and that it should offer succour and shelter to pilgrims seemed only proper. For a long time the early Brothers were left in peace by the rulers of Islam; but in the twelfth century they were beset by that peculiarly Islamic product, the professional warrior (often the offspring of Christian captives), bred from birth to the use of arms and trained to resist to the death every encroachment of the Cross upon Islamic soil. The sporadic, inefficient and uncoordinated raids of the Christian Princes could never make permanent headway against a united, organized professional army, and Christendom itself was already disintegrating into nations whose allegiance could never be counted upon by Pope or Emperor.

But the origins of the Order as a Military and Sovereign body are not all part of a high religious idealism. There was commerce, too.

By the middle of the eleventh century a considerable trade with the East had created the rich city states of Italy and the western Mediterranean. Much of the essentials of gracious living—which was again coming to be understood in Europe—depended upon this trade, and an international police force was not unwelcome. It is, indeed, possible that Brother Gerard himself first found his way to the Holy Land as an auxiliary of the Merchants of Amalfi.

This lovely little city—which boasts the Holy Body of St. Andrew in its cathedral—is now little more than an overgrown fishing village, nestling amongst the glorious mountains of Calabria, but, in the eleventh century, it was one of the principal commercial maritime Powers of the Mediterranean. The eight-pointed cross of the Sovereign Order justly figures in the arms of Amalfi and on the 'Jack' of the Italian Navy.

Gerard has been identified as Gerardus de Saxo, a Patrician of Scala. The earliest hospice in Jerusalem was that founded by St. Gregory the Great in A.D. 600 and this, together with the Amalfitan Quarter was undisturbed in the Arab Conquest of A.D. 638. But the fanatic Caliph Al Hakim razed both hospice and settlement to the ground in 1014. Fifty years later, a kindlier (and more commercially astute) régime permitted the restoraton of the hospice and the re-enclosure of the 'Frankish' Quarter. The hospice was maintained by the Benedictines, of whom Gerardus de Saxo was one.

In 1099, when the Crusaders entered Jerusalem, Gerard broke away from the Rule of St. Benedict and in 1113 obtained a new and more militant constitution from Pope Paschal II.

By 1133 the new Order of Hospitallers had won their first military action and were maintaining and garrisoning hostels or hospitals every twenty miles along the pilgrim routes to the Holy Sepulchre.

Thus, from an Amalfitan Benedictine hospice, there developed Christendom's answer to Islam's 'Slaves of God', and, as the distintegrating forces of nationalism sapped the strength of the West, the Hospitallers and the Templars (who were of very similar origin) remained the sole, thin breakwater against the East.

The Templars succumbed very early to the temptations of power, and were much corrupted by fraternization with their Paynim opponents who were, indeed, no barbarians, but highly cultured men with a wealth of learning and proficiency in the arts which was, only now, coming in to Europe by way of the Moorish Kingdoms of Spain. It was always a chink in the armour of these polyglot international Orders, that they might be attracted by other movements which purported to serve the brotherhood of all men. Such was the fate of the Templars, who were drawn towards Freemasonry and a host of interesting and abstruse heresies like the Catharism of the Albigenses and the Gnosticism which was an eccentricity common to both Christianity and Islam. Ideas not much unlike international Communism were current in their Order and the secret intrigues against established authority which were their undoing have a familiar shape. The Templar of Walter Scott's *Ivanhoe* is probably an accurate portrait. Upon the suppression of the Templars in 1309, the Hospitallers of St. John inherited a good part of their vast properties and were left with a clear field in which to recruit the gilded youth of Europe's aristocracy.

The first four centuries of the Hospitallers' history is a tale of heroism and devotion, of bloodshed and brutality, tempered at the knightly level by the rules of chivalry and undeniably inhuman at the level of the common man. Slavery, torture, starvation, and chains were the lot of the man-at-arms, without the means of ransom, and Christian was as brutal as Muslim. Yet we must avoid the easy trap of judging these men by the standards of our own time—if indeed, those standards are really any better. There were rules of war and a respect for personal courage notably absent from the twentieth century, and there was always the knightly code—more frequently respected than disregarded by Christian and Heathen alike—to diffuse a sense of human dignity. The loss of St. Jean d'Acre was a massacre; but Rhodes was occupied by the Saracens with every gesture of chivalry, the Grand Master and his people being honoured and acclaimed as heroes by their enemies, and permitted to depart with all the honours of war.

The Order was established in England in 1100, in Scotland in 1124, and in Ireland in the same year. The Anglo-Normans—soon to become Englishmen—were active in the Order from its earliest times. Gilbert de Sally was fifth Grand Master in 1163 and Roger des Moulins in 1177. Both were Anglo-Normans.

William de Henley led a gallant band of English Knights to the defence of Acre, and Matthew de Paris has described the setting out of the expedition:

> They started from the House of the Hospital at Clerkenwell and passed through the City with spears aloft, shields displayed and banners advanced, seeking a blessing from all who crowded to see them pass. The Brethren, indeed, uncovered, bowed their heads from side to side and recommended themselves to the prayers of all.

From the siege of St. Jean d'Acre not one Englishman was to return alive.

Englishmen were distinguished, too, at the attack and capture of Rhodes—from the effete and schismatic Byzantines—in 1308. From this date the distinct Sovereignty of the Order, which was to be recognized by all Christian Powers and remains so recognized by all Catholic nations, may be said to commence. This matter of Sovereignty was to prove a fruitful source of controversy and tragedy—for the sovereignty of an international body is bound to involve some sacrifice not only by individuals but by nations; a fact which has been brought close home to us, of recent years.

The position of the Order and of the English Knights, in England, seemed equivocal and fertile of conflicting loyalties at an early date, for, of all the nations of the West, England was the first to lose the sense of Christendom, and English dynastic feuds, Anglo-Scottish wars, were to set brethren of the Order at each other's throats on their home soil while they united to defend it, overseas, against a common enemy.

Scottish feelings can still grow hot after six centuries, at the high-handed sequestration of the English property of the Scottish Commandery of the Order, of Torphichen, by the Grand Prior of England in 1376. 'The whole history of Anglo-Scottish relations', writes a twentieth-century Scot, 'is one of attempts to subordinate the Scots on any pretext.'[1]

English and Scottish Knights not only fought on opposite sides in the Anglo-Scottish wars but took opposite sides in matters of internal policy within the Order. In 1378, during the Great Schism, the Langues of England and Italy supported the Pope in Rome; but the Scots—still smarting, we may suppose, from the sequestration of their English property—joined the Langues who supported the Anti-Popes in Avignon. Two Grand Masters were elected and claimed Sovereignty for a time, until the election of one Philibert de Nailhac as 'Sole Master'.

The history of the English Langue is a great part of the stuff of English history.

In 1368, Brother John Paveley, Prior of Clerkenwell, entertained one Richard Whittington (the cat is not mentioned in the archives) and, in 1381, Wat Tyler, infuriated by the policy of the Grand Prior Robert Hales, who seems to have been the Archbishop of Canterbury's confidante, burned the priory to the ground.

Amongst the escutcheons to be found in the Order's fortress at Budrum are those of King Henry IV, Henry of Monmouth, Duke of Clarence, the Dukes of Bedford, York, and Gloucester.[2]

The Prior Robert Botyell fought against Henry VI at Northampton and John Langstrother, Castellan of Rhodes in 1453, commanded the van of Queen Margaret's army at Tewkesbury in 1471.

The 'Historie of the Arrivall of Edward IV in England in Mcccclxxi'[2] records that:

. . . The Prior of Seynt Johns, called Ser John Langestrother, Sir Thomas Tressham, Ser Gervaux of Colyton, Knights, Squiers and other notable parsonnes Dyvers, whiche alle, dyvers tymes, were brought afore the King's Brothar, the Duke of Gloucester and Constable of England and the duke of Norfolk Marshall of England, theyr judges; and so were judged to death in the mydel of the towne Edmond, Duke of Somerset, and the sayd Prior of Sieynt Johns with many other gentils that were taken and

[1] Lt.-Col. Robert Gayre of Gayre and Nigg, *The Heraldry of the Knights of St. John* (1956). [2] Ibid., p. 199.

that of long tyme had provoked and continuyd to great rebellyon that so long had endured in the land agaynst the King, contryre to the Wele of the Realme.

Amongst the Knights of the English Langue who lost their lives in the defence of Rhodes in 1480 were a Becket, of the family of St. Thomas of Canterbury, and a Newport, a Verdelin, a Weston, and an Irish Burke (or de Burgh). Another Englishman who fell at his post in the final assault on Rhodes is an intriguing figure. He bore for arms: 'de geuelles: a trois leopards d'or' and 'une bordure d'azur a 8 fleurs de lys d'or'. This Knight who wore the Royal Arms of England, with a bordure of those of France is recorded as John Bous or Bowes. He was clearly of royal blood; but his secret died with him at the point of a Turkish spear.

The matter of Sovereignty and of mixed loyalties was of ever-growing import for the English Knights. As the notions of nationality and of jealous, national monarchies slowly but surely eroded the ideal of a united Christendom, they became increasingly meticulous in the colours and badges which they wore when upon the King's business. All of them wore the Cross of the Order in Chief with their own arms; but in the Realm of England, and upon Royal business outside it, they wore only their family badges. Sir Thomas Docwra embarked, we learn, with George Talbot, Earl of Shrewsbury, Captain of Henry VIIIth's vanguard '. . . upon the King's going into France' in 1513, wearing a banner which displayed his family badges and the Cross—not of St. John, but of St. George. He might sit in Parliament as Lord Prior of St. John's and claim precedence as the Premier Baron of England; but he did not flaunt his Order's Sovereignty before his Monarch. But this nicety of protocol did nothing to modify Henry's rapacity. The Knights were loyal Englishmen—sometimes, as we shall see, loyal to the point of arrogance—but when Henry assumed the offices of both Pope and Emperor, they paid with their lives for their devotion to Christendom.

2

It was against a background of four centuries of incessant battle, little luxury, and a surprising degree of adherence to vows of personal poverty, chastity, and obedience, that the weary handful of survivors from Rhodes reached Malta, led by their indomitable Grand Master, Philip Villiers de L'Isle Adam—kinsman of the Dukes of Buckingham—in a vessel commanded by Sir William Weston, in the year 1530.

The Hospitallers were not quite free of the Oriental taints which had destroyed the Templars. They, too, had toyed with strange heresies and were not to be completely exonerated from charges of piracy—privateer slave-hunting was certainly a popular pastime with the young Knights and, in Rhodes, they had already become a considerable Naval Power.

The galleys of St. John were famous throughout Europe. In them, the Knights made the swift, dauntless attacks which recognized no possibility of defeat. Their exploits were published in broadsheets in Naples, in Marseilles, in Venice. They became almost mythical. But strong men were needed for the Galleys.

They were over-crowded with slave oarsmen, fighting men, and crew, cumbered with arms and provisions, so that often it was impossible to lie down to sleep. There was neither shade from the blazing sun nor shelter from rain and sea water. Swept by sudden storms the food would become sodden, useless, the men sick or fever struck. After a successful encounter, the galleys would be still more overcrowded with captives and booty.[1]

In 1530, when L'Isle Adam landed in Malta, the galleys had been scattered and many of the surviving Knights had returned to their now impoverished Commanderies or to the courts of their monarchs. The Holy Roman Empire was torn by dynastic feuds, and the unifying spiritual authority of the Holy Father in Rome was troubled by the unquiet spirits of the Reformation. By 1540 the English Captain, Sir William Weston, was dead of a broken heart '. . . upon hearing of the Dissolution of his Order, in England'. The Act of Suppression of 1540 accuses the Knights of St. John of having:

. . . unnaturally and contrary to the duty of their allegiance sustained and maintained the usurped power and authority of the Bishop of Rome and have not only adhered themselves to the said Bishop, being common enemy to the King their Sovereign Lord and to his realm, entirely upholding knowledging and affirming maliciously and traitorously the same Bishop to be Supreme head of Christ's Church by God's Holy Words . . . thereby to subvert and overthrow the good and godly laws and statutes of this realm their natural country, made and grounded by the authority of the Holy Church by the most excellent wisdom and policy and goodness of the King's Majesty.

To us, the words have an all too familiar ring. Henry may be said to be the prototype of nationalizers everywhere; but to the Knights the pronouncement was blasphemy.

But Europe—indeed, Henry himself—cannot have expected

[1] *The unpublished MS. of a Knight of St. John*, Averil Mackenzie-Grieve.

anything permanent to come of his squabble with the Papacy. Kings and Popes had quarrelled, it would seem more disastrously, before. And the Emperor Frederick of Sicily had said and done ruder things—and gone on a Crusade for penance.

Like the heads of a squabbling family seeking one of the children to watch the door, the Pope Clement XII and the Emperor Charles V needed to look no further than those well-tried sentinels, the Hospitallers.

The Order was compensated for part of its losses in Rhodes, and the Knights rallied to the banner of L'Isle Adam in his temporary Convent at Syracuse. Of all the fiefs within the Emperor's gift, the rocky and barren islets of Malta with the remnant of the Latin Kingdom of Jerusalem at Syrian Tripolis appeared easiest to dispose of without stirring up more national and dynastic jealousies. These, then, became the Order's new bases and Malta became the site of the 'Convent' to which every Knight was bound to repair at the Grand Master's summons.

The Maltese were not consulted and received the news with an ill grace. They had already purchased the right to dispose of the fief only at their own will, through their elected representatives, the *Giurati*, rather than be tossed from one petty princeling to another as the prize for some personal service to an overlord.[1] The Norman[2] and Aragonese nobility had been content in their isolation. Far from the intrigues of the great courts they had ruled over a diligent and frugal peasantry, enriching themselves by tolls and a little piracy at the expense of the seaborne trade of the maritime republics.

[1] Roger of Normandy awarded Malta the status of a Sicilian Municipality—governed by a *Università*. In 1427, the Maltese rebelled against their feudal overlord Gonsalvo de Monroy and petitioned their Monarch, Alphonso V of Castille, to vest the fief of their islands in the *Università*, or elected Council, in perpetuity. Their petition was granted—upon payment of the sum which Monroy himself had paid for the fief. Thirty thousand gold florins: an immense sum for those days. Though the name is rare and no longer counted amongst the recognized nobility, there is still one Maltese family claiming descent from Gonsalvo.

[2] The Maltese national flag: red and white, with the recent augmentation of the George Cross, is reputedly Norman in origin, Roger de Hauteville having, it is said, torn his own banner of red and white quarterings in half and awarded it to Malta. Exactly the same story is told of the origin of the arms of the English family of Waldegrave, though in their case it was the less legitimate William who is said to have made the award. Since the Waldegrave arms were registered in 1320 and the earliest known use of the Maltese shield is on a door in 'Mdina, dated 1350 (there is also a seal of 1400), the Waldegraves had the prior claim to the de Hauteville 'halving'. The George Cross sets the matter right.

As if to carry coincidence to extremes, several of the Waldegraves were Knights of Malta.

They received the Grand Master coldly but correctly, ceremoni-
ally handing over the keys of their walled city of 'Mdina and then
firmly shutting their palace doors against these invading Knights.
The people were less incensed. Their barons had been secure and
comfortable enough within the walled cities; but every peasant in
the fields, every fisherman had been fair game for maurauding
corsairs, and little enough of the tolls levied in the considerable
port of the Borgo upon the shores of the Grand Harbour had
reached their pockets.

The Knights brought bustle and increasing commerce to the
harbours. They erected watch-towers and forts and maintained a
constant cavalry patrol of the coast. And as the rich young aristo-
crats rallied to the Convent, churches, fortifications, docks, ware-
houses, armouries, magazines, mills, and granaries began to spring
up as never before. There was labour enough, and copious crumbs
from the table of the Order, for every Maltese and for all the
polyglot horde of camp followers who now began to gather about
the Cross of St. John.

While the Knights remained, in those sterner days, remote and
aloof from the fleshpots of the undedicated commonalty, each
Langue brought in its train men-at-arms, serving brothers, clerics,
artificers, sea-captains, military engineers, seamen from England,
Spain, Portugal, France, Italy, Germany, Hungary, Scotland, and
Ireland. These mingled with the people and were untroubled by
vows of celibacy. From a barren, forgotten backwater of Christendom's main stream, Malta became a rich centre of Western culture
—and Western vice. The Barons might sulk behind the great
moat of Notabile, but the people exulted in a new prosperity.

The epic of the Siege of 1565 has been told too often to need
repetition here. The Siege of Malta, the sea victory of Lepanto
(to which the Order also made a notable contribution), and the
Siege of Vienna, together broke the force of the advancing tide
of Islam and staved off, anyway for three centuries, an engulfing
of Western culture from the East. The Monarchs of Europe were
now safe to pursue their internecine squabbles, which were to end
in national divisions so deep that only some rebirth of ideals
comparable with those of the Knights is likely to save Europe, a
second time, from the enemy in the East.

To their contemporaries and certainly to the people of Malta,
that first half-century of the Order's rule, which saw the defeat of

the Muslim Armada, the building of Valletta, and all those splendid works which give the Island its unique character, must have seemed the beginning of a Golden Age. We, looking back through the dusty archives, can understand that it was not a beginning, but an end to the age of chivalry, of faith, and of devotion. To be sure, we have had our men of faith and devotion and our moments of heroism—not of individuals alone, but of whole peoples; but the devotion, the loyalty has too often been tragically spent upon narrow, tribal causes and offered upon the altars of deified states.

First amongst the Knights to succumb to the new loyalties were the English:

> The arrogance and insolence of English people became proverbial at a surprisingly early date. Already, somewhere about the fourteenth century, visiting observers are heard to remark plaintively, that the English 'do not like foreigners', and somewhere about Queen Elizabeth's time, we hear the characteristic English compliment that so-and-so is 'almost like an Englishman' . . .[1]

In the Royal Malta Library in Valletta, there is a manuscript, which has been edited and published by Sir Hannibal Scicluna, called *The Book of Deliberations of the Venerable Tongue of England*. At first sight a dusty, minute book, in the crabbed, barely legible, italic hand of the sixteenth century, there emerges from it a document of very human appeal to men of English stock.

From it we learn that no vows could quite suppress the turbulent blood of the young English Knights whose sense of Englishry was already strong in the years before the Reformation. Latecomers to the suavities and social niceties of the Renaissance, they seemed barbaric and undisciplined—men from the fringes of civilization—to their more conventional and smoother mannered continental brethren. They reacted, in a way which seems to us curiously un-English, by being touchy in the extreme about their precedence, hot-blooded and quick to pick a quarrel at any imagined slight to their tongue.

Sir Clement West, we find, placed on his escutcheon '. . . the Lion of England over the eight-pointed Cross of the Order. He moved about preceded by a Mace Bearer, carrying a golden mace, or Staff of Command, with the Royal Arms of England . . . in this guise he presented himself in the Palace of the Sovereign Prince of Malta. . . .' The mace was purloined by the young Knights of another Langue (the whole incident reads rather like

[1] Dorothy L. Sayers, *Unpopular Opinions*.

a Gunroom escapade) and Sir Clement '. . . became furious and imperiously demanded its restitution'.

Again, foreign proxies having been selected to represent the Priors of England and Ireland and the Bailiff of the Eagle in the Chapter General of the Order, West '. . . so far forgot himself as to insult the representatives of the absent English and Irish dignitaries, swearing at them and calling them Saracens, Jews, Bastards . . .'—*dictos procuratores Saracenos, Judeos et bastardos. . . .*' Called upon to apologize, 'West imprecates, swears, throws his mantle of state to the ground, unsheaths his Sword and leaves the Hall in a towering passion'.[1]

The background of the *Book of Deliberations* is the Reformation. Whether by accident or design, the cunning of Henry VIII was achieving a social as well as a religious revolution. With the destruction of the fabric of religious life, there began to emerge a new social structure and a complete transfer of power and responsibility in England. The barons, the knights, and the bishops and religious Orders who had ruled throughout the Middle Ages were destroyed and there appeared a new ruling caste—without pretensions either to faith or to chivalry—men of commerce, heirs to the pillaging of the Church, who were to found great families whose influence, in the end, was to overwhelm the Monarchy itself and to survive well into the twentieth century.

The social, as well as the religious change, becomes most obvious during the reign of Elizabeth I; but the spirit of feudalism was to survive in Malta amongst the English Knights for some years yet.

The first and last entries in the *Deliberations* carry us from the loss of Rhodes to the second year of the Order's firm establishment in Malta—with the virtual destruction of the Muslim threat by that last glorious flame of feudalism, radiant with ancient knighthood and the bright gallantries of the past, the Siege of 1565. The first entry coincides with the death of Martin Luther and the last with Elizabeth's Act of Uniformity.

For those few Englishmen of the English Langue, still vowed to a cause which was soon to seem lost for ever, the background of those years was that of the great Cardinal Wolsey with his imperial state, his role of peacemaker in the Holy Roman Empire,

[1] Mgr. A. Mifsud, *Knights Hospitallers of the Venerable Tongue of England in Malta.*

and his ambitions towards the papacy: the royal hypocrite Henry's sordid matrimonial intrigues and his excommunication; Thomas Cromwell's cynical Dissolution—including the properties of the Order itself—and the stout Robert Aske's Pilgrimage of Grace; the massacre of the Abbots; the war with the Scots, Solway Moss, and the burning of Edinburgh.

How sad and bewildered they must have been, torn between loyalty to an excommunicated monarch, to their roots in the English downland and wood, and their vows to Holy Religion.

Cynical and rascally as were most of the activities of Cromwell, the Protector Somerset's destruction of everything that was beautiful in English religious life was vicious and brutal. With it came the final deprivation of the remaining shreds of the dignity and property of the Holy Religion as the Knights loved to call their Order.

How, we may wonder, did the young exiles in Malta react to the tragedy of the gentle lady, Queen Jane Grey? The unhappy marriage of Queen Mary to the Most Catholic Philip of Spain? While their Catholicity may, in a brutal age when there were no shades of right and wrong, have condoned the burning of the heretics Latimer and Ridley and the vacillating Cranmer, we must wonder how their Englishry sustained the idea of a Spanish king. And the Scottish brethren of the English Tongue? How did they fare with their Sassenach comrades when Mary Stuart assumed the title of Queen of England? How did they feel about Mary's marriage with Darnley? And Bothwell?

News seems to have travelled with surprising speed and, despite the hatreds and the persecutions, the mock trials and the burnings and beheadings, there was still no iron curtain between England and Christendom. It is clear from the *Deliberations* that there was a constant coming and going. The Rule of the Order did not require the Brethren to remain permanently within the Convent. Indeed, many of them spent the greater part of their time in their own bailiwicks and commanderies. Once they had served their apprenticeship and done, as we should put it, their 'sea time', the Rule required only that they should repair to the Convent when the call went out from the Grand Master. Having spent the minimum qualifying period of residence in the Inn— rather like a budding young barrister 'eating his dinners'—and borne arms upon a number of sorties or operational missions, known as *caravans*, the young Knight had established his place on the seniority list and was qualified for preferment within his own Langue.

Thus we find the *Deliberations* signed by a constantly changing body. A name may be absent for several years and then reappear. In most cases we are left to guess that the Knight is absent about the business of his distant Commandery or his King; but, in some, the names are part of the history of England and of Europe and are household words.

In August of 1523 Sir William Weston leaves (in the keeping of the Langue) 'a parcel of silver bearing the arms of Darrel, Boswell, Lancelot, Pemberton, and Barnaby, as well as those of Weston'. The parcel is acknowledged by the Proctors of the Langue, Giles Russell and John Sutton, who were most careful to note that amongst a number of 'Pitchers, Basins and Trenchers' there were 'Nine spoons, of which one is broken. . . .' This was the year in which the Knight Charles Brandon ravaged France as far as the gates of Paris while Wolsey was imposing yet heavier taxes at home. Weston may well have helped in the ravaging of France, while his Cardinal further squeezed the English Commanderies of the Order and his messmates went adventuring against Islam. A muddled age, indeed, for feudal loyalties were not yet dead and nationalities far from clear-cut.

At this time, too, Sir William paid a part of his *pesse*—passage money or mess subscription—and a part only of his 'bill of Dyners', promising to pay the balance on his coming again and should, in those uncertain times, the coming again be doubtful, then the Proctors had his parcel of silver and the nine spoons, 'of which one is broken'.

Weston came again in 1526 and paid not only his own bill, but that of his nephew, Thomas Dingley, from which we may guess that he had not 'broken his back from laying a Manor on it' at the Field of the Cloth of Gold.

Sir William was to die of a broken heart at the news of the Dissolution, and his nephew Thomas a martyr's death in 1535.

Not all the gear of this little company was as sumptuous as the trenchers and pitchers of silver. Much homelier traps are mustered as the gift of Francis Gallearde: 'A tablecloth, two large towels, six little napkins of Diaper: Five great plates, six of a lesser sort: ten small dishes: Six porringers of English fashion: Eleven pottery trenchers: Eight saucers: A pewter winepot of a potyell (or 4 pints): one brass cauldron: a frying pan a little spoon and a gridiron.' We know little of Brother Gallearde; but the record of his gift to the Langue lifts the curtain of time, a little, upon this small band of exiled English Catholic gentlemen in their refectory with their porringers and their trenchers and their 'potyell' of wine. They cannot have been a very gay company, for yesterday's news, brought to the Convent by some new recruit, may have told of their King's attempts to dissolve his marriage to Katherine of Aragon—who is own aunt to the Emperor from whom the Order hopes to hold Malta and Tripolis as fief.

In March 1528 there is a record of a 'Deliberation' in London. It notes the 'scandalous and unseemly' fact that there is no English-speaking priest in the Convent (at Augusta, in Sicily, where the Order was awaiting the outcome of negotiations for a new seat) and 'for the sake of the Novices, who have no other tongue . . .' the English Knights resolve to appoint one or two English Conventual Chaplains. Not far from the scene of this devout Deliberation, Henry Tudor is casting a lustful glance at the black-eyed Anne Bullen and is breaking up the Court set up by the papacy 'because it is too friendly to Katherine'.

In March 1530 we find a very English entry in the book '. . . one of their number is unable to make his caravan being not a man of courage . . .': but the Langue must make clear that he is exceptional and the record concludes '. . . as others of that noble nacion be. . . .'

By December of 1530 an awkward half of the Universities of Europe, to whom Henry had appealed, have declared Katherine's marriage void; but the fief of Malta is secured to the Order and we find John Babington, George Aylmer, Thomas Dingley, and Henry Pole busy with the accounts and the mustering of the Langue's property in the new Convent.

In March 1531 it is decided to 'build up the void room at the southern end of the palace of the Auberge as a sufficient chamber for the Turcopilier' (Commander of the Cavalry—a post vested *ex officio* in the English Tongue) '. . . as the late Turcopilier was content with the same, paying thirteen ducats for rent for a house from his own pocket . . . and having regard to the poverty of the Tongue having no manner of money, handnapery or utensils. . . .' Thomas Cromwell's work was already bearing bitter fruit.

In 1532, Henry has forbidden payment of Annates or First Fruits and has declared himself Supreme Head of an English Church; but the *Deliberations* note that Anthony Bentham volunteers for a *caravan* 'unless the Grand Master L'Isle Adam requires him to be Governor of the City (in Malta), then Thomas Cavendish will go in his stead'. So, while Henry drives England down the sad path of apostasy, the Benthams and the Cavendishes stand guard on the marches of Christendom.

In 1535, Henry is busily making martyrs. St. Thomas More and St. John Fisher lose their heads and these are bad days for any loyal Catholic gentleman. Anthony Russell is received into the Order without presenting the usual proofs of nobility, for he may not risk access to the proofs and the Tongue is content with a letter from a 'Doctor Mabylstone and other creditable parsonnes'.

The Reformation is now in full swing. It has been written that '. . . men felt in England as if a scorpion lay sleeping under every stone . . . Cromwell had reduced bloodshed to a system. With an awful businesslike calm, he ticked off men's lives among the casual notes of the day: Item, the Abbot of Reading: Item, when Master Fisher shall go to his execution, and the other [More]. . . .'[1]

In July 1539, Sir Adrian Fortescue, a Knight of Honour and Devotion of the Order, suffers martyrdom for denying his King's supremacy in matters of Faith—that same King who had made him a Knight of the Bath for his services in the French wars.

Again in July—seemingly a good month for the popular spectacle of hangings, drawings, and quarterings[2]—of 1541, Sir David Gunston (called the 'Good knight' in the *Deliberations*) follows Fortescue on the road of martyrdom.

At about this time there is received into the English Tongue

---

[1] Meiklejohn, *History of England*.

[2] Dover Wilson in *The Essential Shakespeare* writes of Tyburn: 'Here, at no cost except a few hours of waiting to secure a good position, you may see the hangman at his work, of which hanging is the least interesting part. It is a common "traitor" we will suppose, some Jesuit caught in his vestments at Mass, by Master Richard Topcliffe, the head of the Government Secret Police, an expert human ferret and cunning at devising new tortures. The Popish recusant has been dragged to Tyburn upon a hurdle and the hangman, you hear, is in good form, having already shown marvels of skill with his knife upon the traitors before you arrived. For the Elizabethan hangman is an artist and the knife is his chief instrument; the art consisting in tossing his man from the ladder, hanging him but cutting him down before he breaks his neck, so that he may be dismembered and disembowelled while still alive. Indeed there is one recorded instance of a priest who was heard praying while the hangman already had his bleeding palpitating heart in his hand—and skill could hardly go beyond that.'

one Alexander Dundas '. . . a Scottishman' upon condition that
he is '. . . never to ask a Commandery neither of Grace or chevise-
ment [seniority], nor meliorment [improvement of property]
neither dignity within England or Ireland but only the Commandery of Torphichen in Scotland'. The future of Catholic England
is indeed dim; but our English Knights at their deliberations in
Malta must make it crystal clear that no 'Scottishman' may revive
any ancient claim to property or precedence outside Scotland.
Twenty-five years later, we shall see the Scottish Commandery of
Torphichen, which was immensely rich, owning great parts of
Scotland, being cunningly acquired as personal property by a
Scottish Knight.

An entry of July 1545 provides food for conjecture by the
genealogists. It records the acceptance of the Noble George
Dudley (alias Sutton) without proofs of nobility, it being impossible, as in the case of Anthony Russell, for him to produce them.
Cromwell was adept at seizing title deeds and proofs of nobility
quite often disappeared with them. But Dudley, or Sutton, was
accepted upon a statement by 'the Lord Cardinal of England'.
Who was this George Dudley? Almost certainly a fugitive, he
may well have been a connexion of that Warwick whom Henry
sent to the block. Or a kinsman of Queen Jane Grey's husband.
Or of Elizabeth's 'Sweet Robin'. The patronage of the Lord
Cardinal suggests a cadet of no mean House. And the Cardinal?
Wolsey was long dead and the titular Cardinal was Campeggio—
the Italian Bishop of Hereford who refused to pander to Henry's
black-eyed 'Maid of Honour'. More likely Cardinal Pole, himself
a Plantagenet with young relatives already in the Order, and a
blood relation of the Dudleys, as well as of the Tudors. If young
Dudley were, indeed, of the family of Pole, the 'Cardinal of
England', he was in no position to risk a search for his proofs.
Henry's vicious character was nowhere more evident than in his
pursuit of Pole's family. He repeatedly attempted to have the
Cardinal assassinated—at least once during the Council of Trent,
over which Pole presided. Finding the Cardinal beyond his reach,
he then murdered his brother, Lord Montague, and, in 1541, put
his saintly mother (whom we know as the Blessed Margaret Pole)
to death. Pole was elected, but declined the Papal throne in 1549.
He was to restore the Church, under Mary, and to be the last
Archbishop of Canterbury in communion with Rome. He was

Mary's (and Elizabeth's) cousin and a kinsman of the Emperor Charles V, a grandson of Clarence and great-nephew of Edward IV and Richard III. No wonder that Cromwell threatened to 'make him eat his heart'. His successful rivals for the Papal throne were first Caraffa and, later, Delmonte, both members of houses who gave Grand Masters to the Sovereign Order.

Amateurs of historical 'Whodunits' may find much material in the Archives of the Order. The Tudors' determination to exterminate the Plantagenets may often be suspected as the real reason behind their selection of martyrs. Fortescue certainly had Plantaganet connexions and the same is more than possible of Gunston, Nowell, and Waldegrave.

In April 1547 another Scot is received 'of Grace special, being not of the limits . . .'—that is, he was born outside the boundaries of the Langue or was unable to show the sixteen quarterings of nobility necessary for reception as a Knight of Honour and Devotion. He was one Anthony Geoffrey and undertook, like Dundas, not to claim seniority for the purpose of any Commandery save that of Torphichen.

The Scottish Knights were doomed never again to hold a Commandery, for, in 1563, the Knight James Sandilands made the magnificent gesture of 'presenting' the rich Commandery of Torphichen—which was not his to present, for he held it in fee from the Order—to his Queen, Mary Stuart. She cannot have been ignorant of the nature of the gift and we have, in fact, an instance, by no means unique, of a Catholic Monarch joining the Protestant game of 'nationalization'. Mary returned the lands to Sandilands and created him 'Baron St. John'. The record does not tell us what service the traitorous Knight had rendered to deserve his Queen's connivance nor what twist of political expediency prompted her unfriendly act towards a Prince whose Sovereignty she was bound to recognize. Perhaps the bitter shadow of Knox can be detected in the background.

Later, in 1547, we find a hint of some similar doubtful proceedings, for Sir Oswald Massingberd is promoted to be Prior of Ireland, and Nicholas Upton travels to Malta, to renounce his suit to the Priory in private '. . . in order that the affair be kept quiet'. This year 'the Archbishop of Canterbury did eat meat openly in Lent, the like of which was never seen since England was a Christian country', and whatever the affair which was to be kept quiet, we can understand that this was no time for Christian Knights to be openly disputing the title to an Irish Priory. On 3 November 1548, Upton's tact and loyalty is rewarded with the dignity of Turcopilier, on the death of Giles Russell. The entry is interesting as one of the few recorded in Spanish, the language of the reigning Grand Master, Juan d'Homedes.

On 11 July 1548 there is a pathetic entry. The English Langue had found it necessary to pawn, with one Stamati Galante, 'a silver Basin of the weight of nine marks two ounces, with the Arms of John Boswell . . . to send a man into England to obtain some news and to learn the manner in which to proceed in order to recuperate the property of the English Tongue'.

This year the English were burning the Port of Leith and Holyrood as part of the wooing of Princess Mary by Edward VI, and Cranmer was busily translating a number of Catholic uses to form the basis of his first Book of Common Prayer. Small chance, indeed, of recuperating the property of the Sovereign Order.

Boswell's silver basin was redeemed in July 1551 with the 'spoils' of the Turcopilier Nicholas Upton who had died from a *coup-de-soleil* sustained while repelling a Turkish landing in Malta. It must be a matter of constant wonder that these men survived at all, clothed in full armour, wielding a two-handed sword in the heat of a Mediterranean summer, and Upton was no longer a young man. The *spoglio* or 'spoils' of a dead Knight—not exclud-ing the Grand Masters and the Grand Priors—were, in origin, the spoils of war which he had acquired in combat and all passed to the Order, usually to his parent Langue, upon his death. In time, the vow of personal poverty had been allowed to lapse so far as to permit the individual Brother to enjoy considerable personal riches during his lifetime and there are cases on record where a dispensation was granted, permitting relatives, who would other-wise be left in want, to inherit part of the *spoglio*.

There is a passing flash of Maltese local colour in the name of the Auditor who arranged the redemption of Boswell's silver basin. He is described as 'Pietro de Gozon, known as Melac'. While 'de Gozon' is, I think, not in any way connected with Gozo, it is a fact that the name 'Melac' (variously spelt at different times) is a common Gozitan name and one of the oldest of Maltese family names, always supposed to have been connected with the

Punic and Carthaginian cult of Molok or Moloch. Perhaps the nickname was a Knightly joke, a play on the similarity of Gozon to Gozo.

Ten years later, in 1559, things seem a little brighter for the dwindling band of English Brothers. Despite her Act of Uniformity, Elizabeth has no love for the extreme Protestant and it is possible for Brother Pedro Feliçes de la Nuça openly to journey to England, where he collects 'a sum in English money sufficient towards the purchase of a convenient house [in Malta] for an Auberge for the Tongue of England and for the furnishing of the same'.

Nevertheless, it was a false ray of hope. Pedro de la Nuça was a Spaniard and we find him bearing the dignity of Bailiff of the Eagle—a title essentially English and deriving from a Commandery of that name in Lincolnshire which once belonged to the Templars to whom it had been granted by King Stephen. The Lincoln Commandery passed to the Hospitallers upon the suppression of the Templars and was, in its turn, seized by Cromwell. It was the beginning of the end when the empty title to an English Commandery was borne by a Knight of the Castilian Langue.

By 1560 the English Langue, now dwindled to two Brethren in the Convent, Oliver Starkey and James Shelley, is compelled to sell 'all the houses, tenements, and gardens in Malta, belonging to the Tongue'.

Elizabeth was now making martyrs, too. In 1562 there died at her hands the Knight John Nowell and, in 1563, Edward Walgray (or Waldegrave). Twenty years later, by the Bull of 2 December 1583, Pope Gregory XIII converted all titles of the English Tongue into Titular Benefices of Grace '. . . as for all Titles of Infidel Parts'. The Bull marks (for a time) the end of the Langue of England as a juridically constituted body within the Order of St. John.

But the stubborn and arrogant Englishmen were not to pass out unnoticed. Starkey stood beside his friend and master, the valiant La Vallette, in 1565, in one of the last battles of Christendom and sleeps beside him in the crypt of St. John's Conventual Church in Valletta. While Elizabeth ordered prayers in all her nationalized churches for the success of the defenders of Malta, the names of three other Englishmen—not Knights, but gentlemen volunteers—were recorded amongst those who fought in the

Siege. They were John Evans Smyth, Aegidius Russell, and Edward Stanley. Sir Richard Shelley, by this time the sole survivor of his Langue, protests hotly in 1567 against an affront—real or imagined—to the dignity of his office. A Deliberation of October of that year narrates:

> The manner in which Fr. Richard Shelley, Prior of England, was upheld in the ancient pre-eminence of his predecessors over the Prior of Messina at the Convent of Malta in the litigation and dispute that is to say as to which shall precede the other in the Councils, Public Places and other solemn Congregations of the Order.

Commissioners were appointed and the Grand Master ruled in favour of England,

> pointing out with his hand to the one and the other their respective seat in full Council of the Order, of which places that which was assigned to the Prior of England was the more pre-eminent, because it was next immediate to that of the Marshal who is the second Conventual Bailiff in seniority and the other assigned to the Prior of Messina was of a lesser pre-eminence, it being next to that of the Admiral which place amongst those of the Conventual Bailiffs is fourth in precedence.

By the end of the seventeenth century the Englishmen and many of the Germans had left Malta. Knights and ex-Knights fought against their erstwhile Brethren in the Wars of Religion, and families were growing up all over the British Isles, some renegades like Sandilands, others mere beneficiaries of the Dissolution, proudly hyphenating 'St. John' with their patronymics (some of my own kinsmen amongst them). In England ancestral association with the Order is a matter of some pride—even if it be of the 'bend sinister' kind. But in Malta the name Spiteri, a corruption of *Sptari* or *Ospedaliere*—'Hospitaller', is not worn with any great satisfaction and we may trace this reluctance to advertise a general association with the Sovereign Order to a persistent presentation of the Knight of Malta, anyway in his latter days in the Island, as a profligate monk who peopled the country with his natural offspring. The presentation doubtless had political significance for the French as well as for the British during the early years of their occupation. That many Maltese have Knightly blood is indisputable, but the too willing assumption that every Knight was vowed to celibacy (or, as is sometimes wishfully believed, an ordained priest) must be avoided. The Order maintained a considerable body of mercenary troops, as well as its locally enlisted militia, and offspring of these would qualify, loosely, for the nickname of 'Hospitaller', as would some of our English St. Johns.

We have seen that between the Maltese aristocracy and the Order there was no great love lost. Diarchy seems to be the clumsy fate of these little islands.[1]

The Grand Master Pinto de Fonseca might assume an imperial crown and use the style of an absolute monarch; but he was committed by his oath to recognize the ancient institutions of his Maltese subjects. In theory he ruled only with the consent of his Council, in matters concerning the internal affairs of the Order and the defence of the 'Convent'. Matters of civil law were by the same theory the responsibility of the Maltese elected *Università*— the *Giurati* who had been charged since Norman times with the government of the civil population. In fact, the *Giurati* were almost hereditary. The names Inguanez, Testaferrata, Manduca, Apap recur year after year in the Archives. In fact, too, the 'Convent' was the whole of Malta and Gozo and, exactly as with modern constitutions, 'defence' could cover a sufficiently wide field to enable a strong Grand Master to rule as a military dictator. Thus, with a quasi-hereditary Maltese Council, an often subservient Grand Council of the Order and the purse-strings, too, largely under the Order's control, there would seem to have been little enough semblance of democracy.

It would, nevertheless, be false to suppose that the Maltese were consistently oppressed. If most of the Grand Masters were tyrants, they were benevolent tyrants. They ensured, sometimes at the cost of their lives, adequate food-supplies and expended vast treasure on the improvement of water-storage and the importation of the amenities of life. Some of their laws were harsh; but no harsher

---

[1] Diarchy has been described by Sir David Kelly in a reference to Soviet Imperialism (*Sunday Times*, 15 February 1953) as: 'The technique of camouflaging an Imperial Government behind dual—i.e. metropolitan and local—ministries and behind a common doctrine and common party membership . . . so that each nation is ruled by a nominally native group. . . . It can be applied to any country . . . once the wooden horse is within its gates.' The trouble in Malta from the Imperial viewpoint in 1947 as in 1530, has been the absence of what we now call 'common party membership', for this wooden horse has almost always been left standing outside the gates.

I would certainly not impute to the architects of the Maltese Constitution of 1947 any of the Imperialist aims of the Soviets; nevertheless, the death of that constitution is universally unmourned. As Mr. Patrick Wall, M.P. said in the House of Commons, on 16 February 1959: 'It [the 1947 Constitution] caused considerable trouble . . . largely because of the difficulty of running a Diarchy, and of knowing where reserved subjects, such as defence, end, and Maltese subjects, such as agriculture, start. It was a bad constitution . . . and I think the House should be very pleased it has now been abandoned.'

than those of other European rulers. There were, of course, bad men who were bad rulers and good men who were worse rulers. Pinto, an excellent ruler and well loved, would have been the last to claim 'goodness'. He found his finances with a small regard for legality and is reputed to have made away with a large sum in gold which belonged to the Confraternity of the Holy Souls—a society committed to the duty of praying for the Souls in Purgatory. Charged, by his confessor, on his death-bed to set the matter right, he is reported to have said: 'Father, please do not worry, I shall be seeing the Holy Souls shortly, and will explain to them personally.'

Such anecdotes of long-dead Grand Masters are commonly related by the Maltese as one relates tales of a remembered and beloved grandparent. For the people, the Knights are a living memory which survives. Few of the characters and notabilities of the English régime have left such deep marks on the popular imagination. There are still words and phrases in the language which stem directly from some incident of Knightly history. To say that someone 'has the face of Lascaris' is to mean that he has a treacherous look and is not to be trusted. The original Maltese Lascaris was a Phanariot Greek fighting for the Turks in the Siege of 1565. He changed sides and betrayed a projected Turkish assault to the Christians. He was of Byzantine Imperial blood, and his kinsman, the Grand Master Lascaris de Castellar, ruled well and wisely; but his treachery is held in contempt after four centuries.[1]

Grand Master Ximenes de Texada was a noted tyrant.[2] In his short reign of less than two years he succeeded in sowing seeds of disaffection, both within the Order and amongst the people, which were to flower in the too easy capitulation of the Island to the Revolutionary French. It was against his draconian government that Don Gaetano Mannarino led the narrowly unsuccessful rising known as the 'Priests' Revolt'. Mannarino spent twenty-

---

[1] There was also a Lascaris amongst the traitors who surrendered to the French in 1798.

[2] Ximenez or Ximenes let the side down. His family were brilliant and enlightened leaders in Renaissance Spain. The famous Polyglot Bible, containing the Old Testament in Hebrew, Greek, and Latin, the New Testament in Greek and Latin, and the Chaldaic Targum of the Pentateuch was the work of Cardinal Ximenes, Archbishop of Toledo, who compiled it and published it at Alcala in 1502. It has been a boon—or a headache, depending on your point of view—to theologians of all colours.

15. Gozo: Ta 'Pinu

16. Caravaggio's 'Beheading of St. John'

(*above*) 17. St. John's Cathedral: the interior

(*left*) 18. Grand Master de Vilhena

(*below*) 19. The Admiral Leone Strozzi

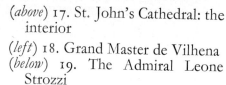

LIONE STROZZI PRIORE DI CAPVA
AMMIRAGLIO   DIFRANEMATA

(*above left*) 20. Grand Master
    Pinto

(*above right*) 21. Grand Master
    de Rohan

(*left*) 22. Mosta Dome

23. Hagar Qim

24. St. Publius surveys his birthplace

two years in chains and Napoleon cleverly released the broken old man and exhibited him as a symbol of French Liberty.

But by far the majority of the Grand Masters were enlightened, Christian rulers who brought prosperity to the people and raised their standards of living much above the general, European level. Great artists, like Caravaggio, Mateo Perez d'Alecio, Paladini, Leonello Spada, Giuseppe Mazzuoli, Mattia Preti, and Favray brought beauty to Malta and native artists like the Gafa's, Zahra, and Buhagiar were nurtured by the Order. The glories of the Renaissance were brought, through the parish churches, into the lives of the people. A body of artificers and craftsmen grew up, second to none, whose traditions have only lately died out and the functional influence of Anglo-Saxon rule has little to show in exchange for their loss.

Resentful of the Knights, the Maltese upper classes yet copied their way of life, built their houses on the plans of the *auberges*, organized their domestic habits, made their clothing, their cooking, and their recreations all upon Knightly patterns. Thus, while there are few truly native dishes, there is a wide and fascinating choice of local versions of foreign dishes ranging from the allegedly English roast beef to the *calamares* of Spain, and the sausages of Germany. The great, old houses had their own bakeries, their cold storage, packed with Sicilian snow, their laundries and their sewing-rooms, and the domestic routine was as strictly ordered as that of a monastery.

In the latter years the Order created its own nobility, rewarding the loyal Maltese commonalty with titles of the Empire which were, later, to be recognized by the British Crown. These families survive and some few have managed to keep their homes intact —museums, in fact, treasure-houses of the period which saw the ennobling of their ancestors—packed with portraits, jewels, weapons, books, as redolent of past ages as any of the great houses of England or Italy.

The Hospitallers, mindful of the fate of the Templars, were always particularly sensitive to any suggestion of a 'Saracen' taint; partly from their memory of the Holy Land and partly from fear of 'fraternization' with their Muslim captives. They suspected that the old Maltese nobility had intermarried with peasant stock of the Muslim occupation and refused, no matter how splendid the family blazon, to admit young gentlemen of Maltese birth to the Order. But the nobles circumvented this bar by arranging that their wives be confined in Sicily, and a number of Maltese, of whose heraldic quarterings there could be no doubt, thus became members of the Order. There was never a Maltese Langue (though one of the conditions upon which Great Britain agreed to return Malta to the Sovereign Order at the Treaty of Amiens was the creation of such a Langue) and Maltese Knights were accepted, as a rule, into the Langue of Italy. Nowadays some Maltese members of the Order belong to the British Association of the Knights of Malta. Others are admitted '*In Gremio Religionis*'.

Many Maltese were admitted 'of Grace' as Conventual Chaplains and two Grand Priors of the Conventual Church second only in dignity and influence to the Grand Master, were Maltese.

By the eighteenth century the Order seemed to be a complete anachronism and new forces of disruption were on the point of completing the fragmentation of Christendom which the Reformation had commenced. But 'the Convent' in Malta was still the venue of many of Europe's young Catholic aristocracy and the Island was one of the richest and most prosperous places in the world.

An eighteenth-century 'description of the Island of Malta', the original of which is in the Royal Library in Valletta, was painstakingly compiled in 1764 by the Marchese Camillo Spreti, a nobleman of Ravenna. Averil Mackenzie-Grieve, who edited Spreti's manuscript, writes:[1]

Behind the fascination of old observances, of traditional ceremonies symbolizing a truly great past, behind the wealth and magnificence, Camillo scented decay. 'Boredom and Idleness, the Father of all Vices', as Spreti unoriginally observes, gripped the city gentlemen. Attached to their National Auberges or Inns, the rich young noblemen perfunctorily performed their tasks, their often empty religious duties, using all their ingenuity and such energy as they possessed in devising fresh means of whiling away the appointed two years until they could become fully fledged knights and candidates for any of the Order's rich Commanderies, scattered throughout Catholic Europe. According to Spreti, gossip, gaming, and duelling were their chief diversions, despite the vows of brotherly love which the Order professed, national rivalry throve. But it must be borne in mind that half Europe was again at war and that even in Malta, high feelings were but natural in a society formed of members of the leading European families. 'Be affable with all', counsels Spreti, 'especially with the French, but do not seek to imitate their Caprices or take them

[1] Averil Mackenzie-Grieve, *The Manuscript of a Knight of Malta*.

into your confidence. Enter as little as may be upon Discourses concerning Sovereigns and Nationalities, especially with the Germans, and always profess Neutrality when the conversation turns upon War. Be courteous to the Spaniards, but do not emulate their pride and contradict neither them nor the Portuguese, and in the company of the latter do not speak in a language they are unable to understand (although, of course, this would be a sign of Bad Breeding in any company), for they are excessively Suspicious by Nature.'

'Avoid the Coffee shops', he goes on, 'for in so doing you will avoid the opportunity of both hearing and speaking Evil of others—perhaps even worse. Since men of every Nation are to be met with there, nothing is easier than to become embroiled in an Affair. By this I do not mean that you should play the Savage and eschew all company. There are many ways of avoiding this and of escaping from the Idleness of the Island, which is very great. The practising of some Instrument of Music, the Study of Books and of Navigation—which is especially suited to a knight—will all help you not to become a Friend of Idleness. Receptions given by the Venerable Baillies are not lacking and there one may pass an evening, but remember, when you are professed to sell no-one your Vow. Never was there such a country for open quarrels as Malta. But, if your soul is dear to you, avoid interested parties and do not allow yourself to be won by gold or promises of reward, for this vile object should never be that of a knight and be guided in all things by the Holy Spirit.'

And of the Order and the people, Miss Mackenzie-Grieve and Camillo have this to say:[1]

One of the most interesting features of Spreti's manuscript, however, is the picture he draws of the relationship of the Order to the Maltese, who, since Charles V had ceded the Island to the Order without their consent, had never ceased to regard the knights as interlopers. So much has been written about the Order that the majority of the Island's population is apt to be forgotten.

Grand Master Pinto, while robbing the Maltese of their ancient civic rights and liberties, bestowed titles freely upon the middle class, encouraged social relations between the newly ennobled and the knights, and—from many travellers' accounts—turned a blind eye upon closer and less legitimate associations. But the exclusive old Spanish families, whose admission to the Order was forbidden, aloof in their dark palaces in the old walled capital of Notabile ['Mdina], would have none of Knight or Noble. 'The Barons are few' Spreti explains 'and not tractable. Knights may be received only with the greatest difficulty into their houses, because they, having suffered various wrongs and discourteous treatment from the same, do not wish to expose themselves again to similar Affronts, and thus it came about that many Innocents must suffer for the bad behaviour of the guilty few. The Counts entertain the knights more often, and among them are families in which one may spend a few hours pleasurably and without offence to God. The citizens, who are either Clerks to the Order, or in some Public Service, or employed by the Treasury as Magistrates, Jurymen, Lawyers, Store-keepers, etc., are the most frequented, but here I do not advise you to go, not because they are lacking in honesty, but for the

[1] Averil Mackenzie-Grieve, op. cit.

reasons which I will give you. One frequents receptions firstly to learn and secondly to pass the time in Honest Diversions. If you go to these Citizens' houses for the first reason, you will, of a truth, be mistaken, for they understand little Italian and speak less. Although it is the foreign language most used by them, they do not know how to string together a serious, well-salted conversation without using Arabic [*sic*] expressions which you will not be able to understand, and, what is worse, in your presence they will often speak with another Maltese of the company in their own perfidious Idiom, which is unknown to the knights, which shows as indeed their behaviour testifies in many other respects, little or no education. And you may be sure that when the Maltese talk in their own Idiom in your presence or that of other knights, they are criticizing your clothes, your appearance, and your speech. . . .

'Camillo's vanity had evidently suffered from the slight regard in which the Maltese hold those who demand deference as a right' is Miss Mackenzie-Grieve's pertinent comment. Describing a gathering, on a Feast Day, for gaming and gossip, in the house of some prosperous *bourgeois*, Camillo records:[1]

On entering the Room you will hear [*sic*] a great silence and see four or six gaming tables surrounded by both men and women, only a few of whom take any notice of a knight's entry or departure, holding the Maltese in greater esteem. I myself have seen a whole company of knights arriving at one of these Routs and the Maltese not so much as looking up to acknowledge their Bows or Compliments, while, a quarter of an hour later, a little Maltese Popinjay came in (for many of them seek to ape the Parisians) and you should have seen the to-do! The scraping of chairs and the curtseying of the Ladies. So you will see that it is not fitting to frequent this Society. Firstly because there is nothing to learn, secondly because there is no diversion to be found there, and thirdly . . . unkindest cut . . . because owing to the antipathy of the Maltese for the knights, one is made to cut a ridiculous figure.

Camillo was making the same error as some of his successors. When the return of Malta to the Sovereign Order came to depend largely (though not entirely, for British strategy had a final say, and the British were already in occupation) upon the goodwill of the Maltese after the Treaty of Paris, the chauvinism of those Knights who, like Spreti, expected the automatic subservience of the 'natives', tipped the balance of feeling against the Order.

But it was the Maltese women—those, at least, who deigned to consort with the Knights at all—who upset Camillo most. 'When the Order first came to Malta', he writes, 'they resembled proud and wayward savages, fleeing Society and never permitting any of our number to see their faces'. He calls them predaceous and

---

[1] Averil Mackenzie-Grieve, op. cit.

perfidious but the more dangerous for their great beauty and their flattering ways of 'luring birds into their cages'.

'Do not', he warns, 'be easily deceived by their apparent Beauty neither dwell upon their frequent and artificial sighs and tears, which may well be Crocodile's Tears, for they are avid by nature and no sooner have they despoiled the poor, blind knight of all he possesses than they will shut the door in his face, only opening to admit other persons whom they may treat in the same way. In this respect never a day passes but that dreadful things befall the poor, inexperienced, young knights. . . .'[1]

To this awful warning, Miss Mackenzie-Grieve adds her comment: 'Spreti is weighing the balances fairly heavily on the side of those hot-blooded young gentlemen.'[2]

The picture which Spreti paints with so charming a mixture of accuracy and *naïveté*—he was undoubtedly a bit of a prig—is, nevertheless, a sad commentary on the decadence of a splendid tradition. New ideals, new ideologies like The Rights of Man were stirring, even amongst the ranks of the aristocratic Knights and the 'Convent' of Valletta, the Auberges, the fine country villas, the churches with their centuries of accumulated treasure were all ripe for pillage by the People's Army of Napoleon.

If, today, we may be bewildered at the wealth of artistic treasure still stored up in the Maltese Islands imagination pauses before the vision of Malta in the last days of the Order. What now survives from that time is a mere remnant left from the looting of the French, the acquisitiveness of collectors, and the shambles of unrestricted war; the ignorant iconoclasm of military engineers, the contemptuous neglect of bureaucracies, and the penal taxation of the custodians of inherited treasures. Add to all these enemies the ordinary ravages of time, and it becomes clearer that Malta of the Knights had few peers amongst the capitals of Europe.

Other things become clearer, too. When we think of Malta as having a standard of living somewhat above that of other Mediterranean, European countries and pat ourselves on the back, we forget that, in the late eighteenth century and at the beginning of the British occupation, the Maltese had long been accustomed to standards which compared favourably with those anywhere else in Europe and were probably superior on the cultural level. For this reason, amongst others, the Maltese long remained 'frozen' in their feudal pattern. British patterns seemed to have little better to offer. They were, essentially, children of Christendom, and it

---

[1] Averil Mackenzie-Grieve, op. cit.   [2] Ibid.

is not improbable that the spiritual values left by the Sovereign Order have made their marks deep enough to resist erosion for some years yet.

3

Points of contact between the Order and England did not cease abruptly with the virtual abrogation of the Treaty of Amiens. Neither did the Order's influence upon European history disappear with the French and British occupations of Malta. Already, before the betrayal of the Grand Master Ferdinand von Hompesch to Bonaparte, a new star of Christendom seemed to be rising in the East, at the Court of the Czar of all the Russias. The dream of a new Byzantium was part of the Russian Imperial and ecclesiastical tradition and the weakly, muddle-headed but well-meaning Czar Paul saw himself as the head of a new, reunited Christian Imperium.

The Grand Priory of Russia was created in 1797—and recognized by the Crowns of England and Naples in 1798. Paul was elected Grand Master of the Sovereign Order (illegally, by a majority only of those Knights who had deserted Hompesch, who was still alive and had neither abdicated nor been deposed). The more astute Russians saw, in the prospect of a revived Russian-controlled Order, the realization of their constant ambition of an irruption into the warm waters of the Mediterranean and the commerce and life-lines of the West. The Treaty of Amiens had stipulated that England should share her occupation of Malta with Naples and Russia and that she should, in concert with these Powers, ensure the re-establishment of the Order. The people of Malta protested vehemently against the return of the Knights, and the promise of the institution of a Maltese Langue failed to mollify the long-embittered Maltese old nobility. They were all full of ingenuous hope in the promises of the new democracy and the Knights were divided. The Holy Father in Rome, though naturally wishing for the Order's re-establishment, could scarcely be expected to recognize the election of a Czar who was head of a national, and schismatic Church.

Officially from tender regard for the feelings of the Maltese, but actually from a somewhat belated realization of the Russian danger (for she had, after all, signed the Treaty), England refused to permit the landing of Russian troops. The sequence of events is muddled and the records of the period notably partisan; but in fairness to the British politicians of the time, it does seem that there were several opinions as to the value of Malta as a naval base, and this was really Great Britain's sole interest. Nelson is on record as having said that the Islands were of small value and Pantellaria was considered as an alternative. Only a comparatively junior naval officer—Ball,[1] who was acting as Commissioner—on the spot seems to have been fully alive not only to the Russian threat but to the possibilities of Malta. He seems, too, to have had a great regard for the Maltese,[2] and was on the best of terms with their leaders. It was to him, perhaps, rather than to anyone at a higher level, that the decision not to implement the terms of the Treaty fell. It was well enough to ensure that the Mediterranean did not become a French lake from the possession of Malta (Napoleon would rather have put England in possession of the heights of Montmartre); but Ball preferred further that it should not become a Russian lake. In the meantime, the Czar Paul was assassinated (it has been said because he had made his submission to the Catholic Church), and the dream of a new Byzantium collapsed.

[1] On 10 January 1810, Admiral Lord Collingwood wrote to his friend, the Duke of Northumberland:
'I am truly grieved that this country shou'd have lost so usefull a servant as Sir A. Ball. I heard much of the Ability he showed in his Government of Malta and the affection the Maltese had for him, from an officer long resident in that Island. I believe the Cabinet have made as good a choice as they possibly cou'd and have done in appointing Sr. T. Keates to succeed him.
'I only lament that such an Active and able officer shou'd be taken just now from the service of our Fleet. But from your Lordship's account, I am a little reconciled to it and believe that the Government of Malta, in the present situation of affairs in the Mediterranean, is an Affair of the first consequence.'
                    The Private Correspondence of Admiral Lord Collingwood,
                    edited by Edward Hughes, Navy Records Society, 1957.
[2] In February of 1799, Ball himself wrote to Sir William Hamilton from Malta:
'The lower class of Maltese who are all attached to us have evinced more patience and cheerfulness under their great hardships than I ever expected from any nation. They have done the duty of soldiers in the severe weather, almost naked, without pay and their only nourishment bread and a small allowance of pork. . . . Capt. Hardy, Col. Rooke and the gentlemen who came from Palermo . . . can give you many particulars of the strong attachment which the Maltese profess for the English. But I am extremely anxious to impress upon your mind and that of Lord Nelson that this has not been effected by any intrigue or insinuation on the part of the English. I have studiously avoided all overtures and have constantly held out to them the necessity of being under the protection of his Sicilian Majesty. . . . I have most zealously obeyed that part of his Lordship's [Nelson's] instructions . . . to strengthen the allegiance of the Maltese to his Sicilian Majesty . . . their legitimate Sovereign.'
                    Nelson's letters to his Wife and other Documents, edited by
                    G. B. R. Naish, F.S.A., Navy Records Society, 1958.

The background of England's occupation of Malta is one of the great 'might-have-beens' of history.

Paul's submission to Rome might have reunited the Churches of West and East and a reconstituted, revitalized Order might have regained possession of the Island—wiser, perhaps, from experience. The 'Hundred Days' might still have ended at Waterloo; but with a Russian foothold firmly in the West, a clash with England would have been inevitable and the Sovereign Princes of Malta could scarcely have survived the issue. If there be any inevitability about history, Malta goes with sea power: a prospect for the future which the Maltese may well view with mixed feelings.

By the Treaty of Paris, in 1814, in accordance with 'the Will of the Maltese and the voice of Europe', the sovereignty of Malta was vested in the English Crown; but the Bourbons had returned to France, and the dormant Langues of the Order, of Provence, Auvergne, and France were revived. There was now no Grand Master; but only a Lieutenant-Master, with his Council—almost exclusively Italian—hopefully assembled, once again, at Catania in Sicily.

It was seen to be necessary that, if the Order was to retain any semblance of its ancient sovereignty, it must somehow be represented at the Congress of Vienna by a body enjoying the protection of a great Power. The German and the Anglo-Bavarian Langues had dispersed. The Langues of Aragon, Castille, and Portugal had been annexed to their national Sovereigns, and Italy was not yet a nation. Thus, it seemed, the only body which might hope to be heard were the three French Langues. A Capitular Commission, headed by the Grand Prior of Aquitaine, was set up by the French Knights and its legal status, as representing the Order, was acknowledged by a Papal Bull of August 1814. With all this talk of sovereignty and international representation it must not be overlooked that the Knights were still a Religious Order, subject in all matters of government to the approval of the Supreme Pontiff. The Lieutenant-Master, one Andrea di Giovanni, and his Council at Catania, submitted to the Capitular Commission in October 1814. His successor, Antonio Busca, submitted in 1824.

Throughout all these muddled proceedings—or so they seem to us, now—we may yet detect a persistence of the ideal of

Christian unity. The Order had for so long represented, in the minds of Europe, the best hope of that unity that it was hard, even for Protestant statesmen, to abandon the concept. Despite religious differences and economic rivalries, the rulers of Europe seem both to have recognized and desired the survival of a Sovereign body which would be above dynastic intrigue and national jealousy. The Order, for its part, had been careful to recognize national rights, even where those rights were, from its own standpoint, *de facto* rather than *de jure*. When, for example, the King of Bavaria had wished to revive the dormant Anglo-Bavarian Langue, offering to endow it with the expropriated lands of the suppressed Jesuits, in 1782, the Order had formally sought the approval of the Protestant King George III of England. That Monarch vacillated for a year—ostensibly awaiting the Pope's reaction[1]—but finally, in 1783, signified his approval, addressing the Order as from one Sovereignty to another.[2]

Relying upon the Bull of 10 August 1814, the French Capitular Commission, under the Grand Chancellor, the Marquis de St. Croix Molay, and protected by King Louis XVIII, deemed itself the legal successor of the Grand Master in Council and, on 14 September 1827, it formally revived the Langue of England and announced its willingness to admit Protestants to the Order in the English Langue; but Catholics, only, in the Grand Priory of Ireland. The Commission cited as precedents the recognition of the Protestant Bailiwick of Brandenburg and the Orthodox Grand Priory of Russia, both of doubtful legality.

A Protestant cleric, the Rev. Sir Robert Peat, was duly appointed 'Grand Prior *ad interim*' of the Venerable Tongue of England on

---

[1] Perhaps the Gordon Riots, in 1780, were still too fresh in his mind for him to risk an appearance of toying with Popery. The avowed object of the rioters was to secure a repeal of the Act of 1778 '. . . for relieving His Majesty's subjects of the Catholic Religion from certain penalties and disabilities imposed upon them during the reign of William III'.

[2] For a Hanoverian, George III was not unfriendly towards his Catholic connexions. After the death of Charles Edward Stuart, his younger brother, the Cardinal Duke of York proclaimed himself Henry IX of England '. . . by the Grace of God but not by the Will of Man'. The Vatican refused to recognize him, always carefully addressing him as 'His Serene Highness Henry Benedict Mary Clement, Cardinal Duke of York'; but there were still plenty of Jacobites who gave him Royal style and it is the more surprising—and greatly to the credit of that maligned Monarch—that George exerted himself, in the most compassionate and delicate manner, to obtain Henry a pension of £40,000 a year when the Cardinal was left destitute by the Napoleonic rape of the Holy See.

29 January 1831, and on 24 February 1834 he took the oath '*de fideli administratione*' in the Court of King's Bench before the Lord Chief Justice of England.[1]

Peat died in 1837 and was succeeded by Sir Henry Dymoke.

The Marquis de St. Croix Molay was now dead and the Capitular Commission, of which he had been the moving spirit, had been abolished. The affairs of the Order now reverted to the Lieutenant-Masters and their predominantly Italian Council. They were less generous in their interpretation of the Statutes than their Gallican Brothers and immediately began to question the admission of Protestants which was, they held, permissible only by specific dispensation of the Grand Master. They did not, at first, question the legitimacy of the revived English Langue; but they emphatically forbade the future admission of Protestants to it, of its own authority. Later, in 1843, the Lieutenant-Master decreed that no Protestant might in future be admitted and negotiations with the English Langue were broken off—though, be it noted, without any formal declaration on the part of the Sovereign Order about the legality of the Langue.

Until 1858 we have the curious (and perhaps encouraging?) spectacle of a Protestant Langue continuing to conduct itself exactly as if it were an integral part of the Sovereign and Catholic Order, acknowledging the Lieutenant-Master as its Superior and the Holy Father in Rome as its spiritual head.

However, in 1858, the English Tongue, despairing of 'reunion' upon their own terms, declared their own Sovereignty, describing themselves as 'The Sovereign and Illustrious Order of St. John of Jerusalem.'

Though Protestant in essence, the English splinter group soon

[1] For some reason which is not readily apparent, the Knights of Malta seem to have aroused English popular interest at this time. In May 1838, 'The Riots of Canterbury' centred around a colourful figure who called himself Sir William Percy Honeywood Courtenay, Knight of Malta. He is described in Ainsworth's *Rookwood*:

'A magnificent, coal-black beard decorated the chin of this worthy—but this was not all—his costume was in perfect keeping with his beard and consisted of a very theatrical looking tunic upon the breast of which was embroidered in golden wire, the Maltese Cross, while on his shoulders were thrown the ample folds of a cloak of Tyrian hue. To his side was girt a long and doughty sword which he termed, in his knightly phrase, Excalibur.'

Courtenay was, in fact, a Cornish wine merchant called John Nicholas Thom who had stood, unsuccessfully, for Parliament in 1832, conceiving himself the champion of the oppressed: particularly in the matter of Excise Revenue. He was shot—having previously murdered two men—while resisting arrest by a body of soldiery and lies buried at Herne Hill, near Dulwich Village.

ceased to have any very definite religious character—except in so far as every such organization, in default of a definitive announcement to the contrary, comes sooner or later within the orbit of the National Church. Its most active and most publicized function, of the St. John Ambulance Brigade, went from strength to strength in England and astutely assuming an 'inter-religious' character overseas, the Brigade soon numbered thousands of devoted members in all parts of the Empire and Commonwealth—Catholics, Jews, Buddhists, Hindus, Confucians, and Muslims.

In 1878 a fresh Constitution declared the English Order, now described as 'The Order of St. John of Jerusalem in England', to be 'national and not Sovereign'. This curious pronouncement left some doubt whether or not the English Order recognized the Sovereignty of its Catholic parent and, despite Geneva Conventions and other international agreements, there was then, as now, much to be said for any organization purporting to serve all mankind, irrespective of creed or colour, being free from national limitations and owing an allegiance, no matter how tenuous, to a non-territorial Sovereignty. Clearly, the Catholic ideal lingered in some minds. But, by 1936, the Order of St. John had become a national institution—in practice, as we see every day, an essential auxiliary to the police forces—and, in that year, another Constitution established by Royal Charter that 'The Crown is Sole Governor of the Venerable Order of St. John of Jerusalem in the British Realm'.

The history and origins of what, for want of a more accurate description, we must describe as the Protestant Order, is, in part, an example of the inherent English addiction to compromise and dislike of rigid definition; but there is something more to the Charter of the Venerable Order than this, and to appreciate its full significance we must go back, once again, to the turbulent and tortuous Tudors.

The Sovereign Order was suppressed and the English Langue dispossessed by Henry, in 1540, and Pope Gregory virtually abolished the Langue in 1583, by converting its titles into 'Titular Benefices of Grace' . . . *in partibus infidelis*. But there was a Statute of Mary Tudor,[1] restoring the Order in England and negotiations

---

[1] Royal Letters Patent of 1557 reinstated the Sovereign Order in England and it is upon these Letters Patent, which remain unrevoked, that the Sovereign Order's claim to be a juridically recognized Sovereignty, in England, must chiefly rest.

for Papal recognition of a restored Langue were well advanced when Mary died.

Elizabeth and her successors failed to revoke Mary's Statute. In Elizabeth's case, she trod, as ever, a slender tight-rope between the hanging and quartering of loyal Knights on the one hand and an appearance of amity with the Catholic Princes overseas. Only in this way could she hope to survive and, despite the Papal ban of excommunication[1]—admitted by Catholic historians to have been a peculiarly clumsy piece of politics—she ordered prayers for the Order and sent a token force of 'Volunteers' to the Siege of Malta. Whatever deep and clever use she intended for the Order, there is no doubt that, juridically, she recognized its Sovereignty,[2] as did most of her successors. George III clearly committed himself to this position and the Rev. Sir Robert Peat, as 'Grand Prior *ad interim*' (there is a wealth of implication in that '*ad interim*') certainly had no doubts in the matter, as he had accepted his appointment as from a Sovereign body.

The Declaration of 1858, together with the Charter of 1936, present the curious spectacle of a Little Reformation, as far as the Order is concerned, some four centuries late. The English official attitude towards the Sovereign Order has remained polite, but cool. While the Venerable Order seems to seek occasion to honour members of the Sovereign Order with its decorations, the latter has lately instituted an Order of Merit with which it can honour non-Catholics as well as its own members.

The English Order is by no means the only splinter group springing from the seedling of the Blessed Gerard's dream. Within Freemasonry—so I am credibly informed—there is a flourishing Order of Malta claiming (with some justice) a kind of apostolic succession from the early Grand Masters. In the Netherlands there is a national Order demanding proofs of nobility, but insisting on Protestant adherence. In Canada and the U.S.A. there are organizations calling themselves The Military Knights of Malta; but in general the Sovereign Order and the Venerable Order divide the Catholic and the Protestant worlds between them. Their labours

[1] The Bull of Excommunication is known, as are all such documents, by its opening words. They were *In Coena Domini* . . . and the phrase 'A Bull in a China Shop' is by some accounts, a corruption of the title of one of history's supreme examples of clumsiness.

[2] By the Bull of Reconciliation of Mary's reign, the Church had renounced all claims to ecclesiastical property: a fact which may have weighed heavily in Elizabeth's acquisitive mind.

are largely complementary, though collaboration in many projects is inevitable.

The claim to Sovereignty without territory, to which the Order seems now to be irrevocably committed, the niceties of protocol and the right to award or wear decorations may seem of small moment—fit matters to concern only victims of the snob appeal of heraldry and pretty ribbons; but the practical value of the claim was lately demonstrated very strikingly when, after the Suez adventure of 1956, Egypt broke off diplomatic relations with Great Britain and France.

British and French subjects were in peril and their property rights in jeopardy. Representations through the International Red Cross and the Swiss Embassy seemed abortive. Curiously, for a body which had for centuries been the implacable enemy of Islam, the Sovereign Order still enjoyed diplomatic relations with Egypt and the Arab world. The Order's Envoy intervened, with notably happy results and some thousands of Maltese, amongst many others, had cause to thank their ancient rulers.

As for Malta and the Order today, I have seen it written (by a Colonial Office official) that 'The Order has nothing to do with Malta.' Politically, I suppose, strictly accurate. In any other context supremely naïve.

At the other end of the scale was an article in a popular women's weekly journal which confidently asserted that the Order (presumably from the centre of some monstrous web in the Vatican) was plotting to regain the Sovereignty of Malta. Could sensationalism go further?

More sensibly, I have heard it whispered (though I speak without authority) that the dream of the Sovereign Order is to return to Jerusalem, in company with all its offspring, Catholic and Protestant alike, and there to set up, in an internationalized city, a great centre of medical and humanitarian services. The Holy Places, too, would be placed once more under the care of the Order.

The Sovereign Order's relations with Islam and with Israel are good. Its influence in the U.S.A. is strong; but there are many political and religious obstacles to be negotiated yet. Nevertheless, if the Order could achieve this dream, it would be a victory worthy to rank with any in its thousand years of history.

IV

THE SOVEREIGN ORDER
AS A NAVAL POWER

THE SOVEREIGN ORDER AS A
NAVAL POWER

'Their goal is such honour as their stout right arm may win
them and they may justly call their own. . . .'
(The Lusiads, Camöens.)

IT is probable that the Knights of Malta were amongst the first
Europeans to see the need for sea power organized on a
national basis, as opposed to being the personal enterprise of
merchants and sovereigns. Their warship construction, under
L'Isle Adam (in 1523) and Perellos (in 1704) was certainly much
in advance of its time. Although L'Isle Adam's great carrack
St. Anne was not the equal, as a fighting ship, of John Hawkins's
ships, like the *Revenge, Vanguard,* and *Rainbow* of half a century
later, she was in the same tradition, and no other Mediterranean
sea power had yet seen the approaching end of the oar-propelled
galley and galleass. Perellos, too, with his line-of-battle ships was
thinking in terms—not surprising in a fellow-countryman of da
Gama and Albuquerque—of an ocean-going navy.

As long as a Christian foothold remained in the Holy Land—
until the end of the thirteenth century—the Order seems to have
possessed little maritime organization and certainly had no permanently armed fleet.

The provision, maintenance, and protection of communications
between western and eastern Mediterranean was, for the most part
undertaken by those seaports which furnished the Mediterranean
and the world with so many of its great sailors—Venice, Genoa,
Pisa, Amalfi (whose most famous son is Flavio Gioia, to whom
we owe the mariner's compass). Christendom in the Middle Sea
depended upon the great maritime Republics almost entirely for
both ships and seamen.

Yet, while still without anything having the shape of a fighting
navy, the Order of St. John turned its energies towards the
provision of its own transports.

These transports, carrying the Religion's officers, troops, and supplies, maintained a regular service during the passage seasons of spring and autumn to and from the seat of war. The return voyages often served to carry the slaves, the booty, and the trophies of war. In 1361, after the victorious assault upon Satalia, the great chain which had closed the harbour was sent to St. Peter's in Rome.

There grew up a system of contracts between the Knights and the maritime Republics, providing for the use by the Order of the great roadsteads during the passage seasons. One such contract, dated 17 April 1234,[1] was made in respect of the city of Marseilles, while a further reference dated August 1246 speaks of a transport by name, the *Comptesse*, which had a carrying capacity of fifteen hundred souls.

During their occupation of St. Jean d'Acre the Knights still hoped for a Christian reconquest of the Holy Land. Their eyes looked landwards. Their hopes were never to be realized, and, with their headquarters in an island from 1291 until 1798, the Knights of St. John maintained an armed fleet.

During the transport period there was no Admiral; but in the contract of the year 1234 there is reference to a *Commendator navium*, and in a Statute of 1300 (dated 5 November at Limassol)[2] the title *Admiratus*[3] is used.

During the first ten years of naval history proper the Admirals were French and Spanish, namely:

Foulques de Villaret	. . .	(1299)[4]
Sanche d'Aragona	. . .	(1300)
Sanzoli de Grasse	. . .	(1307)

Towards the middle of the fourteenth century posts and prerogatives within the Order were allocated definitely to the Langues and that of Admiral was allocated to the Langue of Italy—a decision dictated by the contemporary pre-eminence in the Middle Sea of the navigators and shipwrights of the great Italian seaports. Next in rank to the Admiral was the Bailiff of the Langue of Italy, *ex officio* the 'Lieutenant Admiral'.

[1] Ettore Rossi, *Storia della Marina dell'Ordine*, 1926, p. 8.
[2] Rossi, op. cit., p. 9.
[3] A curious piece of 'Dog Latin' from *Amir al Bahar*.
[4] A letter written from Cyprus in 1299 to William de Villaret speaks of 'Frere Fouque de Vilaret, Aumirail de la maison'.

The powers of the Admiral appear to have given some cause for jealousy. As early as the year 1504 at Rhodes, the Council of the Order had to settle a dispute—almost modern in its nature—touching the right of the 'Flag Captain', or Captain General, to appoint his own junior officers.

The Captain General was next in rank to the somewhat shadowy 'Lieutenant Admiral', and commanded the flagship known as the *Nave* or *Galera Capitana*: under him were the *Padroni* or commanding officers of the other galleys.

In Rhodes the Captains General were appointed for varying terms—stated at the time of their selection—but in Malta an Act of 1548 fixed the duration of office at two years.

In 1704 a further title appeared—that of 'Lieutenant General of Ships' (*Luogotenente-Generale dei Vascelli*)—whose function might better be expressed as 'Rear-Admiral of the Line', for his creation was necessitated by the Grand Master Raymond Perellos's introduction of a *Squadra dei Vascelli* or 'Line of Battle Ships', constituting a practically independent command, only nominally under the control of the Captain General of the Galleys.

The complements of the Order's vessels naturally varied with the passage of time, but they were, nevertheless, manned on similar principles throughout the Order's history. A typical galley would have carried, in addition to her Captain, a Chaplain, a Surgeon,[1] a Pilot,[1] a Secretary,[1] and a number of *Cavalieri Caravanisti*—that is, Knights over the age of eighteen who had served at least six months of their novitiate.[2]

In addition to a Gunner and a Boatswain, with a number of what we should call Chief and Petty Officers, there were others whose especial care it was to supervise and discipline the galley-slaves. Of this number was the fearsome *Agguzino*, with his whip.

The oarsmen of the galleys fell into three categories:

(1) The *Bonavoglie*, who were volunteers, offering their services for a term of years on receipt of a sum of money—which they often dissipated on the waterfronts in a final debauch before embarking, or of which they stood in sore need to recover property or save themselves or their families from

---

[1] These officers were 'mercenaries' and not Knights. Many Maltese held these posts and served the Order with distinction.

[2] The Senior *Caravanisto* was known as 'King of the Galleys' and the second senior as *Cercamare*. Their duties were those of a modern British Officer of the Post List combined with those of a Royal Marine Commando.

jail. Sometimes, too, the money was itself a debt or fine owed to the Order which had not been repaid and which the poor debtor elected to 'work off' at the benches of the galleys. These *Bonavoglie* were somewhat better treated than their fellows, being better fed and permitted to retain their moustaches.

(2) The *Forzati*, pressed men recruited by the usual press-gang methods familiar to us, and within the living memory of our grandfathers.

(3) The *Schiavi*, galley-slaves proper who were almost invariably Muslim and occasionally Jew, though there may also have been the odd Christian convicted of piracy and fortunate to escape the gallows.

But this motley selection were only the 'engines'. They had no choice, once embarked, whether to go ahead or astern in the face of an enemy, whether to live or to die. In the matter of what we may call the 'Upper Deck' complement of their ships, the Order had an uncommon grasp of the essentials of sea power. While the great seafaring nations, Spain, Portugal, and even England, were slow to understand that a fleet could no longer be manned by filling ships with gentlemen adventurers who need not know stem from stern and a company of slaves and jail-birds and nothing more, the Order insisted on its young gentlemen performing their *Caravans*—their General Service Commissions—and learning the hard way about sea warfare before ever they aspired to Knighthood and command. These, with the local mercenary officers, who were specialists in their own trades—Rhodians and Maltese— formed, with the *Bonavoglie*, a permanent nucleus of seasoned, fighting seamen who manned a fleet permanently commissioned as a fighting arm. Philip's Armada and even Elizabeth's 'Ships Royal' were haphazardly manned and commissioned by comparison.

In Rhodes, as well as in Malta, the Knights recruited their upper-deck seamen, their gunners, and their sailing masters from the local seafaring population. In both Islands there was first-class material: Malta, in particular, had been a nest of Christian corsairs when the Knights arrived in 1530. These corsairs operated upon a written warrant from the Viceroy of Sicily; but, like Drake, Hawkins, and Oxenham in the Caribbean, the Maltese were not over-particular about the flag of their victims. The names of two of these worthies have come down in the archives—Colo Fardello and Canga Rossa. The latter was hanged by the Knights for an attack upon a Christian merchantman.

The Order's Board of Admiralty consisted of the Admiral, the Captain General of the Galleys, and four Knights Grand Cross. The Board was instituted in 1596—fifty years after Henry Tudor's first English Navy Board—and possessed a complete Secretariat presided over by a General Secretary who submitted the decisions, proposals, and the Accounts of the Navy before the Council of the Order.

In 1704, when the Grand Master Perellos formed his independent squadron of battleships, a separate Board was set up to adminster this new arm of the Fleet composed of one Knight Grand Cross and four Knights.

2

By the beginning of the fourteenth century the fighting vessels of the Mediterranean had changed little, if at all, since Actium (in A.D. 31), and in inshore fights the tactics of Salamis (in 480 B.C.) were by no means unusual. The galley had remained the principal arm of an active fleet, long after it had become ancient history in other waters. Nevertheless, the 'Round ship' had made its appearance early in the Christian era as transport and merchantman.

These 'round' merchantmen were as fully equipped as their construction and sailing qualities permitted to protect themselves against the pirates and corsairs with which the Mediterranean had always teemed. Thus, during the fourteenth century, the 'Round' fighting ship emerged and we find the Knights using both round and long ships in their naval service. But, for four centuries, the chief arm of the Order's Navy was its Galley Squadron: of ships with beautiful lines, six times as long as the measure of their beam, equipped with 'lateen' sails and great oars or sweeps, and armed with the immemorial weapon of their type, the ram.

Contemporary pictures of the galleys of the Order, brave with their striped sails and their innumerable pennons, gilded and enamelled with heraldic finery, their great sweeps never a hair's-breadth out of stroke, conceal the rugged truth of a veritable hell of slavery for the oarsmen; conditions not much better for the free men of the ship's company and all the hazards of overcrowding, unsuitable clothing and accoutrements, no shelter from the sun, rain, or sea; sodden food, contaminated water, plague, fever, and scurvy for Knight and slave alike.

By contrast with the galleys, the great carracks[1] must have seemed luxurious beyond belief; but they were fair-weather ships and, even in the passage months of spring and autumn, the Mediterranean can muster some very nasty weather.

> The Carracks, of up to two thousand tons, were the largest ships in the world. They had four decks, eight feet high, with poop and prow overtopping the main deck by twenty feet. No tree—unspliced—was tall or thick enough to provide them with a mast. Two hundred men and two big capstans were needed to raise the yard . . .[2]

In bad or gusty weather, the heavy main yard had to be lowered and rehoisted as often as ten or twelve times a day. Good sailers before the wind, the carracks were worthless on the bow line, and, failing the most careful navigation, the winds might carry them to the west instead of to the east. Brazil had been discovered in this way by Portuguese who set out for India, round the Cape.

With the Galley Squadron as the permanent nucleus, the Order's fleets were made up of a wide variety of vessels ranging from the great carracks to the *Fusta*, or light galleass, of the Christian corsairs, in league with the Religion.

The carracks of the Order, while not actually part of the line of battle, filled a very important role, being the transport and hospital ships and in constant demand for conveying the higher officers of the Order to and from the mainland and the outlying posts of the Knights. They were neither so mobile under sail as the galleys, nor so swift, but their weight, stability, and heavier armament made them valuable auxiliaries.

The round ship was much more in favour with the Ottoman navies whose vessels were almost all of the 'galleon', 'carrack', or 'horgue' type—difficult to board and therefore difficult to capture in an age when the capture of an enemy vessel was more to be sought than its destruction. The carracks, therefore, were invaluable in action against the Muslims, and one of them often carried the flag of the Captain General.

[1] 'Carrack' is derived from the Italian *Carricare*—'to load, or take in cargo'. In modern Maltese *karrakka* is a 'clumsy, unwieldy figure'.
[2] Vincent Cronin, *A Pearl to India: the Life of Roberto de Nobile*.

The oldest carrack on record is the *St. John Baptist*. She was responsible for the capture of the Sultan of Egypt's carrack, *Mogarbina*, which later became the Order's *Santa Maria*.

On 1 January 1523 (the same sad date on which L'Isle Adam evacuated Rhodes), there was launched at Nice a carrack almost as epoch-making as the English *Henri Grace à Dieu* of 1515: she was the *St. Anne*, constructed on plans prepared by the Order and effectively armoured against the projectiles of contemporary naval warfare. 'She was sheathed with metal and was perfectly cannon proof.'[1] She was a hundred and thirty-two feet long and forty-four feet in the beam, of four thousand tons burden, and had an enormous freeboard, her after-superstructure rising seventy-five feet above the waterline. She had stowage for six months' victuals, a blacksmith's shop where three smiths might work, a bakery where fifty-six pounds of bread was baked at a 'batch', luxurious saloons and cabins, a council chamber, and a beautifully decorated chapel dedicated to her patroness, St. Anne. Her three masts had each three fighting tops, one over the other. Her armament included fifty long-range guns and a number of falconets and demi-cannon, while her armoury held personal weapons sufficient to equip five hundred persons. Her complement is recorded as '300 besides 400 light infantry and cavalry'.[2]

The carrack *St. Anne* was built by contract at Nice. The carrack *Santa Maria* was captured from the Egyptians. Many of the galleys were the private enterprises of the Grand Masters and of the Knights.

The larger vessels seem to have been built in the European ship yards; but, both in Rhodes and in Malta, dockyards were constructed and maintained by the Order where vessels were repaired and equipped in the Knights' own arsenals and smaller vessels were built.

[1] Captain Windus of the British East Indies Squadron, addressing the London Archaeological Institute in 1862, said '. . . the carrack *St. Anne* of the Knights of Malta was the first armoured war vessel adapted to resist the projectiles of her own time. . . .'

[2] A document quoted by Mr. Demajo called *Essamine del Bombardiero* by Giacomo de Robertes, a Bolognese, and *Capo Maestro* of the Order's artillery, gives the specification of all the guns in use in 1602. They ranged from the Cannon-Royal, which flung a shot weighing over one hundred pounds nearly two miles, to the Falconet, smallest of all, which fired an eleven-pound shot, and the swivel gun, *Petriera* or *Perier* which discharged stones and fire-balls while the demi-cannon fired a five-pound shot a comparatively short range. A detailed account of the *St. Anne* appeared in the *Daily Malta Chronicle* on 13 January 1926—one of a series of articles by Mr. G. Darmanin Demajo.

Before the appearance of L'Isle Adam and his gallant handful of siege-worn followers, Malta had developed a considerable ship-building industry whose beginnings date from the Phoenicians or possibly earlier.

For the first eight years of their occupation of the Maltese Islands the Grand Masters contented themselves with what facilities they had found already established in 1530. In 1538, however, the second General Chapter held in Malta decreed that provision should be made for the construction of a regular Naval Arsenal on the shores of the Grand Harbour, on the side opposite to what is now Valletta, in the locality called then, and still called, 'Il Birgu'—either from the Roman *borgo*, 'a town', or from the earlier Greek *pyrgos*, 'a port'.[1]

This nucleus of a dockyard consisted of storehouses and slip-ways; under stone arches, covered with wooden roofs, the galleys were constructed and laid up for refit. The first buildings of the Knights' dockyard stood close to what is now the naval bakery in H.M. Victualling Yard. From this point the dockyard of the Order spread until it embraced nearly all the foreshore of the Grand Harbour. In 1542 the fortification of the shore establish-ments was undertaken. In 1545 a building, which still stands, was constructed whose first floor was a bakery and whose second floor constituted the first sailcloth factory of the Order—it is now the Naval Clothing Depot. To judge from contemporary pictures and sculpture the sails of the galleys were always striped and bore either the device of their owners the Grand Masters and the Knights or, if the common property of the Order, the eight-pointed cross. Both the galleys and the 'great ships' are depicted flying the red burgee with the white cross of St. John at both the fore and main topmasts. The name of a renegade Moor—one Pietro della Saliba[2]—has come down to us as one of the Order's chief sailmakers. Under him there worked a number of female slaves in this sailmaker's loft above the bakery.

In 1551 the Council allocated the defence of the dockyard and its environs, which had rapidly become a populous city (called then Citta Nuova to distinguish it from Citta Vecchia, the ancient capital), to the Langues of Italy and Aragon. From this date until

---

[1] The Roman *borgo* behind Trastevere in Sassia has been derived by some authorities from the Saxon *burh*.

[2] Possibly 'Peter of the Cross'. *Salib* is 'cross' in Maltese. Saliba is nowadays a common surname.

after the Great Siege of 1565 there was a lull in constructive work, and the next project undertaken was the building of the city of Valletta.

The stone for this undertaking was commanded to be cut from the solid rock on the Marsamuscetto side of the new site, where it was proposed to construct docks for ten galleys in the deep, sheltered cove thus made—the *Mandraggo*. The next major work of excavation in this area was the boring of a number of tunnels at sea-level for use as submarine pens in the Second World War.

Between the years 1631 and 1667 there were built at Vittoriosa the palaces of the Captain General, the Commander of the Dockyard, and various smaller residences for other naval dignitaries. Most of the buildings remain and are occupied by British naval officers and Dockyard officials today. During this period also the great crane was erected.

3

By the commencement of the fourteenth century the spirit of the Crusades was dead—Christian States were often on friendly terms with the Great Muslim-Mongol conquerors, and the Emperor Charles V paid tribute to the Sultan; but the Order of St. John never lost sight of the danger which threatened Christian civilization; it had vowed to fight Islam and it fought it with or without assistance, until Islam fell. The Order was the Christian outpost, the Christian rallying-point, and its fleet the ever-dependable weapon of Christendom.

The earliest independent action on record is that of Amorgo (1312), where Foulques de Villaret—the first of the Admirals—with a small force destroyed twenty-three Turkish coasting vessels. Albert of Schwarzbourg, Grand Commander of Cyprus in the same year, led a mixed fleet, brought up to a total of twenty-four by the reinforcements of one Master Zaccaria, a Genoese corsair, against fifty Ottomans out of Ephesus and defeated them. In 1313 the same Albert of Schwarzbourg with four galleys and four smaller vessels ('*leggieri bastimenti*')[1] of the Order and six Genoese galleys routed eighty Turks.

In the year 1334 an attempt to fan the embers of the Crusades was partially successful and resulted in the Alliance of Avignon;

[1] Rossi, op. cit., p. 11.

the King of France, Venice, the Papal Navy, and the King of
Cyprus rallied about the standard of St. John and utterly destroyed
an Ottoman fleet in the Gulf of Smyrna. That Christendom was
accustomed to regard the Religion as its rallying-point is evi-
denced by the appointment of John Di Briandate, Prior of
Lombardy in 1344, to the leadership of the League, formed in
that year by the Papal States, Venice, Genoa, and Cyprus. With
the assistance of the galleys of Rhodes, under Di Briandate,
Smyrna was captured and the League—seemingly exhausted by
its unwonted effort—left the unenviable task of holding that city
to the Religion. Smyrna was held with difficulty until 1402 when,
in spite of an attempted relief by the Admiral Buffilo Panizati, the
Knights were overwhelmed by the hordes of Tamerlane.

In 1347 the Prior of Catalonia, Fra Arnaldo de Peres Tortes,
burned a hundred Turkish craft at Imbros. Ten years later thirty-
five Muslim pirates were destroyed by the combined fleets of the
Order and of Venice under Raymond Beranger. In 1361 King
Peter of Cyprus, with the assistance of two Papal ships, twelve
Christian corsairs, and four galleys of the Order, commanded by
the Admiral Ferlino d'Airasca, attacked and captured Adalia (or
Satalia), and in 1365, again with the assistance of d'Airasca, this
time with sixteen galleys, King Peter sacked Alexandria.

In 1395 and again in 1399 galleys of the Order penetrated into
the Black Sea and attacked the nests of corsairs which had long
been established there. The 1395 expedition, starting well, ended
diasastrously at the bloody combat of Nicopoli, where the Grand
Master d'Heredia fell, with his surviving Knights, into the hands
of the enemy. The 1399 adventure passed through the Dardanelles
in company with the Genoese Fleet of Boucicaut and was more
fortunate than that of d'Heredia. One galley of the Order was
present, too, at the Battle of Morea, between Boucicaut and Zeno
of Venice, in 1403. It is not clear whether the Order supported
Venice or Genoa; but it is difficult to imagine the Grand Masters
being anything but Guelph in their loyalty.

In this same year of 1403 the Religion made a pact with the
Mamelukes of Egypt. It not only permitted the Order to maintain
its Hospital in Jerusalem but granted free Christian access to the
Holy Places and allowed the Grand Master and his Knights the
freedom of all the principal Egyptian and Syrian ports.

Guelph or Ghibbeline, the Order was here taking a leaf from

Frederick II's book in his conduct of the Sixth Crusade: conduct
which so baffled the Papacy that the Emperor was 'three times
excommunicated. First for not going. Secondly for going and the
third time for coming back.'[1]

Throughout the fifteenth century, the tide of Islam rose steadily
about Rhodes. In 1440 Castelrosso, an isolated advance-post of
the Knights, fell to the Mamelukes—once more in arms against
the Cross—and nineteen Mameluke ships invested Rhodes itself.
Grand Master Lastic was prepared with four carracks and a galley
squadron. They routed the blockading force, pursuing them to
the coast of Anatolia and, landing a force of Knights and Rhodian
mercenaries, fought a battle in which sixty Knights and seven
hundred Muslims fell. Losses amongst the Order's mercenaries
are not recorded.

In the following year the Mamelukes again sought a pact; but
the Order mistrusted them and the offer was refused. In 1444 a
further attempt to invest Rhodes was repulsed by the Order's
Fleet, and, in 1446, the Mamelukes yet again sued for peace. They
feared the onset of their powerful rivals, the Ottoman Turks, and
the Order was willing to weaken its enemies by dividing them.
But this alliance could do nothing to save the effete Byzantines
(for whom Latin Christianity had, in any case, small sympathy),
and Constantinople fell into Ottoman hands in 1453.

Mahomet Fatih—the 'Conqueror'—now launched a determined attack upon Christendom. By 1457 Cos, Lemnos, and
Lesbos had yielded to Mahomet.

In 1459, on the death of King John of Cyprus, his bastard son,
James, sold himself to the Mamelukes and, turning Muslim, he
seized the Crown of Cyprus from his half-sister Carlotta.

The Chapter General held at Rhodes in 1462, realizing how
isolated and wellnigh surrounded by enemies Rhodes had become,
made every effort to place the fleet in the highest possible state of
efficiency. The Holy Father's vain attempt to raise a combined
fleet against the Muslims in 1464 was warmly supported by the
Knights, but not for the first time internal dissension amongst the
Christian States left the Order to face Islam alone.

In 1480 the Turks laid siege to Rhodes, but the Navy of the
Religion rendered a blockade impossible and the enemy was
repulsed and defeated.

[1] Jasper More, *The Land of Italy*, p. 209.

With the death of Mahomet Fatih, in 1481, there followed a few years of respite while his sons fought each other, and while the Mamelukes and the Ottoman Turks competed for supremacy.

The Order under Grand Master d'Aubusson (1476–1503) reached a high level of prestige and efficiency. D'Aubusson was appointed Captain General of the League formed in 1500 by the Pope, France, Spain, Portugal, Venice, and Rhodes. The Order provided four galleys, four ships, and a number of smaller vessels, but the League accomplished nothing for two years. Only Venice and the Order produced the fleets promised. In 1502 the vessels of the League commanded by the Admiral Ludovicus di Scalenghe of the Order, captured a number of Turkish ships carrying rich merchandise and destroyed a Turkish fleet at Samos. In 1507 the Order's carrack (*Grossa Nave*—'great ship') captured the famous carrack *Mogarbina*, and in 1510 came the greatest victory achieved in the history of the galleys of Rhodes. The Mameluke Sultan had planned, with the aid of the Turks, to raise a powerful fleet wherewith to confront the Portuguese in the Indian Ocean. The galleys of the Religion, commanded by L'Isle Adam, and the carracks commanded by Andrea d'Amaral, came up with the Egyptian squadrons destined to swell the great combined Muslim Fleet, off Alexandretta. The battle which followed was merciless, resulting in an overwhelming victory for the Order. The Sultan's nephew, who commanded the Egyptian forces, was slain and the Religion captured 'eleven great ships and four galleys or galleotts'.[1]

The Portuguese incursions into the Indian Ocean and their growing trading-posts on the Indian mainland were rightly seen as a serious menace to Islam. Their victory at Diu, in 1508, and the occupation by Albuquerque of Goa, in 1510, were the eastern leg of a pincer movement which the Sultan could not fail to recognize. He must first dispose of the western, and seemingly weaker, leg of the pincer and the Order's destruction of the Egyptian force at Alexandretta is one of those little-known victories whose repercussions far transcend their apparent significance. The Portuguese were now given breathing-space to consolidate their bridgeheads in India and, incidentally, to bring new life to the small isolated Christian communities in southern India: a process which has at least had notable reactions on Hindu and Buddhist thought.

[1] Rossi, op. cit., p. 30.

But the Order was not long to rejoice over Alexandretta. In 1522 there was launched against Rhodes every vessel, every man, and every engine of war at the command of Suleiman the Magnificent—great-grandson of Mahomet Fatih.

The little fleet of Rhodes was hopelessly outnumbered. There was no hope of facing Suleiman at sea, and the Knights and the companies of the galleys and carracks disembarked to swell the garrison of Rhodes.

At the end of six months the Order, decimated, half-starved, and betrayed most shamefully by that very d'Amaral who had commanded the carracks at Alexandretta, was forced to capitulate.

Suleiman was a generous, high-minded, and chivalrous victor, and on 1 January 1523 the Grand Master, L'Isle Adam, with his heroic following, was permitted to leave Rhodes, not only unmolested but accompanied by a guard of honour and all the ceremonial which seemed to Suleiman the just due of a gallant foe. He took with him the Order's archives and the treasure from the Conventual Church and the Auberges, in the carracks *Santa Maria* (ex-*Mogarbina*), *Santa Caterina*, and *San Giovanni*, together with a number of the surviving galleys and galleotts.

The conquests of Suleiman now extended from Egypt to Poland; but squabbling Christendom made no combined effort to stop him.

L'Isle Adam spent seven weary years wandering from Court to Court, vainly begging help. 'He went to England to interview Henry VIII and was entertained in the Priory at Clerkenwell, where he stayed, until, after a few days, Henry invited him to St. James' Palace for the remainder of his visit. Eventually the King gave him guns and armour valued at 20,000 crowns of which armour only one piece, a buckler, exists now in the Armoury of the Palace [of Valletta].'[1]

During these years the Order found temporary homes in Candia, Messina, Civita Vecchia, Viterbo, Villefranche, and Nice, but it was their fleet—or what remained of it—which held them most together; Councils were in fact held in the specially constructed Council Chamber on board the new carrack *St. Anne*.

Finally in 1530 the Emperor Charles V was prevailed upon to grant the Islands of Malta, together with the Fortress of Tripolis, to the Order. The Knights made every effort to hold Tripolis, but

[1] Chevalier H. P. Scicluna, *A Brief Account of the Order of St. John* (1929), p. 21.

it was isolated and surrounded by Muslim communities. It fell a fairly easy prey to Sinan Pasha in 1551.

L'Isle Adam sailed into the Grand Harbour of Malta in the *St. Anne*, commanded by the English Knight, Sir William Weston, on 26 October 1530. On 21 August 1534 he died. He deserves to be remembered as one of the greatest commanders of the age of chivalry. He was a great sailor and a great leader. He lived by the motto of his house: '*Va oultre. La main a l'ouvre*'—'Onward. Hand to work.'

The Knights had scarcely settled in Malta when the new Admiral, Bernardo Salviati (nephew to the Pope and Prior of Rome), with five galleys of the Order and two of one James Grimaldi of Genoa (a privateer in the pay of the Order) destroyed a Turkish fleet at Modon, sacked the city, and, being forced to retire by the arrival of fresh Turkish forces, returned to Malta with much loot and eight hundred Turks. In the same year Salviati, losing the ship *St. Michael* by stranding, attacked a detached squadron of Khair-ed-Dhin's forces off Tripolis and destroyed it.

In 1532, Salviati commanded the squadrons of Malta and of the Papal Navy which had joined the great Genoese Admiral Andrea Doria in his successful attack upon Coron. Again, in 1537, the Order allied itself with Andrea Doria, now commanding a combined attempt on the part of the Empire and Venice (France was allied with the Turks) to break the Ottoman sea power under Khair-ed-Dhin. An action was fought off Corfu and, although the Knights, led by Strozzi, behaved with desperate valour, the two fleets parted without a decision. Then follows a period of continued combat with the great Muslim corsairs. Christendom was again disunited and France made alliance with the corsairs of Islam—Dragut, Murad Agha, Sinan Pasha, and the renegade Luciali. In 1565 Suleiman the Magnificent looked like repeating the events of 1522–1524. A great fleet under the Ottoman Admirals Piali Pasha and Mustapha Pasha was dispatched against Malta. The ships and galleys of the Order retired into the Grand Harbour, which was secured by means of a great chain manufactured for the Order in Venice against such a contingency. The Knights were not, however, to lose their new base. The siege lasted from 21 May to 7 September 1565. Queen Elizabeth ordered prayers to be read in all the churches for the success of the Knights in their defence of Malta. The Knights and the Maltese people[1] under Grand Master La Vallette fought like tigers, while the smaller vessels of the Navy were able, in spite of the great Ottoman fleet, to keep up a continual communication with the mainland, and even to transport reinforcements from Sicily—though little enough help was forthcoming from the Christian Princes. At last the Turks, having lost an incredible number of their men and their ships, were constrained to retire. The power of the Ottoman Turks had passed its brief zenith and it was the Sovereign Order and its fleet which had chiefly wrought the Turkish undoing.

The effort had, nevertheless, left its mark on the Order. Some of that apathy which so often follows victory set in. In the year 1570 the unhappy Captain General Francesco St. Clement, with four ill-found and under-manned galleys, was put to ignominious flight by a flotilla of the renegade corsair Luciali off the Tunisian coast. On his return to Malta, St. Clement was court martialled and sentenced to be strangled and flung over the bastions into the sea: a seemingly ferocious piece of discipline—yet it was a hundred and seven years later that our own Admiral Byng '. . . satisfied the murderous instincts of those who once more thrust upon the innocent the burdens of their own fault'.[2]

Happier things were to follow.

In 1571, on 7 October, the Galley Squadron of the Order joined Don John of Austria at Lepanto and acquitted themselves nobly. Cervantes, who lost an arm in the Battle, wrote of Lepanto that the action 'broke the pride of the Osmans and undeceived the world which had regarded the Turkish fleet as invincible'.

But the destruction or neutralization of major fleets has never ensured command of the sea. The Mediterranean, with its innumerable islands, bays, creeks, and easily defended roadsteads is ideal for a sea war of attrition against commerce passing through its comparatively narrow confines. The Malta convoys of the Second World War were a repetition—albeit on an altogether vaster scale—of the task which the Order set itself after Lepanto. Religious in impetus, there were, nevertheless, great economic prizes to be won from this effort, for much of the commerce of Europe still passed through the Middle Sea. The survival of

---

[1] 'Toute le Monde sait que les Turcs . . . ne craignent que les corsairs de Malte . . . un de leurs capitains s'ecrivit: Il y a surement un diable dans le corps de chaque soldat Maltais . . .' D'Avalos, *Tableau Historique*, VI, p. 147.

[2] Callender, *The Naval Side of British History*.

French and Italian trade, in competition with the new commercial empires of Spain and Portugual, founded on their American and Indian convoys, depended upon the security of communications with the Middle East.

Throughout two centuries the power of the Order and the prestige and striking power of its Navy grew as fast as the power of Islam waned. The Knights continued to police the Mediterranean, setting free Christian captives, seeking out corsairs and pirates, collecting Muslim (and not a few Jewish) slaves and hostages—many of whom were held to ransom for gold, wherewith to swell the Order's treasury and to finance the fortifications of Malta.

Then came the overflow of the Northern Naval Powers into the Mediterranean. The decline of the Order as a maritime force was inevitable from the moment that these great national Navies became the instruments of a policy and a balance of power in which the concept of Christendom no longer held meaning.

The reign of the Grand Master Pinto de Fonseca (1741–1773) covers the decline which, under a less able, less respected Prince, would certainly have been more rapid. With French Knights in a majority in the Convent, Pinto had his hands full to maintain the neutrality of the Order; and English pressure was growing constantly more determined.

In 1756 the Order could impound the rudder of an English privateer and imprison her captain, a proceeding which led to an exchange of letters with George II, whom Pinto addresses as '*Serenissime et Potentissime Rex*'; and is, in his turn, addressed as '*Eminentissimo Principi . . . consanguineo et amico nostro charissimo.*'

But, despite the appearances, Pinto was powerless to dispute, in 1764, what amounted to dictation by his English 'cousin' in the matter of the imprisonment of the Consul Dodsworth.[1] What we should now call a 'note' was delivered by Captain Harrison, in the frigate *Centurion*, and the Order complied on all points.

4

Amongst the Order's last notable seamen were Suffren, Vice-Admiral of France, known to English history as a brilliant tactician and a worthy and gallant foe, Captain General of the

[1] Joseph Galea, 'English Privateers at Malta', *Revue de L'Ordre Souverain Militaire de Malte* (1958).

Maltese Galleys in 1780; and the able and high-minded Neapolitan Admiral Francesco Caracciolo, who was elected Captain General of the Galleys in 1795.

In 1798 three ships of the Order, returning laden with booty from an action against the Algerines, sailed into the French blockading squadron off Malta. Napoleon seized two of the vessels —the *San Giovanni* and the *San Zaccaria*—which he renamed *Dego* and *Beruse*.

The pick of the Order's Maltese seamen and infantry troops were pressed into service, not all unwillingly: for they had high hopes of Liberty and Fraternity in Napoleon's *Legion Maltaise*, which won great honour in Egypt.

The Grand Master Ferdinand von Hompesch was bundled out of the Island with no ceremony and small respect. On 29 June 1799 the Admiral Caracciolo was hanged at the yard-arm of his own ship *Minerva* at Naples.

If the Order's naval history can be said to end with Caracciolo it is, indeed, the saddest of endings to a magnificent tale.

Having served the Neapolitan Monarchy and their English premier, Lord Acton, after the collapse of Malta, as friend and comrade-in-arms of Nelson, Caracciolo took service (be it noted, with his King's permission) under the Parthenopian Republic.

Upon the defeat of the Republicans by Cardinal Ruffo, with his *Lazzaroni*, the Admiral was given a safe-conduct. But Nelson, bemused as one version has it, by Emma Hamilton's bright eyes and influenced by the bloodthirsty Queen Maria Carolina (sister of Marie Antoinette), allowed his former friend and ally to be judicially murdered by a venal court martial.

In fairness to Nelson it should be recorded that the fog of controversy created by his detractors and his apologists has never dispersed and the truth is difficult to come at. Lieutenant-Commander George P. B. Naish, F.S.A., in his edition of *Nelson's Letters to his Wife and other documents* writes:

> The Cardinal protested, with reason, at Nelson's assumption of over-riding powers. . . .
> Nelson's temper was shown when the rebel Neapolitan Admiral Caracciolo was arrested and brought on board the *Foudroyant* bound and weary. Captain Hardy . . . recognized him and had him unbound and offered refreshment.
> Nelson had him tried by a Court martial of Neapolitan officers and hanged the same evening. . . . He [Caracciolo] had visited Naples by permission,

to try to save his possessions, but the French Marshal Macdonald, who had commanded the Garrison at Naples before the French withdrawal, comments: 'He afterwards fell a victim to the English Admiral Nelson who cruelly and ignominiously caused him to be hanged . . . a death with which I have always deeply reproached myself, as it was I who overcame his reluctance and gained him to our side.'

The Archives in the Royal Library of Malta contain an Italian version of the Caracciolo story, under 'Caracciolo di Napoli' in *Famiglie Celebri Italiane*.

The tragic death of the Order's last Admiral is but part of that curious by-way of history: the English, expatriate hegemony who were the real power in Neapolitan and Sicilian affairs in the early part of the nineteenth century. They impinged for a brief space upon the story of the Sovereign Order, and the ignominious end of the last Admiral to which their policies contributed was typical of the sometimes irreconcilable loyalties which tormented so many of the Knights at this crucial point in history.

V

THINGS THAT GO BUMP

THINGS THAT GO BUMP

'Whatever things we imagine, these same things are real:
They are the only realities. If an old monk came to me and
said "I have seen the Devil; he has two horns and a tail",
I should make reply to that same old monk, and say, "Father,
even supposing the Devil did not exist already, you have
created him. He exists now without a shadow of a doubt.
Take care he doesn't have you!"'
Anatole France, *Dialogues upon Fairy Tales.*

SUPERFICIALLY, the everyday currency of Maltese folk-lore is markedly different from the Anglo-Saxon, but there are plenty of indications of common roots in a remote common past.

The lore of birth and childhood, for example, seems very un-Saxon. I know of no Teutonic equivalent of the Birth Rose—a budding rose offered by a friend to a woman in labour. As the bud opens, so the new life begins and the birth-pangs are eased. And, again, children with red hair are commonly called 'Son of the Wind' or 'Child of the Alcove', possibly no more than the uncharitable reaction of a preponderantly brunette people; but since the term is not applied to blond offspring, the association may be that of the colour red which was sacred to Venus, with 'Love Child'.

The imprisoned spirit called Gawgaw (he is also called Kawkaw and Babaw), who is released to wander abroad only on the eve of Christmas, seeking the life-blood of unrepentant sinners, may be a vampire or the remnant of a disgruntled Mithras whose feast day was appropriated by the early Christians. The Syrians have a similar character called Hagogo.

There is rich ground for the excavations of the comparative ethnologist; but for the amateur who wishes merely to exercise his imagination and his curiosity there is also much of interest. Broadly, Maltese folk-lore is exactly what you would expect: Mediterranean, European with a dominant motif of the classical

179

Latin; Christian upon a substructure of Latin-Hellenic paganism; but there are also many vestiges of earlier mythologies: Semitic, Syriac, Chaldean, and some curious affinities with the Celtic cultures.

The ceremony of the *Quccija* or 'Choosing' is part of a child's first birthday celebrations: a tray or basket is filled with a number of objects representing trades and vocations—a book, Rosary beads, an inkstand, a sword—and the first object towards which the tiny hand is outstretched foretells the little one's future bent. Some ears of corn are sometimes added, nowadays supposed to symbolize a generous heart; but we may guess that originally the symbols were all those of tutelary deities of whom only Ceres survives. We may not be wrong to derive the *Quccija* from an Hellenic source. The custom is also Sicilian and Neapolitan. Nevertheless, it is better not to pursue derivations too far. Anatole France, from whom I have filched the 'motto' of this essay, has wisely remarked (of the Academicians) that 'when they have taken prodigious pains to prove to you that *Peau d'Ane* comes from the Hindu Koosh, and that the tale of Reynard the Fox is of exclusively Japhetic origin, behold, an explorer arrives with the news that he has discovered Reynard among the Zulus and that *Peau d'Ane* is a household word among the Papuans. . . .'

Maltese snake-lore is full of inconsistencies. The guardian spirits of a house—the word used is *Hares*, and I wonder if it may not once have been *Lares*—sometimes appear in the form of a pair of black snakes. These must not be injured and are known to be harmless and friendly. In most other contexts the snake, all of whose native varieties are in fact quite harmless, is loathed and feared as the embodiment of evil, despite St. Paul's apochryphal reputation for banishing the venomous kinds from the Islands.

The idea of a snake as a protecting spirit is widespread. Examples are common in Greek mythology and the African Bantu have the belief.

The benevolent little *Hares* who appears to children and to innocents of all ages would seem to be of quite different provenance. He looks like Puck, or a leprechaun, and he invariably leads his favourites into a land of magic and plenty which is obviously the Country of Cockaigne, the *Paese di Cuccagna*. Giuseppe Cocchiara, the Sicilian ethnologist, described this land:

Nei tempi antichi, quando desiderare serviva ancora a qual cosa, l'uomo, secondo la fantasia popolare, non aspirava soltanto a vivere eternamente

giovane, ma amava, altresi, immaginare un paese lontano dove si mangi-
asse senza lavorare, dove l'abondanza dei prodotti fosse ottenuta senza
fatica . . . cosi il paese di Cuccagna si configurava come un paese lontano
dove l'uomo poteva trovare tutti i beni della terra. . . .[1]

It is towards this Italian vision of the Welfare State that the
Maltese peasant is led by a Celtic Puck.

Another popular little character of folk-tales is Pietru Lagrim-
anti: 'Peter, Son of Tears', for he is born, like Man, from the tears
of the Egyptian Goddess Nu, from the tears of his mother. Like
the Phoenician Cadmus in Ovid's *Metamorphoses*, he does battle
with a great serpent, the Dragon Draganti. He is armed, like Thor,
with a miraculous hammer. Like Orpheus, he releases an imprisoned princess from the Underworld and undergoes countless
trials and adventures which have their counterparts in the *Sagas*,
the *Iliad*, the *Mahabharatta*, and *Tripitaka*.

The fate of the Phoenician Cadmus and his wife who become,
in Ovid's version, a pair of friendly black snakes, may account for
one aspect of Maltese snake-lore. Indeed, the ethnologist needs to
beware of apparently Hellenic sources in Maltese folk-lore. It was
at about the time of the advent of the Sovereign Order (in 1530)
that Ovid, and the *Fasti* and *Metamorphoses* in particular, began to
delight a wide reading public. Europeans from Camöens to
Shakespeare, from Boccaccio to Milton owe much to Ovid, and
the Knights brought with them a lively literary culture to what
had been a semi-literate backwater. Maltese writers—almost all
of them clerics or men educated by clerics—continued to quote
and to produce Maltese versions of Ovid until well into the
nineteenth century. How much apparently indigenous folk-lore is
really owed to this comparatively brief period it would be difficult
to ascertain.

The Evil Eye is commonly accepted as a fact. Its baleful effects
may be discounted by making the Sign of the Cross, or, more
frequently, by pointing the index and little fingers at the source
of the menace. Certain unhappy families traditionally possess this
unfortunate gift and, since the calamitous consequences of their
admiration of your wife, your child, your dog, or your goats are

---

[1] 'In ancient times, when wishes had meaning, mankind was not content to express,
in his popular fancies, the desire for perpetual youth; but he wanted, as well, to enjoy
the vision of a distant land where he might eat without labour, where the abundance
of natural fruits could be enjoyed without effort . . . thus the Land of Cockaigne
appeared as a distant country where mankind might find all the good things of
Earth.'

beyond their control, it is permissible to make the sign of the Horns of Mithras behind your back to avoid causing them hurt or embarrassment.

The Horns of Mithras may still be found over the doorways of many farms and country houses. The Saxon substitute, the horse-shoe (or Crescent of Astarte?), is sometimes seen, too, but I think this is a recent, English import.

Some of the country-folk—who have certainly never heard of Mithras or Astarte—will assure you that the bull's horns serve as lightning-conductors and, for all I know, this may be true.

Witches used to be found in most villages and for this reason you must always burn your nail-parings and hair-clippings for, should they fall into the hands of an Ghagusa who wished you ill, they were potent ingredients for the manufacture of spells. The word *Ghagusa* is also used for the Spider Crab; but whether the witch lent her name to the crab or vice versa, I do not know.

The only certain way of ridding society of these old women was to fling them from the tower of the parish church on the vigil of the feast of the patron saint; but there is, I am happy to note, no extant record of any poor old crone suffering this fate. Malta's record in the matter of the disposal of witches is kinder than England's, or New England's.

Contrary to popular report amongst English visitors, the Evil One rarely makes his appearance in person, and it may be as well to add, in passing, that the statement of a retired Admiral which I have lately read in an antiquarian publication, to the effect that 'The Maltese always have twin church towers with one clock which tells the wrong time, to deceive the Devil . . .' is completely unfounded. In most cases (as the Admiral certainly should have observed) one 'clock' shows the day and the month albeit in the canonical year (which the Admiral may not have understood). In other cases, the second clock is a dummy, added for mere symmetry.

Many Maltese superstitions are exactly similar to the English versions, though those which have a religious significance or origin are nearer, here, to their source—which immediately becomes more obvious for this reason. Examples are the spilling of salt, the open umbrella (presaging a death in the house), the ladder, the number thirteen, the colour green. All have a Christian significance: the salt of Baptism, the Canopy of the Viaticum, the

Ladder of the Crucifixion, the Thirteen of the Last Supper, the
Green of the priestly vestment. There are other 'superstitions'
which border on actual religious observances—reminders or
symbols of a living Faith of the people. Many of these have died
out, or been deliberately suppressed, in northern Europe.

The ancient, pagan Midsummer Fires were enthusiastically
adopted by the Knights, who evolved a whole, intricate ceremonial about the practice which served to remind their subjects of
their Patron, St. John, whom they described with exaggerated
devotion as '. . . the Light that came to bear witness to the Light,
who enlightens every soul born into the world'.

Bread, whose form and ingredients become, at Holy Mass, the
Divine Presence, is very properly treated with great respect.
Before cutting a new loaf you kiss it and make the Sign of the
Cross.[1]

These and many similar customs survive. Not all are capable of
a Christian interpretation and it is surprising that so many of a
plainly heathen origin have lasted so long in so staunchly Christian
a community. But the Bishops and the Grand Masters were particularly benevolent towards local custom and turned a blind eye
upon many harmless pagan survivals. Nevertheless, the old things
are dying and little effort has been made to record them. The
complex magic of a Maltese 'Wake' was already a memory by the
end of the last century, with its wailing women, the breaking and
overturning of the dead man's possessions, the staining of the
doorposts with a mixture of soot and ashes, the cutting of his
vines, and the scattering of hair from his animals over the coffin.

In Gozo it is still sometimes a disservice to your host to admire
any of his possessions, for if he is old-fashioned he will have to
give it to you.

Admiration, perhaps because it is an emotion akin to envy, is
not always welcome. To admire another's health, wealth, or good
fortune is to invite calamity; for the demons are always alert to test
the fortitude of humanity. So you should never say 'How well you
look!' but 'How well you look, God bless you!'

The cloven hoof-mark and the smell of sulphur so well known
to the English countryman are not common experiences in Malta,
where the Old Man rarely makes a spectacular personal appearance;

---

[1] I lately learned that this practice also persisted in the North of England until
very recently.

but his minions certainly 'wander through the world for the ruin of souls' and the Maltese are none the worse for a healthy fear of them.

2

The South European is not usually so ghost-ridden as those of the North. Climate may have something to do with this. Headless horsemen and phantom carriages parade the misty lanes of England; screaming skulls and walled-up nuns lurk in her ancient houses; but weeping madonnas and sacred relics of great potency are vouchsafed beneath the clear skies of Calabria and Apulia.

Miracles happen in Malta, as they do wherever there is the Faith to deserve them. But there is a sceptic strain in the national character which discards sensationalism of a kind which might easily find credence in Sicily. Perhaps English influence has something to do with this and we thus have the interesting paradox of a southern European who is more tolerant of ghost-hunters than of miracle-mongers.

Ghost stories are common; but most have a suspiciously English shape, and I think that some, at least, are English importations, set in a background which is, admittedly, ideal. So much of fear and hate, of passion, love, war, malice, and faith has been packed into these small Islands for so long. Hardly a rock lacks its peculiar record, its own potent *Feng-shui*. Every hill-side has its caves in which men have dwelt, buried their dead, hidden their treasure, since long before Cadmus.

The narrow streets of Notabile, after sunset, deep shadowed between their high, Norman walls, can still ring suddenly to the tread of a mailed foot. And not long since, one of those white, hooded figures of the *Misericordia*—who pray for the souls of the hanged—might emerge silently from the black shadow of a gateway.

Meat enough, indeed, for the English imagination nurtured on tales of the Inquisition and haunted vicarages.

Most popular with the English, because she complies fairly closely with the English rules is the Grey Lady who inhabits a fortress which I will call 'Sant' Anna'.

The fortress has long housed British officers and their families. It is principally of Siculo-Norman origin, with Angevin and Aragonese additions and a great deal of reconstruction by the

Grand Masters. British modifications have been generally careful and have not spoiled the fort's charming character. Situated upon a natural strong-point, there has been a habitation here from the time of the Carthaginians, at least. Its Chapel of Our Lady retains elements of a Temple of Tyrian Astoreth.

The British captain and his family live in the quarters of the ancient Governor of the fortress, in rooms which have been occupied continuously since the time of the Normans in the eleventh century.

The Grey Lady has been heard, seen, and her presence felt by people of very different sorts on countless occasions, over the years. She is not bound to a particular room, or to the immediate environs of the Captain's House; but she does most frequently make her presence known in a particular room, through which she is heard—or felt—to pass, to the accompaniment of all the familiar signs: the cold blast of air, the slowly opening door, the rustle of voluminous skirts, and the light, tapping footfall.

An uncle of mine, who once served in the fortress, and who is not particularly fey or particularly devoted to grape or barley-corn, firmly asserts that he has seen the door open, heard the passing of dainty feet in the direction of a blank wall through which the sound passes and dies away. He also claims to have met the Grey Lady in the long, dark tunnel which used, in his time, to lead to the Water Gate; but since, on this latter occasion he admits that he was returning from a late session at the old Union Club, he does not stress this evidence.

The Lady has been seen, too, in daylight, walking in the gardens of the Upper Bastion. She wears 'a long, grey dress and a sort of tall, pointed head-dress from which hangs a sweeping grey veil'. She is beautiful and sad, but she does not weep, groan, scream, or clank chains. She has been seen by very young children who have spoken of 'the nice lady who came to say "good night" to us'.

In the long succession of British captains' wives, there have been two Maltese ladies—devout Catholics who were familiar with the story of the Grey Lady. They were the first and second Maltese chatelaines to reign in the household since Aragonese times, and the first of them took the matter seriously enough to have Masses said for the restless soul. The results were surprising. The Grey Lady abandoned her quiet and dignified habits and commenced to behave like any vulgar poltergeist: flinging a decorated Christmas-tree to the ground, banging doors, and throwing the furniture about. Though, as far as the children were concerned, she remained a 'nice lady'. The second in succession of the Maltese wives would have nothing less than a solemn exorcism. And the Grey Lady, so the story goes, was seen and heard no more.

Whether or not some sad spirit really troubles the fortress, local tradition identifies the Grey Lady as the light o' love of the last of the Sicilian-Aragonese Captains of the Rod and Governors of the Fort: one Seigneur di Nava.

The gallant Captain, whose private demesne was in the capital of Notabile, is supposed to have maintained a second establishment at his place of duty—a sort of sixteenth-century version of the managing director's secretary—though which of the ladies was his legal consort neither history nor tradition relates; but it is said that the one or the other was observed, by a vigilant Maltese Quartermaster, approaching the Water Gate in a boat at a particularly unsuitable moment. The Seigneur lost his head and intending, it is charitably supposed, merely to hide the superfluous lady, he shouted to his Maltese men-at-arms to 'get rid of her'. Whether he spoke Spanish or Italian is a moot point; but it is conceded that he had none of the 'sort of Moorish' of his men-at-arms and they misunderstanding, and with more discipline than humanity, put an end to her and cast her inconvenient corpse into a convenient *oubliette*. The poor Grey Lady cannot have been popular with the other ranks and was, perhaps, like her lord, a foreigner.

This story, or variants of it, had been current for many years when some restoration work was undertaken in the room through which the Lady most often passed. On all the walls, beneath layers of plaster of indeterminate age, were exposed a number of armorial frescoes in a good state of preservation. There were the expected and ubiquitous escutcheons of L'Isle Adam, Wignacourt, Perellos and, high up on the blank wall through which the Lady had seemed to pass, those of the di Nava family.

Further examination exposed an arched doorway, immediately beneath the arms of di Nava, and beyond this a narrow stairway terminating in the mouth of a deep *oubliette*. At the bottom were three skeletons—two male (the men-at-arms?) and one female, together with some fabric which might once have been grey.

The story is, in parts, a little too much like the *Ingoldsby Legends* to be Maltese in origin, and it has been suggested to me that the Grey Lady has nothing to do with anything as recent as the Aragonese but is originally the Greek and Cretan *Stoikheion*, the spirit of a maiden commonly sacrificed in Homeric times whenever some important building, fortification, or bridge was commenced. The fortress is old enough; but how account for the di Nava arms and the grisly contents of the *oubliette* which are fact?

3

The Black Knight inhabits another fortress, which we will call 'Fort Vilhena'. Here, too, the British captain occupies the house of the ancient Governors and while the Knight cannot claim the antiquity or the widespread credence which the Grey Lady enjoys, I have a personal interest in him, since I had some hand in setting him at rest: or so I hope, for my successors may have displeased him.

This fortress is comparatively modern, having been built between 1723 and 1726. Its chief interest, before the bombing of the Second World War laid a great part of it in ruins, was as an example, the last of its kind, of fortifications designed to resist assault by sea and land forces not yet equipped with high explosives. Its efficiency, even in its ruined state, I can attest. During several full-scale battle exercises it was defended with ease against Royal Marine Commandos—no mean test.

My wife, too, is Maltese, and when I commanded this 'sto ne frigate' we found ourselves occupying the quarters which h ad been the domain of one of her ancestors. It was thus particularly important to us that the tradition of this fortress of the Sovereign Order should be perpetuated and that as much as possible of the widespread war damage should be made good.

We never saw the Black Knight, though it would often have been easy to imagine him, but he was persistently reporte d by both English and Maltese men of my ship's company. He was silent and in no way malevolent; but he had an alarming habi t of appearing out of the empty air, suddenly, in the moonlight, on the drawbridge, in the dry moat, on the battlements and bastio ns; but most frequently in the vicinity of the heap of rubble wh ich desecrated and almost obliterated the site of the lovely little cha pel of the Fort, dedicated by the Grand Master, Anthony Manoel de Vilhena, to his patron, St. Anthony of Padua.

Only a part of the façade and one wall remained and the site had been used as a dumping-ground for all the assorted debris of bomb damage—a common enough part of the Maltese landscape at that time and so widespread that it was difficult to believe that the Islands would ever seem otherwise. We resolved, however, that the site of the chapel should at least be cleared of rubble and that I should press the Admiralty, through my Commander-in-Chief, to restore the little chapel to some semblance of its former charm. This I did, using every course open to me; but financial stringency is a normal state with the Navy—in peace—and English bureaucracy is not nowadays enthusiastic about building churches at the State's charge, of any complexion; and least of all for the 'Romans'. Maltese local resources were stretched to the limit and, in any case, the chapel was in 'foreign' hands. As yet, the chapel remains unrestored—but I overtake my story.

With the benevolent connivance of an excellent Admiralty civil engineer (a pillar of the Scottish Kirk) and the maximum of self-help by our little company—English and Maltese Catholic sailors, Dockyardmen, and officers alike—we were able to clear the site and give its ruins a tidy and dignified appearance.

From the moment of our starting work on the chapel, the appearances of the Black Knight became more frequent. His description began to approximate more and more closely to Favray's portrait of the Grand Master Vilhena which hangs in the Palace of Valletta. My Maltese seamen were now convinced that the Grand Master was personally supervising our labours. They began to see him in their mess—which abutted on one of the remaining walls of the chapel. Their discipline improved noticeably.

While we were anxious to restore the chapel because of its historic associations, we were, of course, more concerned to restore the practice of religion to this ancient setting where it so much belonged and, with this end in mind, I wondered whether there had not been a crypt which might, if it were of sufficient size, suit our purpose as well as the very problematic reconstruction of the chapel itself.

I was encouraged in this by the fact that several local churches of very similar design had crypts whose area was almost equal to that of the floor area of the church. They were usually dry and airy.

My good friend, the Chevalier Galea, a noted Maltese

antiquarian, searched the original *Cabbrei*, or specifications, of Vilhena's reign in the Archives of the Royal Library and came upon the following:

> La chiesa del Forte . . . dedicata a S. Antonio di Padova fu eretta in titolo di cappellania d'obbedienza, 1 Agosto, 1724, e poi eretta in parrochia in virtu di bolle di Benedetto XIII, data da Roma 9 Settembre, 1738 . . . con quelle riserve del vescovo e parroco di Birchircara.
>
> Fu assegnato un vice parroco per servizio della chiesa col titolo di capellano d'obbedienza, 12 giugno, 1732. Nella chiesa vi Sono altri quattro altari (oltre l'altare maggiore) *ed uno sotto di essa.*
>
> | | |
> |---|---|
> | Concezione Immacolata eretti | 23 Settembre 1750 |
> | Sant 'Anna eretti | 23 Settembre 1750 |
> | S. Giuseppe eretti | 18 Giugno 1751 |
> | Assunzione di nostra Signora | 25 Agosto 1751 |
> | Delle Grazie *sotto la chiesa* | 2 Agostò 1752.[1] |

The reference to the altar under the church was proof enough of a crypt and we were now coming upon broken marble tablets, votive inscriptions, and pillars and the like, which enabled us to identify the four other altars, as well as the High Altar. In the event, the crypt was literally under our noses. A flight of steps had been blocked up very recently, it would seem, from the quality of the cement which emerged, to the right of the façade and the main door of the chapel—immediately in front of the Maltese seamen's mess.

I sought and readily obtained the permission of His Grace the Archbishop to open the crypt.

It had indeed, and all too obviously, been entered recently. And not by Christians. The altar had been wrecked and the paving-stones ripped up, exposing human bones—some of which we could identify from medallions and inscriptions as members of the Sovereign Order. A crucifix in high relief and two charming reliefs representing the Souls in Purgatory (smiling happily, in the Maltese tradition, amongst enveloping flames) had been brutally mutilated.

---

[1] 'The church of the fort . . . dedicated to St. Anthony of Padua was raised to the status of a Chaplaincy of Obedience on 1 August 1724, and later promoted to a Parish under a Bull of Benedict XIII, given at Rome on 9 September 1738 . . . together with those (whose privileges) were reserved to the Bishop and to the Parish of Birkirkara. On 12 June [1732 there was assigned a vice-chaplain with the rank of Chaplain of Obedience. In the Church there were, besides the high altar, four altars *and one beneath these*

Immaculate Conception	dedicated	23 September 1750
Saint Anne	dedicated	23 September 1750
Saint Joseph	dedicated	18 June 1751
Assumption of Our Lady	dedicated	25 August 1751
The Graces *under the Church*	dedicated	2 August 1752.'

By now the Black Knight was appearing to the Dockyard work-people, and there was a general conclusion, which I more than half shared, that he was approving our efforts and urging us on.

The crypt was small. Much smaller than we had hoped, being about one-third the total floor area of the chapel; but we pieced together the shattered stones of the altar, reopened a blocked ventilation shaft, and reburied the dead. We relaid the pavement and decorated the walls and the altar in white and gold and the eight-pointed cross of the Order. On the Christmas Eve, soon following, Mass for the Dead was said by our naval chaplain, and Mass has been said daily in the crypt of St. Anthony ever since.

The Black Knight has not, so far, been seen again.

4

Every Maltese town and rural district confers on its natives some peculiar quirk, characteristic, vice, virtue, or historical association. The Gozitan, like the Scot, counts his pennies and is dour and canny. The Senglean is always 'from the Other Side' because the gentry formerly inhabited the Valletta side of the Grand Harbour. He cannot pronounce the letters 'q' or *Ghajn* which is tantamount to dropping your 'h's', and talks 'like an Englishman'. The 'Wharfee' from Bormola, like Taffy the Welsh-man, is a thief. The Hamrunese is *tat-Tsikina*, too ready with a knife and the people of Sliema are *Tax-Xelin*, 'Of the Shilling', for a very curious reason.

A certain house on the borders of the suburbs of Sliema and St. Julian's, of monastic style, though it was never a monastery, enjoys the doubtful attentions of a ghost who restlessly paces its cloistered courtyard with halting, infirm, scraping, sandalled feet.

I have heard him (the tread is male) often, though the fact that the leaves of a lusty banana palm brushed the window of my bedroom may have some bearing on the matter.

In the middle years of the last century this house was the temporary home of a curious little sect, headed by an unfrocked Italian priest who was assisted by a number of other discredited Italian clerics and a Greek. The ex-priest appears to have 'ordained' his followers into a private 'Italian Protestant Church', and their avowed purpose was to 'convert' the Popish Maltese. They had persuaded what now seems to have been a particularly gullible section of the English Establishment to support and almost certainly to finance their venture. All of them seem to have been on the pay-roll of a Protestant college, which, whatever its official connexion with Canterbury, certainly enjoyed the protection of the Protestant Bishop of Gibraltar (who claimed and still claims jurisdiction in Malta).[1]

The leader of this forlorn 'mission' was the pathetic but turbulent Dr. Achilli, to whom Cardinal Newman referred in his lectures on *The Present Position of Catholics in England*. Newman, representing Achilli as though boasting about the unsavoury achievements which had led to his unfrocking, said: 'I am that Professor of the Protestant College at Malta, who with two others was dismissed from my post for offences which the authorities cannot get themselves to describe.'

A contemporary English account of Achilli appeared in *The Dublin Review* of July 1850, in an article by Wiseman:

> From Corfu, we are informed that Dr. Achilli proceeded to Malta; and, if we are rightly informed, it was at the invitation of Dr. Tomlinson the so-called Bishop of Gibraltar. [Dr. Achilli has already left the Church, and had by now declared himself a Protestant. Dr. Tomlinson was presumably the Anglican Bishop of Gibraltar.] Here an Italian college, manned by apostates, had been established. Among them was a certain Saccares (who appears to have gone, like Dr. Achilli, to fish in the troubled waters of republican Rome), Desanctis, and others of the same stamp. Among these Dr. Achilli received the appointment of Professor of Divinity with a salary of £150 per an. There surely never was a luckier man. Professorships seem to drop ripe into his mouth; but how strange it seems, that he never keeps them! We have seen how, in his youth he had three of these birds in hand, and gave them all up for three in the bush; and, of course, lost them all. And here is another professorship of the highest science bestowed upon him. And yet, like the former ones, he soon lost it. What was the cause of this? We regret that, since information reached us on this subject, we have not been able to make the full enquiries which would have enabled us fully to verify it; and we have been most careful not to set down anything, for which we have not vouchers, or authentic and formal information. The matter, then, which wants clearing up, is this. It is said, that the conduct of persons connected with this college, became so notorious and scandalous, that Dr. Hatfield, the superior, was desired to make a full investigation, that the result was (we are told), that he publicly advertised in the Maltese papers, that Saccares had no further connection with the college; and that further, at this very same period Dr. Achilli ceased to be professor and left the college. We trust that some one, able to reach accurate information, will investigate this history; we give it as related to us and shall be glad of further light.
>
> In 1848, Dr. Achilli was in England. . . .

[1] A story is told of a Bishop of Gibraltar who called on Pope Pius IX. His Holiness —famed for his humour and affability—greeted the Anglican with the remark, 'I understand that I am in your Lordship's Diocese.'

Wiseman's article was a review of two books about Achilli—who certainly created a stir and seems to have fancied himself in the roll of Titus Oates: *The Imprisonment and Deliverance of Dr. Giacinto Achilli* by Sir G. E. Eardley, Bart., and *A Brief Sketch of the Life of Dr. Giacinto Achilli* by P. Dixon.

What actually happened in Malta is nowhere very exactly recorded and this may have been one of the most difficult points in Newman's defence when a libel action was brought against him. Offences by Achilli in various towns in Italy seem to have been fully established; but Newman is on record that, when he visited Malta, he 'never met a single Maltese'. Had he done so, he might have gleaned an even less favourable impression of Achilli.[1]

The Protestant Mission used to dispense to the poorer sort of the people of Sliema copies of the Protestant Bible, a loaf of bread, and one shilling. Henceforward to be born in Sliema was to be 'Of the Shilling', and it is easy to understand why the older generation who remembered the origins of the nickname did not much relish it.

The Mission inevitably failed, bringing nothing but discredit upon those who seemed to have sponsored it, and I do not know what eventually became of Achilli and his companions.

Neither do I know whether it is Achilli or one of his disciples who paces the cloistered patio so restlessly—or whether it is simply the banana tree—or a story put about to protect the fruit in the very extensive gardens of the house.

5

The Ghost of St. Paul's Steps, a rambling pretty little hamlet on a windswept hill-top, was of rather different calibre, though he or it also consisted principally of a noise. But this noise, unlike the dainty footfalls of the Grey Lady or the halting shuffle of the apostate priest, was loud, boisterous, and cacophonous.

Here there used to stand a pair of houses obviously the beginning of a row or street which never materialized. They were isolated, some way from the nearest outskirts of the village, empty, dilapidated, deserted. The villagers returning from the fields always gave them a wide berth and avoided the area altogether after dark.

[1] For these details of the Achilli story I am indebted to Monsignor H. Francis Davis of Oscott College.

Only one of the pair now survives. It has been modernized and was, when I last saw it, inhabited by a family of heartily sceptic N.A.T.O. Americans. Its twin had been demolished early in the Second World War by one of those stray bombs, jettisoned by a hard-pressed German or Italian over open country.

When the bomb fell the former occupants of the two houses had long since fled in disorder, pursued by unreasoning terror of a noise which came from nowhere. For many nights they had been disturbed by the roistering clamour of what could only be a hearty stag-party, coming as each family thought, from an upper room of the neighbouring house. The party would start regularly at midnight and continue until dawn. There would be loud laughter, singing, the clink of bottle against glass, fuddled talk, oaths, shouts, culminating with the first light in an eldritch scream and then, sudden silence.

The father of each family, both patient and easygoing men, was at length impelled to tax his neighbour with this nightly and unseemly roistering.

Both pleaded complete innocence and it was arranged to conduct a joint search of both houses as soon as the noise should be heard again. Neither family had at first any intention of solving a mystery and each distrusted the other. Sure enough, that very night, as midnight was slowly counted on the bell of the parish church and the womenfolk, as was the universal custom, began the prayers for the dead, the noise commenced and the search started. Both houses were quite empty. They were surrounded by fields with a few stunted oranges and carobs at the back, offering no cover to any human movement in the bright moonlight.

The two families had stood in a puzzled, anxious group before their doors as the menfolk had conducted their search. Nothing was seen, no light, no movement; but the din went on. The families fled, incontinent, to the house of the parish priest and, on the morrow, in comfortable daylight, they collected their belongings, piled them on to flat carts, and were gone to seek shelter with brothers, mothers, cousins until new dwellings could be found. No one ever lived in the two houses again; but in 1941 a solution was offered to the infernal bottle-party by the stray bomb which demolished the greater part of one of them and exposed, in the thick wall between, a bricked-up spiral stairway (of the kind delightfully called *garigor*). At the top, which had been blanked off at roof-level, lay a huddled mummy, still clothed in the remnants of the finery of a village Teddy Boy of the nineteen-tens.

The inevitable Old Woman of the village claimed to recognize a notorious Bad Boy who had suddenly gone to Australia with several of his boon companions, when she was a girl.

He had been the only son of a prosperous farmer, spoiled by a doting mother and much given to gambling and the bottle. There had been one other child, a little girl who was, the Old Woman said, the only person in the world for whom the Bad Boy cared. That little girl had been the mother of one of the families who had lived in the twin houses.

6

A house in Valletta which stood empty for many years used also to be pointed out as a place to avoid after dark. It was one of those splendid old seventeenth-century palaces, built by the Knights in their hey-day, with a great iron-studded door, graceful balconies, and elegantly proportioned windows in the best tradition of Melitan Baroque.

Alone amongst the houses in that street, it retained the original brass dolphin door-knocker which is a collector's piece and nowadays rarely appears except in poor copies.

During more than a half-century, it is said, only two people ever crossed the threshold of the House of the Brass Dolphin, and they, strange to tell, were English naval officers making their first visit to Malta.

They had been to Floriana, to the flat of a married shipmate. It was a fine summer's night of brilliant moonlight and they had elected to walk back to the Customs House by way of Valletta. It was late and the silence of the moonlit streets was only broken by the occasional, distant hoof-beat of a *karrozin* horse (there were few cars and no taxis in those days) or by the hurried footfall of a belated diner-out.

As they reached the deep shadow of the Porta Reale they were, as it seemed to them, accosted by a black shrouded figure which, in their unfamiliarity with the Island, they did not at once recognize as a Maltese lady wearing a *faldetta*. In those days every

Maltese woman who wished to be thought 'respectable' wore the *faldetta* in the street, with a black silk dress, ample lace petticoats, and a collar or *jabot* of lace, a costume which had persisted, unchanged, for centuries. This the young officers were not to know, and their astonishment was not lessened when the hooded figure addressed them in a cultured voice, in French. Fortunately, both had sufficient of that language to understand her and to make intelligible, if halting, conversation.

The lady apologized charmingly for addressing them; but she could see that they were gentlemen and she explained that she had foolishly locked herself out of her house. All her servants had been sent off to their village *Festa* and would not return until the morning. She knew that it was possible to spring open the shutter of one of the lower windows, but was doubtful of her ability—and clearly embarrassed by the prospect of trying to do so—to climb the wall by way of the cornice of the doorway, an operation which would be simple for two such strong young gentlemen as she had the honour of addressing. Would they help her?

Whatever else she might be, the hooded lady was no common street-walker. If the operation be a 'pick-up', it was a complex and unusual one—though why she had preferred to accost a couple of complete strangers rather than return whence she had come, or wake her neighbours, remained unexplained; but the night was theirs until 'Hands fall-in'; *dghaisas* from the Custom House plied at all hours and the lady was charming and in apparent distress.

The three of them set off in the direction of Strada Sant' Ursola, and Saint Ursula seemed to smile mischievously from her niche at the street corner.

The brass dolphin shone brilliantly in the moonlight, and this was clearly the house of people of consequence.

The burglary presented little difficulty to two young, agile men. It was a matter only of one mounting the other's shoulders and, under instructions from their charming companion, springing the latch of the window-shutters with a pocket-knife. The young officer scrambled through, alighting on a thick carpet, and found, in the moonlight which now flooded the room, a silver candelabra. Lighting the candles, he descended a wide staircase, rich with oil-paintings and trophies of arms, to the great door. The key—a huge affair which turned, nevertheless, with ease—*was on the inside of the door*.

The lady was profuse in her thanks and pressed them to take a glass of wine before returning to their ship. Now convinced that there was no catch, the young men gladly accepted and followed the lady into a room of baronial magnificence, where she poured them each a glass of some excellent white wine.

While they made somewhat stumbling conversation, the young men were able to appreciate that they were in a household of considerable wealth. The cut goblets from which they drank, the tapestried walls, the embroidered upholstery of the furniture, the silver engraved with a princely escutcheon were all of another and more spacious age. But the lady herself, divested of the unflattering *faldetta*, was by far the loveliest thing in a room full of lovely things. She had the copious black hair, coiled heavily on her neck, the finely cut features, large candid black eyes, and the milk-white complexion of the Maltese aristocrat. Her hands, too, were singularly beautiful and she wore, on her right hand, a single diamond of immense fineness. About her neck hung a heavy Maltese cross in gold and white enamel.

As they chatted, their broken French causing the lady no small amusement, she apologized for having no English. She seemed, indeed, surprised and puzzled that they should be English. She had known at once that they were foreigners and assumed that they must be French.

One of the young men asked if he might smoke. She seemed taken aback, but nodded her consent.

By now they were thoroughly intrigued; but they could not in decency extend their curiosity beyond a second glass of wine, and bidding the lovely lady as continental an adieu as they could muster, they made their way back through the now moonless streets from which, it seemed, some magic had departed, to the Grand Harbour and to their bunks.

There was still much that puzzled and intrigued them. Why had she chosen to seek the aid of two strangers? The blue lamp of a police station had shone clearly a few yards from the Porta Reale. Why should a household of such obvious opulence be deserted by all its staff at once? And with the huge key inside, how had she got out? The burglary had seemed too simple. Why had she assumed they were French? But her manner, her speech, nothing about her had suggested any hidden motive. She had volunteered no name, and though charming and friendly in the extreme, she

had given no hint or opportunity for a further call at the House
of the Brass Dolphin.

But one of the gallants had left his cigarette-case in the house—
not, he assured his companion, the obvious stratagem. If the
excuse had been deliberate, would he be sharing the opportunity
of a second call?

On the following day the operation of retrieving the cigarette-
case was planned with some care. They sought advice about the
official calling hours in Maltese society. Clean linen and best
'poodle-faking' suitings were indicated.

Full of conjecture, they made their way up those steps which
Byron had cursed, past the smiling saint, and there stood the
house, somehow less imposing in daylight. Dingy, dusty, with
plaster flaking off the façade, and scraps of paper and rubbish
blowing about the doorstep. The brass dolphin which had shone
so brightly in the moonlight they now saw to be green with age
and neglect. The great door stood firmly shut.

A rusty bell-pull hung by a heavy chain. They pulled with no
result beyond a protesting squeal. And again, harder, to be
rewarded with an unconvincing tinkle somewhere a long way off.
They waited some ten minutes, now and again tugging at the aged
chain until a final tug parted the corroded contraption and an
embarrassed young man narrowly escaped landing flat on his back
in the roadway. But the ringing within the house was at least
peremptory and certain to raise some response if the house were
not, as they now suspected, deserted.

The sudden sunset was followed by brief twilight. The young
men were now intensely curious. And the shutter by which they
had entered on the previous night stood ajar.

They now transferred their attentions to the brass dolphin. The
knocker was stiff; but a firm knock reverberated in what certainly
sounded like an empty house. It was now dark. Perhaps the lady
had left the house? The servants had not returned? The cigarette-
case was a good one and the shutter stood open. With little effort
the young officer cocked his leg over the sill and dropped into the
room—on to the bare stone floor of an unquestionably empty
room. He fumbled his way, lighting matches, to the door. There
was the great key. It grated and complained as he turned it to
admit his friend. Together they explored a completely deserted
house. Dust and cobwebs lay everywhere; but, in the centre of the

room, where they had taken their glass of wine, was the cigarette-case. And, in the thick dust of the stairway, the two sets of their own footprints.

I passed the house not long before Kesselring's blitz. The brass dolphin was quite black and the broken chain of the bell dangled forlornly out of reach. One of the shutters of a lower window stood ajar.

A block of Welfare-Cubist flats now stands on the site, and for all I know the brass dolphin decorates the pillar-box red door of a too-too elegant little Mews flat in Chelsea.

The secret of the lovely lady is buried with much else of Valletta's aristocratic past.

VI

RACE AND LANGUAGE

RACE AND LANGUAGE

'All Generalizations are false: including this one.'
(Heracleitus)

I HAVE had much to do, in my time, with Civil Servants of all grades who are, in fine, the men who call the tunes to which our Colonial and Commonwealth administrators dance. Contrary to popular imagination, they are an intensely hardworking race who take themselves and their responsibilities very seriously. I have greatly admired them and have not often found it possible to be brusque with them—save on those all too frequent occasions when they have used such phrases as 'Europeans and Maltese . . .'; '. . . Maltese and other non-Europeans'.

The conviction that the people of Malta are something other than European is deep-rooted, even amongst university graduates. But it is useless to lose one's temper about it. The obvious retort to an objection is, 'Well, then. What are they?' And the answer is too long and too involved—alternatively, it's not supposed to matter in these enlightened days. The fact that it does matter a great deal is one of those inconvenient facts to which one is supposed not to refer in official dockets or administrative circles.

But what are they? Many of them look like Sicilians and they talk a language which is sufficiently like Arabic to be mistaken for a dialect of it. Geographically, they are on the very fringe of Europe—or Africa, depending on which way you turn the map. It is only of recent years that the connexions between race, language, and geography have been seen to be tenuous and misleading and the ordinary man still uses these convenient rules of thumb whenever for one purpose or another he wishes to pigeonhole his fellows. Perhaps the most notable exponent of this kind of fatal generalization was Adolf Hitler; but he and his Aryan myth had their precursors amongst serious students who should have known better.

The Maltese case is only one of many examples of people whose racial and linguistic roots are quite separate.

To say what the average Maltese looks like is almost as difficult as to describe the average Englishman, or, indeed, that shocking monster 'the Average Man'. Morant, in his *Races of Central Europe*, wrote that there are bigger differences between individuals within a country than between the average types of different countries and, further, 'It is possible that pure races have never existed except in the imagination of some anthropologists.'

Most Maltese have black or brown hair and eyes; but many have red or blonde hair and blue, green or grey eyes. Most are below average European height and grow portly at an early age; but many are tall and thin. There are whole villages and isolated families of 'pure' Germanic appearance: others who might be Arabs, Jews, Berbers, Celts, or just indeterminate Anglo-Saxons. More than one family of my acquaintance, of unexceptionable parentage, be it added, ranges from Spanish brunette to ash-blonde Scandinavian in a single generation. And, despite official disapproval of 'mixed' marriages, there is scarcely a family of the upper classes or of the nobility which has not some English, Irish, or Scottish blood.

Nevertheless, there is an identifiable Maltese type—commoner in Gozo and the country than in the urban areas—which we may accept as representing the native stock. He is of middle height, barrel-chested and sturdy, with wavy brown hair and peculiarly attractive green eyes. He is of cheerful disposition and has a vast capacity for hard manual labour. Self-reliant, independent, quick-witted, and friendly once he has overcome his Islander's distrust of strangers, he is much slower to arouse than his Sicilian or Corsican cousins and, although he once shared their tradition of the Vendetta, he does not bear personal grudges. In complexion, the countryman is deceptively dark, for he spends all his days in the open and is tanned from birth by a fierce sun. His natural skin tint is a good deal lighter than the olive of the Italian or the Spaniard.

I am not the first to remark that the Maltese woman is often taller than her menfolk and her 'milky' complexion (no longer as fashionable as it used to be) has been remarked by connoisseurs of such matters from the sixteenth century, at least.

The Sieur du Mont, whose *New Voyage to the Levant* was

'. . . done into English and adorned with figures', at Westminster in 1696, wrote:

> The habit of the women in this place is as melancholic and dismal when they go abroad as it is wanton and lascivious when they are at home. In the streets you see nothing but a long black veil instead of a woman, which covers them entirely from Head to Foot, that such a sight would cost a low Briton at least twenty Signs of the Cross; for the women in this city look just like so many ghosts wrapt in shrouds, stalking about the streets. But if they are ghosts in the streets, they are Angels at home; for though the peasants are tawny the women who live in the City have the fairest complexions in the world. I can only give you an account of their Summer Dress since I never had occasion to see 'em in the Winter. They wear a fine white Smock, plaited at the neck like a man's shirt, but the opening is so wide that it leaves their shoulders and Breasts entirely exposed to the view of the Ravished Beholder; the sleeves are very large and tucked up to the neck-band of the Smock to which they are fastened with a Pin, so that one may see their whole Arms. This Smock is almost their entire Habit for they wear nothing above it but a very little Pair of Boddice about their waist under their Breasts, which being not above a span long serves only to set off the fineness of their Shape and rather exposes than conceals those alluring charms that strike the eyes and the hearts of the Spectator with a sweet but irresistible violence. The men's habit is not very different from ours. Almost all the Maltese are served by Slaves. . . .

Popular works of reference consistently derive the 'lower orders' from the Phoenicians and their kinsmen, the Carthaginians, and it is a fact that the earliest clearly identifiable antiquities are Punic in character. The famous 'Cippus', the Rosetta Stone of Punic studies—one of a pair of decorated phallic columns excellently preserved—was found in the Island, bearing an inscription in Punic with a Greek translation. The Punic version, transliterated into modern Maltese, makes sense and this is, I believe, a unique example of an inscription some four thousand years old in a tongue which is still spoken and written.[1]

Punic colonies in Malta are discernible from 1500 B.C. onwards. Evidence of Greek influence is curiously slight, but there are not negligible remnants of Egyptian culture. The widespread Punic elements merge through Carthaginian to Roman; but it has been

---

[1] There are, in the new Museum of Valletta, five of these Cippi in various states of preservation and of various standards of execution. The most famous is a column—almost certainly phallic in import—with an acanthus-patterned base bearing, in Greek and Punic, the legend: 'A Vow from Abdosir and his brother Osirxamar, sons of Osirxamar to the Lord Melkart, Lord of Tyre. . . .'

The Greek version reads:

'. . . Dionysius and Serapion sons of Serapion of Tyre to Hercules Archigetas.'

The columns were discovered, sometime before 1694, in the region of the Temple of Tyrian Hercules (or Melkarte) at Marsaxlok. One was presented to Louis XVI of France in 1780 and is now in the Louvre.

the habit of local and visiting historians—not, I think, without political bias during recent years—to label everything Punic which was not demonstrably Roman. The late Chevalier F. W. Ryan, himself a Celt but an admirer and amateur of all things Maltese, was an early protagonist of the Phoenician theory, basing himself, as was then the widely accepted premiss, upon the equation of Race and Language. He wrote, in 1910:[1]

> The Maltese are a homogeneous race, distinct from their African or European neighbours in language and character, and with national customs of which they are tenacious and proud. They are descended from the Phoenicians, who colonized the Island a thousand years before Christ. From this stock they inherit their native tongue which is neither English nor Italian, but akin to the ancient Hebrew. Many races have ruled Malta since the coming of the Phoenicians but few have sent settlers to the Island in sufficient numbers to crush out the primitive inhabitants, and so down to this day the Phoenician strain predominates. Some ancient families, indeed, especially amongst the Nobility, are of foreign extraction bearing Italian, French, Spanish, or other Surnames; they came to the Island long ago, inter-married with the natives and are now more Maltese than the Maltese themselves. Environment has, no doubt, in part done this, as well as the use from infancy of the Maltese tongue, universal as the language of domestic life both high and low in the Island; hence the Maltese present a study in national development in many ways unique . . . In local records may be read in microcosm the history of Europe; while the archaeological remains present a complete picture of the various stages of Western civilization.
>
> Here, Hamilcar surrendered to Titus Sempronius Gracchus when Carthage ceded her command of the Great Sea to Rome. . . . Napoleon declared "Peace or war depends on Malta. I would rather put you [the English] in possession of the heights of Montmartre than of Malta".

And Ryan goes on to eulogize the Phoenicians and to discover, in the character of the Maltese of his time, clear evidence of their descent from these 'Foremost of Barbarians' [i.e. non-Roman] who were the only political rivals of the Greeks, who came into the narrow waters of the western Mediterranean from the strip of land between Lebanon and the sea, from the cities of Tyre, Sidon, and Arvad. They were the Canaanites of the Old Testament, worshipping Baalim and Astoreth with their foul and bloody rites, burning their children in the fire. The oldest mariners in the world, the most efficient traders, far in advance in material arts of the Greeks who learned much from them, including their alphabet, they were, according to Rawlinson, 'pliable yet with an iron fixedness of purpose; possessed of a deep and forceful yearning for dreamy ease together with a capacity for the hardest work.

[1] F. W. Ryan, K.M., *Malta*, 1910, p. 3.

They loved abstract thought and had an intensely spiritual conception of the Deity. . . .'
Ryan[1] finds all these qualities in the Maltese:

Hard work has made the Maltese merchant the most flourishing in the Mediterranean at the present day [1910], while the successful trader in Tunis and Alexandria and other Eastern ports is often found to be a Maltese whose hope, generally realized, is to amass a competence and return to end his days in his beloved Malta. A traveller in the eighteenth century notes the adventurous merchants from Malta who travelled to America, no mean performance in those days, returning with fortunes; and a good Knight, with perhaps affectionate exaggeration, would have us believe that, so famous were their woollens, half Europe at one time wore Maltese socks and went to bed between Maltese blankets . . .[2]

He traces the 'yearning for dreamy ease' in the midday siesta (though admitting that early rising may account for this) and the 'abstract thought' in the rich metaphors of the Maltese tongue 'like the late Dr. Mizzi'—he did not live to witness the explosive oratory of Dominic Mintoff. The 'intensely spiritual conception of the Deity . . .' was certainly not far to seek and, although we may think that affectionate exaggeration and Celtic imagination play some part in his conclusions, Ryan certainly had a fair case.

The linguistic and cultural traces of Phoenicia are clear enough, and Malta's association with Carthage may have been very close indeed. The Phoenician names Hannibal and Hamilcar were commonly found amongst Maltese many years before the 'Punic fashion' can have prompted any deliberate flourish of racialism, and Ryan says that he knew a family in a remote village whose surname was Hamilcar, who claimed descent from the great Carthaginian.[3]

Particularly valuable to the supporters of the Phoenician tradition is the area about the naval air stations at Hal Far and Kalafrana. Though little now remains of it, there stood in the region of St. George's Bay, apparently well preserved until 1681, a splendid Temple of Melkarte, the Punic Hercules. The Roman historian Ptolemy, writing in A.D. 196, refers to it as 'a temple of great renown in the times of antiquity . . .' and, in 1528, the

[1] F. W. Ryan, K.M. op. cit., p. 15.
[2] Rabelais, of all people writing during the first years of the Knights, has several references in *Gargantua* and in *Pantagruel* to the whiteness and excellence of Maltese cotton and Maltese wool.
[3] It is relevant that purity of race was already a myth before the time of Herodotus who notes, in his *Histories*, that the mother of Hamilcar, the son of Hanno, the great navigator, was a Sicel (whom we might now call a Celt) from Syracuse.

Auditor and Surveyor to the Sovereign Order who was conduct-
ing a reconnaissance for the Grand Master writes of 'this immense
temple of Hercules ... three thousand paces in circumference ...
with many great stones of a stupendous size'. In 1681 'certain
great hooks and hinges of brass' were removed from the demolished temple and used for the embellishment of the Church of
St. Lorenzo in Vittoriosa.

In this same area, within the limits of the headland called
Benghajsa and, significantly, in a field called (as was often the
custom, by the nickname of its owner) Tal-Berqa, an inscription
was unearthed, in Punic characters, which greatly excited the
savants.

The inscription suffered, as such things do, a variety of trans-
literations and translations. The tombstone—this much is clear—
is first recorded by Canon de Soldanis, Keeper of Antiquities of
the Sovereign Order in 1761. His version was in Latin, and we
have to wait until 1810 for an English version by Sir William
Drummond which, with respect, seems peculiarly inept. It reads:

> The Grave to be locked up Room
> In the House of Eternity
> Inertness to the Mother of Disgrace
> The pious Hannibal, son of
> Barmelek to be deposited in that grave.

Sir William seems to have been in no doubt that the tomb was
that of none other than the incomparable Hannibal, conqueror of
Spain and Italy, who all but made Europe a Semitic dominion,
and there is some evidence to support him. Local tradition had
always pointed to the area around Marsaxlok as the home of
Hamilcar and the birthplace of Hannibal and Hasdrubal and the
field in which the inscription was unearthed was called *Tal-Berqa*,
which means, in Maltese, 'Lightning' and is the same word as the
Punic patronymic of Hannibal—'Barca'.

The German savant Gesenius produced a Latin version of the
inscription which read:

> *Conclave domus alternae sepulchrum*
> *Depositus est Pius in hoc claustro*
> *Spiritus remissionis mater ignominiae*
> *Hannibal filius Barmeleck.*

25. Townswoman: nineteenth century

(*above*) 26. Maia the Earth Mother

(*left*) 27. Inscribed base of the Melkarte Column

(*below*) 28. Temple of the Cretan Dionysius

(*above*) 29. Neolithic Venus
(*right*) 30. Agrippina
(*below left*) 31. Market Boy: nineteenth century
(*below right*) 32. Egg Woman:
nineteenth century

33. The Last Faldetta

But the Maltese archaeologist Vassalli, adopting the obvious expedient of transliterating the ancient Punic into Maltese, got a slight variation of the last line which produced '*Hannibal Bin Batt Malik* . . .' from which he deduced a far-fetched connexion with the Battus, whom Ovid, in his *Fasti* (III) makes a contemporary of Aeneas's Dido, Queen of Carthage. Battus, according to Ovid, was the ruler of Malta, who sheltered Dido's sister Anna. The sister's charms were interesting Aeneas too noticeably for the contentment of the jealous Queen, and she fled from her sister's wrath to the little provincial Court of Malta and its king, Battus. But we are here in the realms of myth, and all that emerges from Hannibal's Tomb is the possibility that that great soldier, who took his own life rather than submit to Rome, in Bithynia in 183 B.C., was brought back for burial in his birthplace—on the perimeter of what is now a British naval airfield.

It has always been in the interests of Britain and of those who served those interests to wean the Maltese from any lingering loyalty to the Knightly tradition or to the feudal ties with the Holy Roman Empire which preceded the Grand Masters. Such loyalties were essentially Latin and continental and we may suppose that there was always more than enough, for British taste, of those loyalties in the Maltese religion. Hence, in part, what we may call the 'Punic Build-up'—a policy which gave the Maltese people pride of race as scions of a great culture—elevated their language to classic status, and tended to minimize any sense of kinship with other European Powers who might, at any moment, be Britain's enemies.

Yet the 'Build-up' is not as completely spurious as some Fascist apologists would have had us believe. In the *Times Educational Supplement* of 11 November 1933 we find:

The common tongue of Malta is as pure as Welsh and even more ancient. It is, indeed, apparently a linguistic survival of a civilization that, perhaps eight hundred years before our era, existed in Southern Spain under the combined rule of Greeks and Phoenicians, the Empire of Tartessus at the mouth of the Guadalquivir. Phoenician colonists from Tyre had been subjects of that Empire from about 700 B.C. Two centuries later the Carthaginians controlled the western Mediterranean, and there can be little doubt that it was in that period that the islet south of Sicily which we call Malta, the Melita of St. Paul, was colonized. St. Paul calls the common people of the Island a barbarous people—people, that is, who spoke neither Latin nor Greek and we have evidence, late evidence but conclusive, of the actual tongue. In 1523 the Knights of the Hospital of St. John of Jerusalem, expelled from Rhodes, were offered Malta as a dwelling-place

by the Emperor Charles V. The Grand Master sent a commission to this
barren island and found that there were about 12,000 inhabitants who
spoke 'a sort of Moorish', in fact the tongue of the lost Empire of Tartessus. This is confirmed by Dr. Zammit, the archaeologist of Malta, who
in a learned paper published in 1913, gives the native tongue and blood a
Phoenician or Punic origin. The word 'Moorish' in 1523 connects the
language with southern Spain; the actual speech is Carthaginian or Phoenician in origin. Such a tongue is worth preserving as perhaps the sole
linguistic vestige of a world that is far older than Rome.

The Punic colonization of the Maltese Islands is a matter of
history and there can be no denying the Punic structure of the
language and a great deal of Punic tradition; but the bland assumption that Maltese history and the Maltese race begins with Phoenician (or Carthaginian) colonization is too easy. The megaliths of
Hal Tarxien and Hagar Qim, together with the innumerable other
Neolithic (and perhaps earlier) remains scattered thickly throughout the Maltese Islands all antedate the Phoenicians by hundreds
if not thousands of years. There are, too, remains which, while
clearly not Punic, are as clearly contemporary with those which
are. In other words, a Maltese race and a Maltese culture existed
long before the coming of the Phoenicians and survived, parallel
with them, while adopting their language. And it is a fact that
vestiges remain, in spoken Maltese, which philologists have been
unable to relate to any of the known influences—Semitic or
Indo-European—which have shaped the tongue.

Attempts to identify the 'First Maltese Race' have never been very
zealous, and an amateur may therefore be allowed his conjectures.

In the so-called Cart Tracks we have evidence of human activity
demonstrably earlier than the disappearance of the land-bridges
which once divided the Mediterranean at its centre. The tracks
remain a mystery about which a whole literature has developed
and it is improbable that we shall ever know what kind of men
made them, or, within centuries, when. Suffice it here to note that
a human race lived, dreamed, and had its being in these Islands
some ten thousand years before a naked and manless England
emerged from its womb of ice.

The cavern called Ghar Dalam—'The Cave of the Unknown'[1]—

---

[1] *Dlam* means 'Darkness' and I suppose that *Dalam* means 'Darknesses' or
'mysteries'. The word is not in general use. It has been suggested to me by a Maltese
scholar that *Dalam* means 'Elephants' in an ancient Syrian dialect. If this really is so,
we have the fascinating position that the cave, which was called Ghar Dalam by the
local people long before it was excavated, was known to contain the bones of elephants, although they were buried in a clay deposit many feet below solid rock. Can a
tradition possibly have survived so long?

has yielded the bones of pigmy elephants and a single human jaw-bone which may be Neanderthal. In Malta, as elsewhere, much evidence of the past which might now have been conclusive has been destroyed through ignorance, indifference, or superstitious fear. More than one country-field is called Ta' Ggant, and the farmers will tell you that Guzé's grandfather unearthed 'the bones of a giant'—and burned them. For it is well known that the remains of pre-Adamites are evil things. British military con-struction, too, has often obscured or destroyed antiquities of great value (though, to balance the account, it should be recorded that soldiers—and Sappers in particular—have contributed much by careful research).

However, Neanderthal settlements are common enough about the northern shores of the Mediterranean—Gibraltar is parti-cularly rich in this respect—and we may be entitled to assume that the rude flint-scrapers and the rough hand-axes which come to light in the so-called cave-tombs of the Maltese hill-sides were left by that unprepossessing fellow whom we call Neanderthaler.

Whether or not we put him forward as a candidate for the title of First Maltese Race is a moot point. The convinced evolutionists have doubted whether he was really *Homo sapiens* at all. Certainly he was an unlovely character, if the anthropologists' reconstruc-tions are to be credited; but he spoke, used fire, and buried his dead in a manner which suggests faith in a resurrection. On this latter count alone, we should not be ashamed to have him for ancestor. He is supposed by some authorities to have been exter-minated by an incursion of the comparatively highly cultured Cro-Magnons who wore clothing of a sort, used the bow, and made stone implements of amazing precision. Implements of this type, too, have been unearthed in Malta—though the nearest source of the flint from which they are fashioned is now distant from Malta by hundreds of miles of sea. Cro-Magnon may have floated logs on rivers; but he was definitely no seaman. The wheel was undiscovered until as late as 2000 B.C., and we know that Cro-Magnon used sledges. Perhaps, then, 'Cart Track Man' and the first Maltese was of that yellow-haired, grey-eyed, long-headed type which has been set upon a pedestal ever since a cynical French aristocrat, the Comte de Gobineau, pulled the legs of the Revolu-tionary pedants by inventing an Indo-European race which, as Toynbee has it, '. . . brought forth the religious genius of

Zarathustra, the Buddha, the artistic genius of Greece, the political genius of Rome and—fitting climax—our noble selves . . . !'

In 1949 an arrow-head of obsidian was found amongst the rubble which had covered the Temple of Hagar Qim for centuries. There is none of this very hard black flint in Malta; but there is plenty in Crete, and it is now known that the Cretan culture extended back to Neolithic times. The oldest levels of the temples of Hal Tarxien and Safflieni belong to a culture midway between the rudely decorated megaliths of Hagar Qim and the fine craftsmanship of the First Minoan culture. The low relief decoration and carved animal portraits are distinctly Cretan in character, as are the female figures traditionally called *Kabiri* and obviously associated with the worship of the Great Mother. The hair-style, the long, full skirt, and the uncovered bosom are characteristically Minoan. It is suggested that *Kabiri* is a latinized plural of *Kbir*— 'Great'. Hence, the 'Great Ones'. I have sometimes wondered whether there is not some connexion with the cult of Cybele—'L' and 'R' being commonly interchangeable. Herodotus refers to a cult of 'the Cabiri'; but he was too much the gentleman to risk giving offence by embarking upon religious discussion, so that we are left with only a vague notion of a fertility cult, and this the Maltese prehistoric faith clearly was; but Appolonius Rhodius also refers to the *Cabeiri*, who were, we gather, servants of Persephone who saved sailors from shipwreck. No more ideal site for their shrine than that of Hagar Qim can be imagined. Their cult, too, was Cretan in origin. At Hal Tarxien some of the finest, low relief carvings include a procession of long-horned goats. The wild goat with enormous horns is a symbol peculiar to the Cretan cult of Dionysius-Zagreus.

The Great Mother and the Bull figure largely in the art of these early Maltese and the themes of resurrection through the medium of a female deity as well as a Mithraic Bull are common in Maltese folk-lore, in guises which are unmistakably pre-Christian and pre-Roman. Of the old Cretan worship it has been said that not only is a prevailing spiritual essence discernible, but something in its followers akin to the faith that, for the last two millenia, has moved the adherents of successive Oriental religions, Iranian, Christian, and Islamic. . . . She (the Goddess) has clearly the power of giving life beyond the grave to her worshippers. The general conclusion is that we are, at Minos, in the presence of a large monotheistic cult in which the female form of the Deity held the supreme place. The comment is equally true of the Maltese Temple of Hal Tarxien.

To our shame, Italian interest in the archaeology of Malta has always been more careful and more intense than England's. The Italian savant Luigi M. Ugolini in his *Malta—Origini della Civilta Mediterranea* (1934) goes to vast lengths of enthusiasm. He describes Malta as a centre of a culture that goes back to the eighth millenium B.C.

Ex Oriente Lux, he says, should be replaced by *Ex Medio Lux*. As Crete had snatched cultural priority from Asia, Malta was to snatch it from Crete. He bases his conclusions on the material from the temple sites of Hal Tarxien, Hagar Qim, Mnajdra, and Gigantija (in Gozo). A great protagonist of the Cretan culture, Ugolini nevertheless believed that Malta, in the earliest Neolithic period, was literally the cultural and spiritual centre of the world. Very similar, though less emphatic, conclusions had been reached by Sir Themistocles Zammit and Dr. Ashby; but no one hitherto had quite gone to the enthusiastic lengths of Ugolini, who would have us believe, in effect, that Malta is really the cradle of civilization.

So far, then, as it is possible to define an Aryan or a Semitic race, the probability is that our original Maltese were a people of Aryan race and culture and language, until the decline of the Minoan thallasocracy and the rise of Phoenician sea power in about 1400 B.C.—in other words, the Islands were the home of an Aryan or Indo-Germanic stock for nine or ten thousand years. There followed two comparatively brief periods of Punic or Semitic ascendancy under the Phoenicians and Carthaginians, until the failure of Hannibal once more left the field clear for the Aryans. They predominated for eight centuries until the Moors and their Berber ancillaries (who are, be it noted, not of Semitic stock), under the Ummayad Caliphate occupied Malta—and a great part of southern Europe.

In A.D. 1090 the Moors were driven out by the impeccably Aryan Count Roger of Normandy (cousin of England's William).

The Roman period is as clearly attested as the Punic. Roman villas, baths, roads, sculpture are all as common in Malta as in Sicily, and the Roman occupation added more Aryan stock to the original race, for the Italic tribes—Oscans, Umbrians, Sabines, and Latins—were close kin to the Celts. More recent admixtures

—Norman, Aragonese, Angevin, French, German, English—still
further tipped the balance in the Aryan direction, so that, for what
it is worth (Neanderthaler was a European!) we may confidently
conclude that the Maltese today is of predominantly Aryan and
European stock, and no more mixed than most of us.

2

The matter of language is, perhaps, not so clear.

That Punic—or Aramaic—was spoken and written in Malta by
1000 B.C. seems clear from the 'Cippi' and from other evidence
like that of Hannibal's Tomb. St. Paul confirms for us that neither
Latin nor Greek was the tongue of the common people (he would
have had no difficulty in preaching to them in Aramaic). And the
Knights found them talking 'a sort of Moorish'. It has been
seriously contended that the origin of modern Maltese is no more
ancient than the Moorish occupation which covered a brief two
centuries during which Arabic was imposed upon the people by
their rulers. While it is perfectly reasonable to assume that the use
of a related tongue by ruler and ruled influenced the common
speech, the fact remains that Maltese contains Aramaic elements
which are absent from Arabic—except in the dialect of that tongue
most remote from Malta and where the original Aramaic survived
longest, in the Lebanon: where the people claim, with justice, to
be Phoenicians.

The language of the Gospels, in the rare instances of directly
recorded speech by Our Blessed Lord, is Aramaic. And every such
speech, allowing for the vicissitudes of differing alphabets, is also
Maltese.[1] Compare:

Aramaic	Maltese
(through Greek)	(through English)
Talitha Cumi	*Tifla Qum*
Ephtha	*Iftagh*
Eloi, Eloi, Lama	*Alla, Alla, Lala*
Sabachthani.	*Sabaqtni.*

We begin now to see the roots of the famous 'Language
Question' and its startling effect upon Anglo-Maltese relations
and local political thought.

[1] I lately came across an essay, by Annibale Preca, published in Malta in 1880,
called '*Saggio intorno alla Lingua Maltese come affine all'Ebraico*', which convincingly
propounds the theory Chaldaean=Hebrew=Aramaic=Maltese. Preca gives a
wealth of fascinating affinities between Hebrew and the Maltese current in his day.

Generations of Maltese, seeking a pride and an individuality to which recognition of their very ancient language seemed to entitle them, sailed under the banner of Punic origins. Devoted scholars succeeded in keeping alive—some would say artificially —their Aramaic speech and in presenting the language, which had certainly not been written between the dawn of the Christian era and the middle of the eighteenth century, as a language of literature. Historians, lexicographers, lawyers, and poets have all contributed, during the last century and a half, to build up a mass of written material of varying merit in this Aramaic revival, whose current orthography is the third or fourth attempt at standardization.

That Maltese is, indeed, a living tongue with a continuous spoken history of some thousands of years cannot be doubted; but neither can the claim that it has been and continues to be diluted and debased by foreign importations. There are so many of such imports in common use by the urbanized Maltese that a stranger may be forgiven for thinking the language nothing but a mixture. Nevertheless, the import is invariably so 'Punicized' as to become unrecognizable. In the argot which we may call Stewards' Maltese (which contains, perhaps, twenty-five per cent of Sailors' English) the words 'knife' and 'fork' are readily enough recognized; but I defy any Englishman to recognize *Najfijiet u Frieken*, which is the Semiticized plural of those homely words. Another strange Semiticization common amongst Maltese Servicemen is *Pajplih*—for what we now call 'Blanco' and was originally 'Pipeclay'.

Malti Safi—'Pure Maltese'—is taught in all the schools, and the lengths to which the purists will go have had the usual quaint results. Since 'airfield' is foreign, a 'pure' native word must be found, and the word *Mitjar*—a 'Flying Place' has been created from the root *tajra, it-tajar, it-tir*—'a bird', 'flying'. No one uses it except the poor schoolboy or the candidate for a Government appointment.

Sometimes, however, the purists are defeated. For obvious reasons, the ancient Aramaic has no word for 'chair', and the long-established usage has been *Siggu*—a corruption of the Italian *seggio*. The peasant, and pure, usage is quite plainly 'a place to put your bottom', and the purists retreat in confusion.

Admirable as is the brave struggle to save so ancient a language from extinction, the Maltese have fallen into the usual trap of failing to understand that if a language is to live it must constantly assimilate. There is no more marvellous an instrument of human expression than the English language—and none more filled with foreign importations. In the event, the semi-literate inventors of *Najfijiet u Frieken* have more of the essence of the matter than the scholarly inventors of *Mitjar*.

During what may be called the Italian Ascendancy in Malta, the use of Italian words was fashionable and a generation grew up interlarding its Aramaic mother-tongue with massacred Italian.

Since the peasant used only one spoon, the Punic *marfa* was good enough for him; but his urbanized daughter found it smarter to use *kuccarina* for teaspoon, *tazza* for glass, and so on.

The fashion has now changed and 'to discover' is *ghamel if-findout*, and things are not *kollox sewwa* but 'Okay'.

Either way, some murderous corruptions were spawned, and it may be a long time before they cease to jar or to excite ridicule.

Only once has a third theory of Maltese cultural origins been seriously advanced. Its inventor, in more senses than one, was the architect of the famous Mosta Church, one Giorgio Grognet de Vassée. His fascinating manuscript, called *Atlantide*, may be seen in the Royal Malta Library. In it, he proves to his own satisfaction that the Etruscans whose origins are still, admittedly, obscure, were the inhabitants of a now drowned land of Atlantis of which the Maltese Islands formed part; further, that the Maltese language was Etruscan and thus triumphantly senior to any Aryan or Semitic root. Grognet de Vassée became so obsessed with his theory that he faked an Etruscan 'Rosetta Stone'.

The fake deceived many scholars, for a short time; but detection came and Vassée was broken-hearted for he sincerely believed in his theory.[1]

The muddled association of race with language has continually bedevilled the Maltese scene. For obvious practical reasons, the

---

[1] The last century was prolific in archaeological fakes. One famous Egyptian fake was the work of a Maltese, Abbate Vella and another of a Syrian called Shapiro— though experts now wonder whether Shapiro's Aramaic 'Dead Sea Scroll' may not have been genuine.

I do not think there is any possibility that Vassée's 'Etruscan' inscription was genuine; but there is certainly some justification for his Atlantis proposition. Robert Graves, in his *Greek Myths*, has the following note:

'. . . the country of the Atlantians, mentioned by Diodorus Siculus . . . living to the Westward of Lake Tritonis. . . .

If then, Atlantis was Western Libya . . . (it) apparently once covered several thousand square miles of the Libyan lowlands; and perhaps extended northward into the Western Gulf of Sirte.'

people of these islands have always wished to avoid being labelled 'African', and while 'Punic' sounds better to prejudiced ears than 'Semitic' their language cannot, certainly, be called European. This sort of thinking has always inspired the defenders of Latin (recently Italian) culture, and it is the same rather silly snob complex which motivates the preference for speaking mutilated English in a family circle where Maltese comes more naturally.

The English Imperial authorities paid scant attention to what must have seemed a very unimportant domestic squabble until it became apparent that there were political implications dangerous to the British connexion. By the time England began to take a serious interest in the years after the First World War, the Italianate school had held the field for more than a century—and for sound enough reasons. Maltese Law was based principally upon Italian versions of Canon Law, of the Codes of the Grand Masters, and an Italian version of the Code Napoléon. It was practised by Italian-trained, Italian-speaking advocates.

Italian had been the language of polite society throughout the seventeenth and eighteenth centuries, and had continued to be so used under British rule. It was the language of music, poetry, art, and literature. Cultured Englishmen saw nothing wrong with this arrangement during a century when they, themselves, affected a certain Italianity and were much enamoured of the great figures of the *Risorgimento*.

Arguments for the use of Maltese as an official and legal tongue were met with the objections that this interesting but frozen survival could not be made the efficient vehicle of the Law and that it lacked all practical value internationally and, anyway, no one really knew how it should be spelled.

Such arguments were to be considerably weakened by the immense labours of patriots like 'Dun Karm' (the pen-name of Monsignor Psaila), who was responsible for a complete literature and for a body of poetry which goes far to demonstrate that Maltese is still capable of expressing the most complex of abstractions as well as the most earthy of exactitudes. We are forcibly reminded that another tongue of the Aramaic family, the classical Arabic of the Qur'ān, is regarded by millions as the veritable voice of Almighty God and that it was in Aramaic that Our Lord conversed with His Blessed Mother.

None of these considerations, however, served to stir England into any very decisive stand until Mussolini's efficient propaganda machinery began to influence the matter. The scales were now heavily weighted on the side of Latinity.

Fascismo, with its marching songs, its flattering uniforms, its generous scholarships, its cheap and excellently presented publications, and its arms, eloquently held wide to welcome Mother Italy's lost children of Roman Melita, found a ready response.

In those days a Maltese of Italianate background might go to bed a loyal citizen of the British Empire and awake to find himself wearing the label of an anti-British Italian Fascist. If he persisted in his English loyalty he was in danger of the alternative charge of treachery to his Mediterranean Motherland—*Italia Irridenta!* Many of the priesthood were innocent sufferers from this hysteria, for hysteria it was, though some small danger to the British connexion may possibly have existed.

Belatedly, Great Britain awoke to the international nuances which had always been inherent in the Language Question. She began to counter the Italian cultural drive with Rhodes scholarships, the British Council, more equitable conditions for Maltese Servicemen, British Trade Unionism and, most pointedly, with open recognition of the Punic legend. The Maltese were not fellow-Latins of the Hellenic-Roman tradition—they were now to be pure descendants of those magnificent rivals of Rome: Hamilcar, Hasdrubal, Hannibal, and the great navigator Hanno. The most improbable myths were dug up—Phoenician settlements in Cornwall—St. Joseph embarking in a Phoenician trireme as a ship's carpenter—even the 'English Celtic' Church reared its long discredited head.

The scholars of Aramaic were astonished to find themselves much cultivated and every encouragement was given to the propagation of *Malti Safi*, from which suspicion of Latin adulteration must be expunged. The orthography was revised so that the very un-Latin 'K' might replace the un-Punic 'CH' and the English 'J' cast out the Latin 'GI'. Streets and villages with time-honoured names were clumsily and hurriedly renamed and Gilbert and Sullivan rated a higher snob value than Verdi and Puccini.

And the Maltese countryman went on talking his own tongue in much the same form as St. Paul had heard it about that welcome fire of sticks from which the snake had emerged nineteen hundred years ago.

But the Language Question is not dead. A major political party is still referred to, in the English Press, as 'pro-Italian', and some of its supporters, still confusing language with race, refuse to submit to a synthetic background which they can only see as Arab-Semitic-African.

Certainly, no Maltese need be ashamed of his language. It was the great vehicle of Syriac civilization, linked by the cultures of Tyre and Sidon with the Minoan world and the Hellenism which is the parent of all European culture. Its script was used in India by Asoka for his Prakrit text and provided an alphabet for the Manchu Emperors. A variant of it is listened to daily by the millions of Islam as the veritable Voice of God and it was the common speech of those Galileans who gave to the Gentile world the message of eternal life.

The bounds of Aramaic speech encompassed, perhaps, more of mankind than we shall ever know. It was never the monopoly of any race, and no Maltese need fear that he is an African because he uses it.

3

All the evidence seems to point to a preponderantly Aryan stock speaking a unique survival of one of the world's oldest and proudest tongues.

It is not very difficult to see how this may have come about.

We know nothing of the speech of Cro-Magnon—who may have made the Cart Tracks. The language of Minos is too obscure, although I believe there is some evidence of Syriac origins and a Mycenaean script. With the Phoenicians and Carthaginians we are on firmer ground, and their language had a thousand years to take root. It was, at that time, the language of commerce, the lingua franca of the seas, and the men who spoke it were almost the only callers in the harbours of the Maltese Islands so that, even supposing the native stock to have spoken, originally, some quite different tongue, perhaps of the Indo-Germanic family, it would not be strange if Punic superseded it. More cogent than this, Polybius and Aristotle assure us that the Carthaginians were unique amongst their contemporaries in having a system of government which had no dominant caste. Their constitution was already one in which '. . . the masses had acquired the decisive voice in their society'. The retention, by native stocks in danger of domination by foreigners, of a 'secret' language is a common phenomenon; but the danger of obliteration, by Punic settlers, whose society knew nothing of caste, was absent. For every practical reason the Maltese would have adopted the highly developed, accurate, widely understood, and easily recorded speech of the Phoenicians and Carthaginians. In much the same way as they have (regardless of the Language Question) adopted English.

But from Roman times onward to our own day the Maltese have lived in danger of obliteration, as an identifiable people, at the hands of a dominant foreign caste and their one certainty of survival has been the retention of what had become their secret, native speech. And the less the outside world understood of it, the more effective it became for this purpose. Much the same factors have informed the survival of Welsh, Gaelic, and Erse.

No single foreign dominance has, so far, survived long enough to evict the Punic tongue and, while each ruling caste has contributed words, structures, and images to the native language, and while succeeding generations of Maltese have had to be bilingual or trilingual, Maltese has retained its identity in a manner which is truly amazing.

To summarize, then, as far as race and language can mean anything in the formation and survival of a people, I would tabulate my amateur findings thus:

Race	Language
500,000 B.C. Neanderthal	?
20,000 B.C. Cro-Magnon (Aryan)	?
10,000–2,000 B.C. Minoan (Mycenaean) (Aryan)	? Syriac
2000 B.C. Phoenician (Punic) ⎫ 200 B.C. Carthaginian (Punic) ⎬	Aramaic
200 B.C.–A.D. 700 Roman ⎫ Greek ⎪ (Aryan) Goth (Vandal) ⎪ Roman-Byzantine ⎭	Hellenic-Latin — Teutonic
A.D. 700–1100 Moorish	(Semitic) Aramaic root
A.D. 1100–1800 Norman ⎫ Angevin, Aragonese ⎪ Sovereign Order ⎬ (Aryan) (Italian-Spanish- ⎪ French-Portuguese- ⎪ English-German) ⎭	Latin-Teutonic
1800– English	Teutonic

And to approximate, the factors seem to produce known racial affinities of the order of ten parts Aryan to one part Semitic and the known linguistic affinities of five parts Aramaic to one part Aryan.

But this is, admittedly, a conclusion based on a series of guesses, and some more convincing evidence is necessary. For this we have the report of an ethnological survey carried out under Imperial Government auspices between the two world wars. The report concludes:

'The Maltese Race or Races may be derived roughly as follows:
(a) First Maltese Race (Early Stone Age)
    Mediterranean and akin to aboriginal British.
(b) Second Maltese Race (Late Stone Age)
    Armenoid or Indo-Germanic.
(c) Third Maltese Race (1500 B.C.)
    Punic.'

Scientific measurements of skulls and long bones from both long dead and living subjects indicate a predominance of the Indo-Germanic or Aryan type. The data preclude the possibility of this predominance being due to later admixtures of Nordic types, and we are left with the interesting conjecture that although the Semitic Phoenicians and Carthaginians were able to impose their language upon an Aryan stock, they were less successful in imposing physical change upon the earlier people.

The same investigation showed a complete absence of any Negroid strain except in isolated and imported instances, for example, amongst the bones of Turkish slaves.

4

For those who may find merit in the thought, it is possible, then, to picture the Maltese as 'almost an Englishman'. I will content myself with having persuaded my Civil Service friends that he is a European whose closest affinities are with his Italian neighbours. The blending of Nordic with Mediterranean stock has produced some very fine results, and the potentialities of the Maltese race remain largely unexploited in its modern ambience. The Italian proverb *'Inglese italianato, diavolo incarnato'* is a kind of compliment which is not irrelevant.

VII

FESTA—1926

FESTA—1926

'From quiet homes and first beginnings,
Out to the undiscovered ends
There's nothing worth the wear of winning
But laughter and the love of friends'.
(Hilaire Belloc)

IT was dark when I left the bus. The rest of my journey must
be made on foot. I was not sorry for the opportunity to
stretch my legs after a fourteen-mile journey from Valletta.
Certainly the driver had not lacked skill. The roads are excellent,
but there remain narrow streets in the country towns, twisting
and turning abruptly, to discover a herd of goats or a game of
football. The hazards had been taken at a speed and with a gay
insouciance which testified both to skill and to a minute knowledge of the route.

My companions did not share my anxiety, which must have
been evident at every lurch of the bus. Their faith in St. Christopher and the pilot sustained them where my heretic imagination
could only conjure up visions of a road strewn with casualties.
They were poor folk but very merry. Every departing passenger
had some titbit of news to impart or some joke to retail. They
examined me frankly but without rudeness. In spite of their
evident poverty, or perhaps because of it, my companions of this
bus ride had a natural grace and an irrepressible gaiety which, in
those days before I came to know them better, I found surprising.
I have not ceased to wonder—it is merely that I am no longer
surprised.

The little knot of passengers had dispersed, laughing and
shouting their 'Good nights' in the vernacular of the countryside.
A low moon, round and cheerful like a laughing, peasant face,
splashed with gold the still waters of the Bay of St. Paul. My way
lay inland, along a good road at first, and then by a narrow cleft
between high rocks, over the crest of a range of little hills. The

long shadows of a stone aqueduct beside the road fretted my path.
Everywhere there was stillness and quiet.

Once I passed a small, square farm-house in which there were
lights and cheerful voices. Then, again, there were only the
shadows, the moon, and a purple stillness.

Near the crest of the hill the road bent round a rugged pile of
limestone. I had hardly noticed, as I walked, that there were no
more precise stone walls and geometrical, cultivated fields. It may
have been the changing and deepening shadows which drew my
attention to the almost wooded nature of the hill-side. Thick
clumps of bushes and low trees grew close to the road and left
only a few patches of the high rock to gleam, silver in the moonlight. There were other things I noticed now, at this bend in the
road. There was a clean, sweet smell in the air. It might have been
thyme, or even heather. Somewhere near my feet there was running water. There, at the road's edge, ran a considerable stream.
It went babbling down the hill-side for all the world like a
Dartmoor brook. Cresses grew in it, and I could make out some
yellow wildflower growing thickly on its banks. The illusion of
a Dartmoor track was very strong until I remembered that it was
November and that here was I, coatless and quite warm from my
walking.

Still the illusion persisted. There was something in the shape of
the hills, in the form of the outcrops, in the stillness, in the very
air, which had about it the same quality of faerie as lies on a Tor-
side dotted with hut-circles. I did not then know that I stood very
near a spring as old as time, whose waters had sustained the
ancestors of the men who piled the burial-mounds of my native
moor.

I had pondered long enough. There was a definite nip in the
air now. I walked on and, as I came round the bend in the road,
it was as if I had walked into another land. The valley which lay
spread out before me was so unexpected in this island of arid
rock—as I had been led to believe. The description with which
I had been furnished and which had led me so far had been fair
enough; but this island within an island, of trees and running
water, seemed too fair to be true.

The villa which was my destination stood on the opposite hill-
side. Its many windows were bright with light. Voices carried
across a pool of shadowed trees. A little above the villa, and to its

right, was another building which I knew for the chapel. The road which joined villa and chapel was embroidered with lights whose flames bobbed and flickered in the gentle evening breeze. I took them for candles; but I later saw them to be earthenware lamps, exact replicas of the Roman lamps which you will see in museums and filled, as the Romans filled them, with oil and salt. Herodotus describes just such festive illuminations at the Egyptian city of Saïs in 500 B.C.

The voices from the house ceased and a new sound mingled with, rather than broke, the pleasant quiet. As I went down into the valley the sound grew clearer. I reached an iron gate which was flung wide open. Coming down the hill from the opposite direction was the procession, intoning a slow, melodious chant. At the head marched one bearing a Crucifix. Priests, monks, and a concourse of men, women, and children whom I took for peasants followed. By the light of the great candles which they carried I was able to study their faces. On every face—and there were faces of many kinds—there sat content.

The central figure—the priest carrying the Reliquary—was to be my host. He had the carriage of a soldier and the face of a kindly Augustus.

I sat on my small suitcase in the shadow and watched them file through the gates. It was my first experience of these matters. I half believe that I had expected something awe-inspiring; but these folk, slowly marching behind the banner of their Faith, were like soldiers trooping their colour, only that they looked more as if they enjoyed it.

After Benediction in the little chapel, with its Spanish campanile, I met the family—the nieces and nephews of the good priest who was both shepherd and squire of this happy valley. They made me so much at home within five minutes that I have never thought of any of them since by so distant a name as 'friend'.

The villa was a rambling affair. Its older parts must have known St. Paul. The new portions were no older than the early seventeenth century, and the great dining-room—more than half the width of the house—had lately been added.

All was bustle and preparation for the Feast on the morrow. Servants there were in plenty, and to spare, but everyone lent a hand. Everyone talked at once and all waited on each other.

In the kitchen there were the gifts of the peasants—chickens, eggs, vegetables—for at the season of the Feast all make their offerings to the villa. I have called them peasants—how often is an 'alien' gently but firmly rebuked for talking of 'peasants': 'We have no peasants in England!' It would have been better had I said 'tenant farmer', for these stout toilers have a pride and a tradition in their different way comparable to those of our own yeomen.

Presuming upon my host's good nature, I stayed some time in the kitchen. All the cooking was achieved in a tiled stone range, over charcoal. Only once before had I seen such a range—in the dead city of Pompeii. The charcoal is kept at white heat in the saucer-shaped grates by hand-fans, cunningly wielded in front of the round vents with which each grate is separately provided. In order that the sturdy, barefooted kitchen-girls might not be kept at a distance from their work by the flat front of the stove there were, at intervals, footshaped hollows at the base of the tiled range.

Above the laughter and chatter of the barefooted cooks in this Pompeian kitchen there rose the steady beat of a motor which generated the estate's electric light. This archaic kitchen, then, was maintained neither from necessity nor from a lack of knowledge of better things. A same blending of old and new, a hesitation to discard the well-tried friend for the chromium-plated modern, I saw everywhere in the valley.

Before supper there was every sort of *vinetto*, from the good new wine of the country to pink gin for my own vitiated palate. The priests and the friars drank sparingly but with evident enjoyment. The Franciscans, who had come for the procession and would sing High Mass on the morrow, were shy with one exception. Fra Piu, with his Puck's face and his well-filled brown habit, would have served excellently as a model for the merry monk. He was plainly something of a public character and court jester. My host would rebuke him, with mock severity, and Fra Piu would feign deep concern, only to convulse the company with some new quip.

I understood not one syllable, and the jokes lost their point when translated; but I laughed as heartily as any, for the laughter was of that fine, infectious quality which is its own excuse for more laughter.

How many we sat down to supper I have forgotten. There

cannot have been less than twenty of us. First, my host, his somewhat stern, fine features relaxed in a constant boyish smile of good
humour. Then Pappa and Mamma. He, cheerfully stout and an
unashamed gourmet; she, petite and still consciously attractive at
fifty. Their six children—the three nephews and three nieces—
completed the family. Then there were the two visiting priests
and the Franciscans.

Conversation, partly from courtesy to me and partly because
the younger generation spoke that language among themselves,
was carried on mainly in English; but there were at least four other
languages being spoken at one time around that very hospitable
table. All, as far as my tongue-tied Englishry could tell me, were
spoken perfectly. The Franciscans spoke English slowly, in the
stilted fashion of men with a wide acquaintance with the English
of books and little with its colloquialisms. The priest used Italian
to some extent. All lapsed frequently into their native Maltese.

My neighbour, a lovely brunette whose clipped and accurate
speech had been learned from the patrician Mothers of the Sacred
Heart, was at pains to translate everything. From her I learned the
first of many lessons in the ways of these strange, new, and
entirely charming folk; but such things as are held in high esteem
outside the valley none of the family ever told me.

I was left to discover that my host's soldierly bearing came
from more than forty years' army service, that he had a distinguished war record, that he was rich but lived frugally and gave
unstintingly. Pappa, an unassuming and indulgent father, had
been honoured by all the countries in Europe, and stood high in
the counsels of princes and governors.

The food was as new, as strange to me and, if such a thing were
possible, as delightful as the people. Few soups in the world are
as good as Maltese soup. None is better. That soup smelt like the
gipsy's stew in *The Wind in the Willows*: 'Also smells—warm, rich,
and varied smells—that twined and twisted and wreathed themselves at last into one complete, voluptuous perfect smell that
seemed like the very soul of Nature taking form and appearing to
her children, a true Goddess and Mother of solace and comfort....'

The fish I would never have recognized as the despised
lampuka. Cooked as those laughing girls had cooked it, with a
sauce in which I detected, amongst many unknown flavours,
capers and thyme, it was not unlike the best of Dover soles. There

were *cervelli* in a rich jacket of beaten eggs, the tenderest of casseroled capons, endives, stuffed paprika—all richly flavoured and cooked with butter. There were pickled tomatoes, very hot, fresh white lettuces, tender young sweet turnips, eaten as we eat radishes, and something that looked like celery but had a sharp, sweet taste. Amongst the cheeses were small, round goat cheeses, pickled and seasoned with black pepper, called *gbejniet*, they told me.

I had never tasted Maltese bread. It is made from a coarse glutinous grain, and though it has what we should call a bad colour, it is rich in nourishment and has an excellent flavour. Its thick, brown crust is crumbed with fine seeds whose nutty taste gives it a distinctive character.

There were French and Italian wines, but I thought the 'raw' product of the valley's own grapes at least as good. They called it *imbid*.

We went early to bed.

They had put me in a room facing down the valley, with a little balcony, from which I could almost touch the feathered needles of a tall pine. The moon, higher now in her purple track, shone most wonderfully through the delicate lace of the tree, while her second self danced on the water of a softly playing fountain beneath my window. In the valley was a dim, green place of trees, and the scent of oranges came up to me and mingled with the sweet, homely smell of the mountain pine.

The only sound was a distant song of running water. My cabin, penned in by the towering bastions of the Grand Harbour, echoing at intervals to the heavy tread of a sentry's boots and the raucous hails of the quarter-master, seemed far away. Yet it was to that other life and not here that I belonged. Soon I must escape the witchery of that bright-eyed Calypso who had been my neighbour at supper; but I vowed, as I fell asleep, that I would return to this valley of laughter and simple Faith.

The sun, streaming through latticed windows, aroused me soon after dawn. A pink haze lay over the Bay of St. Paul and on the hill-sides. There were silvery-grey olives and deep green carob trees on the hill-side where I had paused last evening. In the valley the dimness had flowered into a kaleidoscopic brightness where groves of lemons, tangerines, and oranges divided a number of little fields into a crazy patchwork. The earth was red, like Devon earth. No artist could have exaggerated the morning colours of the valley. A score of different greens were there. The hue of the orange leaves, the sheen of palms, the darker leaves of the root crops and, peeping through, the many yellows of the fruit and the red-brown of the soil.

Even the patches of barren rock were gay with gentle narcissi and the fierce flame of prickly pear in flower. There were purple convolvulus, too, and flowering rock-plants unknown to me.

Early as it was, the house was astir and there was a grateful smell of fresh-roasted coffee.

There came a knock at my door. It was dark Calypso, bearing a tray with a steaming coffee-pot and slices of new, nutty bread. The maids, she said, were much too shy to enter the room of a strange young man. I was glad of their shyness.

The family were to attend Low Mass at seven o'clock. Afterwards they would breakfast. I might like to go for a walk and meet them after Mass at the chapel. There would be High Mass later, at ten. I finished the coffee, bathed in soft spring-water, dressed, and stepped into a world of gay sunlight.

Goldfish capered in the fountain and sparrows held shrill argument in the trees. The sound of running water led me down a flight of winding steps into the heart of the valley.

As I followed a narrow track, beaten hard by generations of bare, peasant feet, there was a flash of blue against the green of the thick foliage overhead. Had someone told me twenty-four hours earlier that there were kingfishers in Malta I should have laughed. The stream rose somewhere deep under the hill, reaching the light at the mouth of a small cavern and bubbling gaily and untrammelled for some way until it reached a square marble pool where the Romans had harnessed and confined it to a network of aqueducts carrying its sweet water all over the valley.

In the marble tank was a golden carp nearly two feet long. He was not too old to bully the smaller fish nor to chase the blue dragon-flies as they paused in their erratic play.

As I came up again to the high ground I saw the hills and the roofs of the chapel, the villa, and the small, square homes of the farmers a-flutter with bunting. Jacks, the white and yellow Papal flag, the red and white of the Maltese national flag, were everywhere. On the chapel road I examined the earthenware lamps with their tallow fuel. They are called *musbieh*.

In the small priest's house adjoining the chapel the family

awaited me. The good Father who had just said Mass (for my host would celebrate the High Mass at ten) was breakfasting. His breakfast had been sent up from the villa, and he seemed much concerned that he had nothing to offer me under what was, for the time, his roof, save his own simple meal. I had difficulty in refusing it.

The peasants were gathered in groups about the doorway of the chapel, where crimson draperies and green palms proclaimed the *Festa*. They gossiped happily of crops, the weather, animals, and market prices, as farmers will the world over.

The older men wore suits of dark cloth, open-necked shirts, and stout sandals. One only, an old man who was the obvious doyen of the tenants, wore a hat of black felt. The rest wore cloth caps. The younger men had no coats, and wore their waistcoats un-buttoned over their bright shirts. Around their waists they had striped cummerbunds of many folds.

The women had voluminous skirts, blouses which would have been gaudy in another place, and the inevitable black silk *faldetta*. Only the girls and the children wore shoes and stockings—un-comfortably, I suspected. The little girls were very much in their Sunday best. Much time and trouble had been spent on them, I guessed. My charming Calypso explained how all the bright linens of the little frocks had been hand-spun by busy mothers. The uncomfortable shoes had been bought with hard-saved pennies, and would be handed on to younger sisters from *Festa* to *Festa*. The bright ribbons in the well-brushed hair were carefully hus-banded, too. The hair had occupied much attention. Two days before the feast each little girl's head had been subjected to a vigorous scrubbing and the fine hair twisted, still wet, into the stiffest of pigtails. This morning it had been released, tied with ribbons, and brushed out. The victims looked as if they thought the uncomfortable process well worth suffering.

They were a sturdy lot, these peasants, broad of shoulder and deep of chest, burned nut-brown by the fierce summer sun, with curling hair and wide, grey eyes. They had the slow, certain movements of dwellers near the soil and the ready laughter of contentment. Not all were dark. There were girls with hair as golden as a Norwegian's, and few of them had dark eyes. The family joined them in their gossip, laughed with them, and shared their family concerns. There was no air of district visiting. The

Senjur was father to his people in a sense other than spiritual; more, he was brother to them.

The eldest nephew, who had got a Blue at Oxford, was having some private joke with a group of chuckling ruffians of his own age; his modulated Oxford periods were no more; he used the broad gutturals and eloquent gestures of the country. Pappa, who had lately addressed an international audience at the Sorbonne, was having a heated argument with an old farmer—about the price of pigs, I gathered.

Here, on the one hand, was a stronghold of feudalism—'lord' and 'lady' are the nearest equivalents to the *senjur* and *senjura* by which the peasants knew and addressed the family, with uncovered head, yet, without loss of either affection or respect, this friendliness and freedom of intercourse was possible.

Outside the valley, I did not always find this quality. What is called progress is killing it.

Breakfast was an English meal, except that English coffee is never as good. The native honey, too, was excellent. My host did not eat with us as he had not yet said Mass. In spite of the early hour at which he had risen, fasting seemed to cause him no discomfort, and he was very far from young. He smoked though, interminably, pungent Turkish cigarettes. If this be vice, then it was his only one, for in the many years during which I was to enjoy his friendship I could discover no other.

Sacks of nuts and packages of a sort of nougat, which they called *Qubajt*, were being got ready for distribution to the peasants. No feast of the Saint who is patron of the valley would be complete without nuts.

There were the prizes for the afternoon's races to be allocated, sorted, and ticketed. The *Xorti*—'Lucky Dip' was the nearest I could get to it—to be prepared. The banners (*palji* they called them), which would be the much-coveted prizes for the donkey-races, to be unpacked.

Soon it was time for the High Mass. The chapel road, the two main roads, and the countless footpaths were full of hurrying, laughing country folk. Some came on foot, some rode in gaily painted *karrettuni*—flat carts without springs or seats, upon whose jolting wood whole families sat in seeming ease. Every mule and donkey wore his *Festa* costume. Their manes and tails were plaited and beribboned. About their necks they wore collars of bright reds, blues, and yellows. Their harnesses had been polished so that the sunlight clothed them in flames and, as they trotted, their plumes of feathers waving and their brilliant mule-cloths swinging, there was the music of dozens of little bells. They carried their happy burdens blithely churchwards as if they, too, were holding a *Festa*.

At the earlier Mass there had been only the tenants of the valley. Now there were folk from all the surrounding countryside— uncles, aunts, cousins, relations by marriage—many from considerable distances and one urbanized young man from Valletta, with a waisted coat and pointed shoes.

The little church was filled to its crimson-draped door. Numbers of men and boys knelt outside; the later arrivals must have been as much as fifty yards distant from the door, yet they genuflected towards the hidden altar before kneeling on the hard and rocky roadway.

Inside, the air was murmurous with the quiet prayers of the peasants. I found myself kneeling beside a figure of the Christ, crowned with thorns. Time had mellowed the original, peasant Christ. At His feet lay a little bunch of wild flowers, such as a child might gather.

The black hoods of the women, the bright shirts and sashes of the men, the prayers that sounded like Arabic, held a suggestion of the East. I could not help thinking that these people were of the sort to whom the Master had first spoken, in a speech very like theirs.

In front of me a mother rocked her baby in her arms as she prayed, '*Sliema Ghalik Marija . . .*' to the Mother and then, '*Missierna Li Inti Fis-Mewwiet . . .*' 'Our Father . . .' To her the Holy Family needed no preaching. Her daily life, her home, the donkey which had brought her here this morning, were all such as They had known. There was no dread mystery for this woman, with her child held close to her breast as she prayed.

The altar was splendid with flowers. The three little acolytes were proud in their red cassocks and snow-white cottas. Incense from a single thurible wreathed slowly about bowed, dark heads. The moving prose of the Latin rite had its full dignity in the deep male voices of the friars. Very priestly, very fatherly, was the sincerity of my host as he offered Mass. . . .

Ite Missa est. Benedicat vos omnipotens Deus,
Pater, et Filius, et Spiritus Sanctus . . . Amen.

The Mass is over. By twos and threes the people file out into bright sunlight.

The sacks of nuts and the packets of sweet nougat have been brought up from the villa. The people file past by families, and Mamma distributes the simple gift, measuring carefully by handfuls. The peasants take each one his share with as much gravity and gratitude as if the nuts had been of gold. A toddler is sharply rebuked for an attempt to get a second helping. What if his greed should deprive some other small person of his share? No one could tell me the origin or the exact symbolism of this custom. It was very old, they said.

As we went down to our lunch the peasants who did not live in the valley were gathered by families on the open hill-sides, preparing the meals which they had brought. Some lit fires and warmed cans of thick *minestra*, others had stews and *ravjuli*; but most were content with round loaves, anchovies, olives, tomatoes, and oil. As I watched them with their loaves and fishes, squatting in groups on the hill-side, I remembered again that other people who had been well content with loaves and fishes on the hill-side by Galilee.

Lunch at the villa was as gay and delectable a meal as supper had been last evening. Fra Piu, undeterred by the presence of a Canon and the Superior of His Order, who had joined us, was in great form.

We were all happy. Happiest of all was my host, whose boyish smile was ever at its broadest when he could make others happy.

The races, in the afternoon, run over a stony, uphill stretch of the chapel road, were some of the strangest I have ever seen. The division of the entrants into their proper classes, by age, presented much difficulty. They counted their age by tens. One oldish man could get no nearer than 'five tens since the year of the great storm'. Luckily the family knew the tenants well enough to hazard fair guesses in every case.

They removed their sandals and ran in bare feet. The waisted young man from Valletta, with his pointed shoes, was left at the post.

The donkey-race was the event of the day. The sturdy little brutes, well groomed and glossy with good feeding, were led to the post by proud owners and mounted by the smallest of little boys, ridden on a snaffle without saddle or stirrups. I had been told that these people were not always kind to their animals. I saw no sign of cruelty or of anything but a real affection between man and beast. Dark Calypso assured me that some of the men thought more of their animals than of their womenfolk. Such things were, I replied gravely, not unknown in my country.

When a donkey stumbled on the stony track there were many willing hands to help him. Eager supporters swarmed on to the course and almost carried their fancies past the post. Very irregular, it seemed; but as they all did it and no one minded it mattered little.

There was more excitement over the *Xorti*. Tickets were distributed and prizes drawn from a tub. Very sensible prizes they were—things much valued by the people, but classed as luxuries upon which they would not themselves spend hard-won pence —knives of English steel, cloth for dresses, *Festa* shirts, leather belts.

More guests had arrived at the villa. Suave Maltese society, svelte Italians, the Services—all very charming folk, but I could not help thinking that few of them had any sympathy with the life of the valley. A distinguished Admiral presented the prizes. Little Zeppu would treasure that damask banner to show to his grandchildren and tell them how he had got it from the hands of a live English Admiral.

Cocktail-time at the villa, with expensive cars drawn up by the fountain, Paris frocks, and the clever, cosmopolitan talk over dry Martinis, seemed to jar on the simple realities of the valley. The sudden dusk fell, and my dark Calypso escaped with me to a hilltop where we watched the fireworks which so pleased the peasants. With each new rocket there was a distant 'Eeee' of delight. They called for *trikki trakki*—crackers that sound like machine-gun fire —*Mignuna*—literally 'The Mad One', a sort of rocket, until there were no more to be had.

The night was quiet again as the last car purred townwards. The lamps of the *karrettuni* jogging homewards winked on the road. There was the trilling of a guitar and a man's voice raised in plaintive song. It was one of the *ghanja*, country songs, he was singing, Calypso said. Each village has its bard, who memorizes these endless, traditional stories, told in rhyming verse, of old wars, loves, and hates. Calypso told me the story of the *ghanja* as its wailing notes faded in the distance and the quiet moonlight.

There was something about it of 'Magic casements, opening on the foam. . . .'

As I looked down into the dimness where the kingfisher was and the ancient carp in his Roman tank, I knew that the valley would always call me.

Walking in the good rain across '. . . the brown, splintered, haunted moor', a voice has said:

> . . . I know an island
> Where the slow fragrant breathing nights creep past;
> And there, 'twixt lowland and highland,
> A deep, fern-shrouded, murmurous water glimmers;
> There I'll come back at last,
> And find my Friends.

VIII

SONGS

SONGS

'A wildness which is not without its romantic beauty and harmony. . . .'

(G. P. Badger)

ATALE is told of the poetess who was quite overcome by the beauty of a Polynesian song, appropriately rendered by a bronze faun whose guitar correctly 'stabbed the night's brown savagery with pain'. On asking that the song be translated for her, her faith in beauty was rudely shaken by the discovery that it consisted simply of the reiterated statement, 'Oh! Lord, I am so drunk. Oh! Lord, I am so drunk.'

I feared something of this sort when I first asked the meanings of some of the quaint chants which I had heard in the Maltese countryside. The trilling of a distant guitar. Silver moonlight and the purple and gold curtain of Maltese night. Strong peasant voices. Haunting, half-Oriental airs, something between the *Cante honda* of Andalusia and the rhythmic wail of Tunisia. These were deceitful trappings, well calculated to clothe even a primitive bawdiness in spurious beauty.

But the beauty was there. It took a little finding. Often what sounded like an impassioned love-song turned out to be an unflattering portrait of a local politician. A song which seemed to hold all the sadness of centuries told only the tale of a wedding-feast which gave all the guests indigestion—sparing few details!

The peasant of Malta is an incurable rhymester. No incident is too trivial to be recorded in rhyme. Not long ago two peasants would carry on a long conversation in rhyming quatrains for the mere fun of the thing. The very ancient origin of this pastime (the technical name for which is 'Amoebaean') is beyond dispute. Virgil, in *Eclogue*, III, 59, has the line:

'*Alternis dicetis; amant alterna Camenae:*'
'Alternate song delights the Muses'

and E. V. Rieu, in his Essays on the *Eclogues*, adds that Virgil here 'comes nearer than in any part of his book to the type of extemporary contest with which we can suppose the real shepherds of the ancient world to have amused themselves during the long days among Arcadian or Sicilian hills'.

The ease and speed with which rhyming and punning lampoons were produced to be sung in the fields and village streets is only comparable to the English and American facility for producing topical stories of the variety known as 'smut'. Here is what was said of the matter by an English observer one hundred years ago:

> The Maltese have the peculiar talent for poetry which is natural to all those nations who speak the Arabic [*sic*] language. The taste for this kind of composition has very much degenerated in the cities, but in the country it is met with in its original purity of style and expression. I have often stood and listened to individuals seated upon two opposite trees, or engaged in some kind of labour, singing answers to each other in rhyme, without any previous meditation. This the natives call *taqbeel*. The subjects vary according to circumstances, sometimes partaking of the nature of epic poetry, and sometimes of satire upon the faults or character of each. The tunes set to these are in general somewhat wild, as is the music of the Maltese in general, but a wildness which is not without its romantic beauty and harmony. In this respect, few will fail to admire the singing of the natives as they join in small companies, each taking a part, which they maintain throughout the whole performance.
>
> I here subjoin two songs for the amusement of the reader, with a rough English translation, in order that he may judge somewhat of such amorous effusions [Maltese originals omitted].

> Beloved, I'm about to leave you,
> I sigh that I take you not with me.
> May God give you now resignation,
> And preserve you secure in my love,—
>
> And preserve you secure in my love,
> That you ever remember me;—
> Remember, I always have loved you;
> Since the time I was but an infant—
>
> Since the time I was but an infant,
> My heart has always been drawn after you
> And I can work in no other light,
> But the light of your beautiful eyes.—
>
> In the light of your beautiful eyes,
> I have always directed my steps;—
> Beloved I'm going to leave you,
> I sigh that I take you not with me.—
>
> How sore does the pain come upon me,
> When I think I must soon depart;
> But if Heaven be propitious, my dear,
> We shall yet enjoy one another.

The following verses, which were furnished me by a Maltese lady, I insert chiefly for the sake of giving the reader an idea of the manner in which matrimonial alliances are entered into by a portion of the towns-people. The four persons introduced in the song are the young man, the *Hottaba*, the mother of the young woman, and the young woman herself. In order to render the piece intelligible, it will be necessary to premise that it is not customary for a young man unacquainted with the lady with whom he has fallen in love to declare his passion in person neither would he be allowed to enter into her parents' house; but he employs a third, generally an old woman, who takes upon herself the office of endeavouring to bring about the match. This character is called a *hottaba*, and is always possessed with an exquisite gift for flattery, a specimen of which will be readily noticed in the song; I give a literal translation, in order better to preserve the native idiom and phraseology.

Introducer.
> Would you know what a maiden does,
> From morning until evening?—
> She adorns her head with curls
> And seats herself in the balcony.

> She seats herself in the balcony,
> And sets about making love;
> When she sees her mother coming,
> She begins hemming her handkerchief.

> The young man walks up and down,
> To see if the old woman is there,
> He traverses (the street) from one end to the other,
> As he does not wish to remain with the smell.[1]

> He meets with an old grandmother,
> And says: 'Woman will you help me,
> I care nothing about money,
> So as that you are able to serve me?'

The bargain is struck, and the brokeress goes to the house of the young woman, and meets with the mother.

Hottaba.
> Madam, I think I know you,
> When quite little you lived near me,
> How oft I bore you, how oft I lov'd you,
> How oft I fondled you in my arms.

> Madam, I think I know you,
> I think you have several maidens,
> For as I was passing through the street,
> I saw one standing at the door.

> Madam, tell me what ails you
> For you appear very melancholy?

Mother.
> Do you know what they say of my daughter
> That she is already in love.

[1] A Maltese idiom for expressing failure in an undertaking.

Hottaba.

> Be easy, Madam, be easy,
> People's tongues say many things;
> Your daughter is a good girl,
> Whoever takes her will gain a fortune.

Mother.

> Come down, my daughter, come down,
> Here's a grandmother desires to see you,
> She is a very old woman,
> And with her words she will console you.

(The daughter descends and the old woman addresses her.)

Hottaba.

> A message I have brought you,
> And wish one hastily in return,
> For the beloved of your heart has sent me,
> Who with pain is now quite ill.

Daughter.

> A message you have brought me,
> A hasty answer I will not give,
> For my mother knows this young man,
> And will not have him for my husband.

Besides the above, the Maltese have also a large number of proverbs, or adages in rhyme, many of which preserve their strict original. These are still often used in conversation, but without any new additions, as the taste for such compositions has greatly degenerated since the introduction of the Italian language.[1]

There is also a considerable body of verse by such patriots as 'Dun Karm' (the philologist and linguist Monsignor Psaila) which strives to present the native genius within academic patterns. Such native poets have striven, too, to redress the degeneration to which Badger refers in his *Itinerary*.

Although Badger was wrong to write as if the Italian language were a comparatively recent import in 1840, it is true that the process of latinization had long been obscuring the essentially Semitic shape, anyway amongst the lower orders, of thought and imagery.

As far as I am able to judge, these national poets have fallen between the two stools of Maltese purism and Italianate structure (which is also English structure). Their work has also been much trammelled by the almost puritan attitude of Maltese Catholicism. A Maltese John Donne would be unthinkable even today. Or, if he existed, his work would never see public print. Once exclude Profane Love from the poet's vocabulary, then nothing

[1] G. P. Badger, *An Itinerary of Malta and Gozo* (1840).

short of the inspired genius of a Hopkins or a St. John of the Cross can flourish, and no one pretends that Malta has yet produced either.

Bradley in his *Malta and the Mediterranean Race* concludes that the Maltese are unoriginal. He says '. . . in their art they are clever and ingenious copiers, but in their work there is no restraint, no impelling artistic power, no reserve'.

If he is to escape from a unique, archaic intellectual environment, the Maltese must copy. It is well enough to pontificate about 'impelling artistic power' when there is no economic pressure: a pressure so acute in this case as to spell survival or starvation. Even poets are sometimes influenced by such thoughts, and painters, sculptors, and lesser craftsmen must at least buy their materials. So the general run of Maltese artificers has copied.

If we are to seek the true and original thought of the people we must then look to the simple, spontaneous productions of the holiday mood, the idle moment, amongst the unlettered peasantry.

I have attempted to render one or two of these little songs into English. That I have failed to do them justice I have no doubt at all. My aim was to show the kind of thoughts which are continually being crystallized in neat verse, and translated into swinging, wailing song by people who can neither read nor write, and who do not know that poetry is written in books. These songs which I have tried to express in English were first told to me by someone of the peasant class—shyly, apologetically, as is the way of such simple people when speaking of their own folks.

Imagine, if you will, a hill-side honeycombed with low, dark cave-dwellings. There is little vegetation here and a pitiless sun beats down upon unkind rocks. Within the cave-dwellings there is little that is pleasant but a welcome coolness and darkness. Here is a song of the people who call the caves 'home':

> They say my beloved is not comely.
> Very lovely he is to me.
> He cometh in by the doorway
> And the cave is bright.
> He goeth out by the doorway
> And the road is beautiful.

The Maltese maid who first put that thought into words can never have read or heard the Canticle of Canticles, yet is there not a distant echo of the same feeling? Indeed, a surprising amount of Biblical parallel is to be found in the Islands generally. The country scene, with its clustered, flat-roofed houses; its cave-dwelling, cave-tombs, and rock-hewn stables; its riot of spring-time colour, followed by the naked glare of summer, is strangely like the Holy Land. This is a land, too, which has the same air 'of having known too much'.

I have no knowledge of Hebrew verse or its structure and my translations are simply translations. Neither the rhythm nor the rhyme bear any relation to the original; but I have a suspicion that renderings by a Hebrew scholar might, in most cases, better convey the feeling of the Maltese originals.

Returning to our songs, here is a song of mourning:

> Here, by your moonlit tomb, I kneel and pray
> And yet, you are not dead.
> You are a bird, who,
> From the broken cage which was my heart,
> Is fled.

The picture of a fountain playing in the villa courtyard while the sun-baked fields wait for water is, perhaps, more common than it should be. Here is that picture used to describe the impatience of the maid at her lover's shyness. It is still not unusual for the shy lover to serenade his love.

> First love is shy. Courage has taken wings.
> To call his courage back, the lover sings.
> He is the distant fountain, sighing.
> She the parched field, for water dying.

Rhyme is used, too, to record the often cynical advice of Age to Youth. The following might, perhaps, be called 'Disillusion':

> When first I loved you, dear, the Wind,
> Whispered strange, lovely things to me.
> Now I'm grown old—and deaf.

Then there is this quaint simile:

> Pay not your court, young man,
> To all sweet maids.
> They're not like patches on your trousers' seat
> Which you may change at will.

There is a proverbial truth here:

> As the bitter almond
> Though the shell be cracked, sour is the nut.
> So is a maiden,
> Though her heart be won, her mind's fast shut.

Here is a lament which shows European (possibly Italian) influence:

THE FORSAKEN MAIDEN

You were the lightning. I was the riven skies
You were the tempest, I was the tree that dies.
Dark like the heavens my eyes, my tears the falling
    rain.
The storm and the brightness are passed.
Your love was too swift to last.
She will be smiling, clad in her trailing white.
There will be laughter and dancing, that bridal night.
I shall go up, alone, to the Hill of the Lonely Dead
And dig with my hands a place for my restless head.
There with the waters of Death
I shall still my sobbing breath.

There are many more of these little songs and countless longer chants of the epic kind. They await an abler pen than mine to render them into worthy English.

That there is a Khayyám somewhere hidden amongst the hamlets of those sun-drenched Islands may be too much to hope. If this were so, I am, alas, no FitzGerald. Perhaps, though, these lines may some day catch the eye of an idle English poet who may find the peasant songs not unworthy of his pen.

APPENDIX

A Note on Maltese Spelling

THROUGHOUT these essays I have attempted to render Maltese words in a form which will be at least recognizable to a Maltese.

Since the only dictionary available to me is one which uses an archaic orthography (based upon Italian phonetics) I may have erred dismally in the sight of the exponents of *Malti Safi*, or 'Pure Maltese'; but since, too, most of my Maltese friends take truly Elizabethan liberties with their spelling—if and when they write Maltese at all—perhaps I shall be forgiven.

To avoid typing and printing difficulties in England, I have not attempted to use the Maltese alphabet.

The difficulty of devising an 'English' alphabet for a Semitic language will be obvious, and I have also touched, in these essays, upon the shifting political bias which has further complicated an already confused problem. Nevertheless, an anglicized alphabet has been devised and since 1934 has been slowly but surely stabilizing (different versions of the same word nowadays rarely appear in the vernacular Press and all textbooks and reputable periodicals are standard). It is now possible for an Englishman with little or no knowledge of the language and only a superficial acquaintance with Italian vowel-sounds to make a fair shot at reading and pronouncing Maltese proper names, public notices, and the like, provided always that he does not expect the spelling always to have English values or the stresses always to be on the same syllables as they would be in English.

If he neglects these provisions, he may find himself wondering, as did a friend of mine, 'Who on earth is this chap Tid Hoakes? He seems to own the Island!' He was referring to the common traffic sign *Tidholx*, which means 'No Entry' and is pronounced 'Titholsh'.

The Maltese alphabet is sufficiently English in appearance to trap the unwary. It may be taken to consist of thirty-one letters, the symbols extra to our alphabet being:

Dotted C—English 'CH' as in 'chain' or Italian 'CI' as in 'Ciano'.
Dotted G—English 'J' as in 'jelly'.
Ticked H—English aspirate.
Digraph GH—Semitic *ghajn*—no equivalent.
Dotted Z—English 'Z' as in 'zest'.

But, since 'J' can, for all practical purposes, serve as either 'I' or 'Y' (but never as 'J' in 'jelly') and since undotted 'C' occurs only in foreign words, or as an out-of-date (Italian) alternative to 'K', we can reduce the alphabet to twenty-eight symbols—or twenty-nine, if we count the diphthong 'IE'. Of these, in addition to the five described above, three others, which look harmless enough have significations completely different from their English sounds. These are:

Q—which represents a sound peculiar to the Aramaic family of languages: an 'articulate pause', like a suppressed cough.
X—which is the English 'SH' as in 'shine'.
Z (undotted)—which represents 'DZ' or 'TS' as in 'adze' or 'hats'.

The digraph 'GH', or Hebrew letter *Ghajn*, is pronounced as a whispered 'Ah' at the back of the throat and is said to be inaudible to the English ear; but try listening to a Maltese and an Englishman each pronouncing *Ghajn* ('a well'), and the difference is quite distinct.

The aspirate 'H' is almost identical with the English aspirate, though it has, perhaps, a slightly more grating sound. It only becomes embarrassing when it occurs in the middle of a word before a consonant or at the end of a word, when it closely resembles the 'CH' of the Scottish 'loch'.

Vowel sounds are Italian rather than English and there is a troublesome diphthong, 'IE'.

'R' is strongly rolled, as in Scotland.

The stresses are almost always on the penultimate syllable, unless the word ends in a double consonant preceded by a short vowel (*Marsamxett*) or a single consonant preceded by a long vowel (*Maktur*); but since many imported words and proper names break the rules, and since there is a widespread habit of abbreviating tails, the only sure guide is mimicry.

Perhaps the greatest source of difficulty for a foreigner is the Maltese uncertainty about 'Q' and 'K'. Many of them either cannot or will not pronounce the 'articulate pause' (a speech habit long regarded by the *Senjuri* as non-U and equivalent to dropping one's aitches). As a result, place-names are often spelled alternatively with 'Q' or 'K', for example, *Ta'Qali* or *Ta'Kali*.

Because the official alphabet now in use (that of the *Ghaqda tal-Kittieba tal-Malti* or Society for the Writing of Maltese) is only some twenty-five years old, many proper names and most family names retain the older, Italian spelling. This, too, can be confusing to the foreigner: 'Scicluna' ought now to be 'Xikluna' and 'Caruana', 'Karwana'.

Since the task of dotting 'G's and crossing the 'H's on a standard keyboard is too much to ask of any typist and too expensive for most printers outside Malta, I have contented myself with spelling which omits the 'extra' symbols. Provided, however, he remembers the different values of 'Q', 'X', and 'GH', an Englishman will not be far wrong without the dots and ticks and a Maltese will, I hope, recognize the words, misspelt as they are.

This note is, of course, a great over-simplification. In the matter of phonetics alone, I have omitted the rules for the interchangeability of surds and sonants (F:V, B:P, D:T) whose relation to each other will be familiar to students of Pitman's shorthand. Neither have I embarked on assimilated articles, dual, numeral, and perfect plurals, hollow verbs, anomalous verbs, and quadriliteral verbs.

A proper study of the Maltese language is a long and laborious business and only rewarding, since it has no 'practical' value outside the Islands, to those who find such matters worth while for their own sake.

This note is really only an apologia for the absence of dots and ticks; but it may, incidentally, assist the visitor to make some sense of a language which might otherwise look like gibberish, and stir him to further interest. There is, after all, no harm in trying to 'get the names right'. The Scots heart warms to a Sassenach who can pronounce 'Dalziel', or the Welshman's to a visitor who can say 'Cymrhydiceirw'.

BIBLIOGRAPHY

ADAMS, A. L. *Natural History of the Nile Valley and Malta.*
AINSWORTH, H. *Rookwood.*
AMARI, M. *Storia dei Musulmani di Sicilia.*
ARDOINO, N. *Gli Uccelli di Malta.*
ASHBY, T. *Journal of Roman Studies.*
BADGER, G. P. *Description of Malta and Gozo.*
BARTOLO, A. *The Sovereignty of Malta.*
BOISGELIN, L. DE. *Ancient and Modern Malta.*
BONELLO, V. *The Madonna in Art.*
BORG, J. *Semina in Malta.*
BORG, J. *Descriptive Flora of the Maltese Islands.*
BORG, P. *Lepidoptera of the Maltese Islands.*
BOSIO, G. *Istoria della Sacra Religione.*
BOSREDON, R. *Journal du Siège et Blocus de Malte.*
BOTTARELLI, G. and MONTERISI, M. *Storia Politica e Militare del Sovrano Ordine di San Giovanni di Malta.*
BRADLEY, R. N. *Malta and the Mediterranean Race.*
BRAUN, H. *An Introduction to Maltese Architecture.*
BRES, O. *Malta Antica Illustrata.*
BROCKMAN, W. E. *Maltese Memories.*
BRYDONE, P. *A Tour through Sicily and Malta.*
BUSUTTIL, V. *Holiday Customs in Malta.*
BUTCHER, M. *Elements of Maltese.*
BUXTON, L. H. D.; Ethnology of Malta and Gozo (*Journal of the Royal Archaeological Institute*).
BUXTON, L. H. D. *The Anthropogeographical Study of Malta.*
CALLENDER, G. *The Naval Side of British History.*
CALLEJA, J. *Works of Art in Malta.*
CARLISLE, EARL OF. *Diary of Turkish and Greek Waters.*
CARUANA, A. A. *Pagan Tombs and Cemeteries in Malta.*
CARUANA, A. A. *Phoenician and Roman Antiquities in Malta.*
CARUANA, A. A. *Sull'Origine della Lingua Maltese.*
CARUANA-GATTO, A. and DESPOTT, G. *Malacofauna Marina delle Isole Maltesi.*
CARUANA-GATTO, A. and SOMMIER, S. *Flora Melitensis Nova.*
CASSAR-PULLICINO, J. *Maltese Folklore.*
CHADWICK, G. *Water-Supply of Malta.*
CESCHI, C. *Architettura dei Templi Megalitici di Malta.*
CREMONA, A. *A Manual of Maltese Orthography and Grammar.*
COCCHIARA, G. *Il Paese di Cuccagna.*
COOKE, A. J. *The Architecture of the Order of St. John.*
DAL POZZO. *Historia della Sacra Religione di Malta.*
D'AVALOS, C. *Tableau historique et politique de Malte.*
DAVY, J. *The Ionian Islands and Malta.*
DEBONO, P. *Storia della Legislazione in Malta.*
DE DOMENICO, F. S. *An Island Beleaguered.*

BIBLIOGRAPHY

DE HELLWALD. *Bibliographie Methodique de L'Ordre Souverain de St. Jean de Jerusalem.*

DELAVILLE LE ROULX, J. *Les Hospitaliers en Terre Sainte et à Chypre (1100–1310).*

DESPOTT, G. *Ornithology of Malta.*

DE VERTOT. *The History of the Knights of Malta.*

DOMEIER, W. *Observations on the Climate, Manners and Amusements of Malta.*

DU MONT. *Voyage to the Levant.*

FERRIS, A. *Storia delle Chiese di Malta.*

FERRIS, A. *Storia Ecclesiastica di Malta.*

FLOWER, A. S. *Notes on Renaissance Architecture in Malta.*

GALEA, L. and MURRAY, M. A. *Maltese Folk Tales.*

GAYRE, R. L. *The Heraldry of the Knights of St. John.*

GERRARD, F. *Malta Magnificent.*

GRAVES, R. *The Greek Myths.*

GRECH-DELICATA. *British Malta.*

GRECH-DELICATA. *Flora Melitensis.*

GRIFFITHS, G. D. *A Journey across the Desert.*

GULIA, J. *Corso di Entomologia.*

HARDMAN, W. *A History of Malta 1798–1815.*

HORNELL, J. *Report on the Fishing Industry in Malta.*

HUGHES, E. *The Private Correspondence of Admiral Lord Collingwood.*

HERODOTUS. *The Histories.*

LAFERLA, A. V. *The Story of Man in Malta.*

LANFRANCO, G. G. *Rare Fungi in Malta.*

LANFRANCO, G. G. *Local Hawk Moths.*

LANFRANCO, G. G. *Midsummer Wild Flowers.*

LANFRANCO, G. G. *The Mantids of Malta.*

LANFRANCO, G. G. *The Mackerel Family round Malta.*

LAURENZA, V. *Malta nei Documenti Angioini.*

LLOYD, H. *Briefed to Attack.*

LUKE, H. *Malta. An Account.*

MACKENZIE-GRIEVE, A. *The Manuscript of a Knight of Malta.*

MACMILLAN, A. *Malta and Gibraltar.*

MAUROIS, A. *Malte.*

MICALLEF, A. *Diritto Municipale di Malta.*

MIEGE, A. *Histoire de Malte.*

MIFSUD, A. *Origine della Sovranita Inglese su Malta.*

MIFSUD, A. *The Knights Hospitallers of the Venerable Tongue of England in Malta.*

MORANT, G. *Races of Central Europe.*

MORE, J. *The Land of Italy.*

NAISH, G. B. R. *Nelson's Letters to his Wife and other documents.*

OVID. *Metamorphoses.*

OVID. *Fasti.*

PRECA, A. *Malta Cananea.*

PUDNEY, J. *Ten Summers.*

RABELAIS. *Gargantua and Pantagruel.*

RITCHIE, L. *The Epic of Malta.*

ROBERTS, E. L. *Birds of Malta.*

ROBERTSON, J. C. *Report on the Water-Supply of Malta.*

ROSSI, E. *Storia della Marina dell'Ordine di Malta.*

RYAN, F. W. *Malta.*

SAYERS, D. L. *Unpopular Opinions.*

SCHERMERHORN, E. W. *Malta of the Knights.*

BIBLIOGRAPHY

SCHERMERHORN, E. W. *On the Trail of the Eight-pointed Cross.*
SCICLUNA, H. P. *A Brief Account of the Order of St. John.*
SCICLUNA, H. P. *The Book of Deliberations of the Venerable Tongue of England.*
SCICLUNA, H. P. *The Church of St. John in Valletta.*
SPRATT, T. A. B. *Geology of Malta and Gozo.*
SUTCLIFFE, E. J. *Grammar of the Maltese Language.*
TALLACK, J. *Malta under the Phoenicians, Knights, and English.*
UGOLINI, L. M. *Origini della Civilta Mediterranea.*
WARING, G. *Letters from Malta and Sicily to a Young Naturalist.*
WELDON, E. C. *Drama in Malta.*
WESTON, F. *Walks in Malta.*
WIGNACOURT, J. *The Odd Man in Malta.*
WILSON, D. *The Essential Shakespeare.*
ZAMMIT, T. *Prehistoric Remains of the Maltese Islands, Phoenician and Roman antiquities in Malta.*
ANONYMOUS (1791). *Malte par un Voyageur François.*